Vienna's
Golden Autumn
1866-1938

To Arif, Anna and Rebecca

Vienna's Golden Autumn

1866-1938

Hilde Spiel

Weidenfeld and Nicolson
New York

Acknowledgments

Thanks are due to my daughter Christine Shuttleworth for her invaluable assistance in making this book acceptable to English and American readers and in preparing the index, to Barbara Mellor for conscientiously and cheerfully editing the text, and to the many who helped in supplying or checking facts, among them Sir Ernst Gombrich, Professor Hanns Jäger-Sunstenau, Professor Gerald Stourzh, Dr Harald Leupold-Löwenthal, Dr Rüdiger Engerth, Dr Jutta Schutting, Elisabeth and Charles Kessler, Henriette von Overhoff and my son Anthony Felix de Mendelssohn.

Published by Weidenfeld & Nicolson, New York
A Division of Wheatland Corporation
10 East 53rd Street
New York, New York 10022

First published in Great Britain in 1987 by
George Weidenfeld and Nicolson Ltd.

Library of Congress Cataloging-in-Publication Data

Spiel, Hilde.
  Vienna's golden autumn, 1866–1938.

  Bibliography: p.
  Includes index.
  1. Vienna (Austria)—Social life and customs.
  2. Vienna (Austria)—Intellectual life. I. Title.
  DB851.S65 1987   943.6'1304   87–2190
  ISBN 1–55584–136–8

Designed by Joy FitzSimmons
Color separations by Newsele Litho Ltd
Typeset, printed and bound by Butler & Tanner Ltd.,
Frome and London

First Edition
10 9 8 7 6 5 4 3 2 1

Endpapers: The annual Corpus Christi procession in Vienna.

CONTENTS

Foreword 6

1 The Rewards of Defeat *7*

2 Private Faces in Public Places *25*

3 The Rise of the Bourgeoisie *38*

4 Idyll, Pageantry and the Great Outdoors *52*

5 Ornament and Austerity *62*

6 'Quite forgotten peoples' lassitudes' *83*

7 The World in a Dewdrop *100*

8 Not Life But Apparition *121*

9 Thinkers and Dreamers *133*

10 The Holiest of Arts *160*

11 *In Vino Veritas* *178*

12 Conflagration and Afterglow *193*

Bibliography *237*

Index *241*

Picture Acknowledgments *248*

FOREWORD

In the last two decades a number of studies have been undertaken, by European and transatlantic scholars, of the intellectual, social and political background to one of the most fruitful periods in modern history: Vienna around 1900. When this book was commissioned by its London publisher early in 1983, none of the great exhibitions documenting the era in Venice, Vienna, Paris and New York had taken place, nor had any of the accompanying literature as yet reached the public. Though the flood of commentaries since let loose should have discouraged me from continuing the present work, I found several reasons strong enough to make me carry on undaunted. While many of the now existing publications had been painstakingly researched and were presented with profound acumen, they seemed to make undue demands on the average reader's capacity to take in a great many complicated facts set out in a rather academic fashion. In some cases, as in that of the catalogues issued on special occasions, the variety of contributors did not further an overall and unified view of the manifold efforts that had led to Vienna's cultural heyday. Moreover, to my knowledge, few of its interpreters shared my advantage of having been born and bred in that city, where my family have lived for generations and where I had met and been befriended by many of the eminent people who played their part in the final years of its prime. I hoped to perform a useful task in attempting to give an authentic yet at the same time readable account of the age; to trace the interrelation between the arts, the movements in philosophy and psychology and the ideological currents; and lastly, to analyse more precisely the intricate hierarchy, vastly differing attitudes and outstanding achievements of writers, artists, composers, thinkers and politicians of wholly or partly Jewish descent, without whom this explosion of talent would not have happened. In describing not only the events leading up to it but also its aftermath in the First Austrian Republic, it was my intention to portray a hitherto little-explored chapter in Vienna's cultural history.

I

THE REWARDS OF DEFEAT

No great period of aesthetic refinement and artistic achievement can be viewed in isolation. To explain its rise and decline we should not merely define the social and political background of the time, but also delve deep into the past and follow a path, albeit a dwindling one, into the future. When attempts are made to describe the magical two decades in Vienna between 1898 and 1918, the reader is sometimes left wondering how that seemingly sudden flowering of talent came about – especially in the fields of literature and philosophy, which had lain barren or borne little crop in previous centuries.

There are good reasons, later to be expounded, for starting a more detailed account of Austria's cultural revolution with the year 1866, and for ending it not with the downfall of the Habsburg monarchy after the Great War, but with the German annexation of the First Austrian Republic in 1938. The true history of Vienna, of course, goes back to the twelfth century, when the dukes of Babenberg held court there in splendour, when the greatest of minnesingers, Walther von der Vogelweide, mourned the early death of the fairest of them, Friedrich the Catholic, and when the foundations were laid for St Stephen's Cathedral. Yet its role as the centre of an empire may be said to have begun in 1556, when Emperor Charles v of Habsburg, on whose realm 'the sun never set', abdicated his throne in favour of his son Philip.

This future adversary of Elizabeth I of England, and husband for a short time to her sister Mary, continued to rule Spain as well as Naples, Milan, Burgundy, the Netherlands and the colonies overseas, from his family seat in Madrid, yet he was denied the highest rank in the Holy Roman Empire of the German People. It was his uncle Ferdinand, younger brother of Charles and archduke of Austria, whom the German prince-electors chose to be their emperor. And Ferdinand, having settled in Vienna after taking over the Habsburg homelands from the Danube to the port of Trieste in 1521, now bestowed on his residence the status of imperial city – an honour that it was to retain for the next three hundred and sixty years.

Paradoxically, this elevation cost the town of Vienna dear, for now it could no longer harbour any hope of ever regaining the autonomy it had once enjoyed, along with cities such as Nuremberg and Strasburg, by being subject only to the imperial crown. On his arrival, Ferdinand had installed a local bureaucracy to administer the city. The burghers had risen in an attempt to regain their privileges and, after their revolt had been put down, had witnessed the beheading of eight of their leaders. Thus, in these early days the city was deprived of – and soon altogether lost – that civic pride so well illustrated in Richard Wagner's *Die Meistersinger*. Confined between a powerful nobility surrounding the court and lower orders destined to serve their superiors in the army and in every branch of civilian life, no strong and self-assured middle class was to develop and thrive until after 1866.

There were compensations, all the same, in being the capital of the Holy Roman Empire. After the Turks had been cast out from central Europe for ever in 1683 and Hungary had been firmly included in the Habsburg realm, Austria, no longer constituting the easternmost and frequently endangered bulwark against Asiatic aggressors, could settle down during long periods of peace to more pleasant pursuits. The three great 'baroque emperors', Leopold I, Joseph I and Charles VI, set about embellishing their city, first by calling in Italian builders like Carlone, Martinelli, Canevale and Burnacini, then by encouraging talented Austrians, such as Lukas von Hildebrandt and the Fischer von Erlachs, to put up splendid palaces and churches inside Vienna or on its fringes. The aristocracy followed suit. Other forms of art too were being promoted: the new entertainment invented in Venice and Naples, simply called opera, was introduced and staged with singular pomp and circumstance, and exquisite collections of paintings were gathered by the imperial patrons. But while music and architecture flourished, the written word did not.

'It takes a great deal of history to produce a little literature,' said Henry James. In Vienna, for so long the centre of world politics, a surfeit of history rather prevented the spread of poetic invention and contemplative thought. While in England the Tudors were followed by the Stuarts and the House of Orange by the Hanoverians, while in France Valois, Orléans and Bourbon battled for the throne, Austria, under its one and only dynasty, the Habsburgs, was busy ruling a large part of Europe from its far-away capital. Three centuries passed after Ferdinand's accession before the first stirrings of a literature written in German were noticed in Vienna. After the death of Charles VI, however, a new monarch, willing to be led by learned advisers, opened the door to a measure of scientific advancement and a more serious preoccupation with creative writing, at least for the stage.

As the emperor left no male issue, his daughter Maria Theresia succeeded him by dint of a Pragmatic Sanction laid down by Charles even before her birth, in defiance of the ancient Salic law. As explained by Shakespeare's tiresome Archbishop in *Henry v*, that law went back to 'certain French' in Saxony

> ... who, holding in disdain the German women
> For some dishonest manners of their life,
> Establisht then this law, to wit, no female
> Should be inheritrix in Salique land.

In fact, though Charles's sanction was hotly contested and his daughter was finally confirmed merely as Archduchess of Austria and Queen of Hungary (while her husband and later her son were granted the imperial crown), nothing was further from Maria Theresia's life style than 'dishonest manners'. A benevolent and malleable, though bigoted woman, she led the Habsburg homelands into a period of prosperity, and of financial, judicial, administrative and educational reform; although she had to go to war more than once, her aim was always a peaceful settlement, especially with her main enemy, Friedrich the Great of Prussia.

Maria Theresia hated unconverted Jews. When the banker Baron Diego D'Aguilar lent her money to help her finish the building of her castle, Schönbrunn, she denied him an audience, but sat behind a screen listening to the final clinching of the deal. Yet when, after his baptism, Liebmann Berlin, the descendant of a rabbinical family and teacher of oriental languages, pleased Maria Theresia's husband with his cabbalistic and alchemical studies, she ennobled him by granting him the title of 'von Sonnenfels'. Later she made his son Joseph – who had also been born in the old faith but received into the new one – her state councillor and influential consultant on home affairs.

The younger Sonnenfels helped abolish torture as an instrument of the law, for which he is still commemorated by a statue in front of Vienna town hall. He also reorganized the police force, gained the merchants a certain freedom of trade and, as official censor, allowed into the country most of the writings of the French and English Enlightenment. His fight against the Viennese harlequin comedy in favour of German classical drama, however, was none too kindly received by theatre-goers in the capital. Not only Joseph von Sonnenfels, but also Count Kaunitz, Maria Theresia's foreign minister and most powerful intellectual mentor, admired Voltaire and the Encyclopédistes in France, thereby preparing the ground for the more drastic reforms of Joseph II, Maria Theresia's son and Austria's most enlightened if still absolute monarch. In his era, which lasted no more than a decade from 1780 to 1790 but gave rise to the liberal movement of the nineteenth century, a number of decrees were issued from the throne granting hitherto unheard-of concessions. These included religious freedom and tolerance for Jews and Protestants, a form of divorce, the secularization of monasteries and an end to serfdom. Yet 'All for the people, nothing through the people' was the motto of this idealistic autocrat.

A further loosening of censorship under Joseph led to a flood of pamphlets, brochures and 'sixpenny booklets', Austria's poor equivalent of the great works of prose and drama then emanating from Weimar and Jena, Hamburg and Berlin. 'Now that we have gained freedom of the press, everybody scribbles as well he can,' complained an anonymously published *Lament of the Gracious Ladies of this Day and Age*. Some minor poets and scholars were trying to follow the flights of fancy of the poet and novelist Wieland or, for better or worse, they imitated the odes of Klopstock, a German theologian and writer of rhymed epics which were more venerated than widely read. Others emulated French playwrights or the comedies of Lessing. Yet no work of philosophical interest or literary value was produced at that time to match the genius of Gluck, Haydn or Mozart. Then, after the beneficial but all too brief reign of Joseph's brother Leopold, his son Franz came to the throne in 1792, and literati and scholars in Austria had to settle down to more than forty years of reactionary thought and censorship.

A surfeit of history, and the final victorious outcome of the war against the emperor's adversary son-in-law Napoleon Bonaparte, further postponed the emergence of a literature comparable to that written in the dozens of the German dukedoms and palatinates still ruled, ostensibly, from Vienna. The years from 1804 to 1806 at least put an end to that outworn farce. First Franz II decided to raise the Habsburg homelands from a dukedom to an empire, elevating himself, under the name of Franz I, to the rank of first Emperor of Austria. Two years later, having recognized the submission to Napoleon of a number of German princes newly united in a Federation of the Rhine, from the balcony of the Church of the Nine Choirs of Angels in the middle of Vienna he solemnly proclaimed the end of the Holy Roman Empire which since Charlemagne had existed for more than a millennium.

Napoleon went, came back and went again, leaving behind an Austrian archduchess and a small son soon to be bereft of their French imperial and royal status. Meanwhile, the Vienna Congress had been held and Europe

WIR Joseph der Zweyte, von GOttes Gnaden erwählter Römischer Kaiser, zu allen Zeiten Mehrer des Reichs, König in Germanien, zu Jerusalem, Ungarn, Böheim, Dalmatien, Kroatien, Slavonien, Galizien und Lodomerien; Erzherzog zu Oesterreich; Herzog zu Burgund, zu Lothringen, zu Steyer, zu Kärnten, und zu Krain; Großherzog zu Toscana; Großfürst zu Siebenbürgen; Markgraf zu Mähren; Herzog zu Braband, zu Limburg, zu Luxenburg, und zu Geldern, zu Würtemberg, zu Ober- und Nieder-Schlesien, zu Mayland, Mantua, zu Parma, Placenz, Guastalla, Auschwitz, und Zator, zu Calabrien, zu Baar, zu Montferat und zu Teschen; Fürst zu Schwaben und zu Charleville, gefürsteter Graf zu Habsburg, zu Flandern, zu Tyrol, zu Hennegau, zu Kyburg, zu Görz und zu Gradisca; Markgraf des heiligen Römischen Reichs, zu Burgau, zu Ober- und Nieder-Laußnitz, zu Pont à Mousson und zu Nomeny, Graf zu Namur, zu Provinz, zu Vaudemont, zu Blanckenberg, zu Zütphen, zu Saarwerden, zu Salm und zu Falckenstein; Herr auf der Windischen Mark, und zu Mecheln ꝛc. ꝛc.;

The 'Great Formula' used by the rulers of the Holy Roman Empire of the German People.

Map of the expanded city of Vienna in about 1873 (drawn by J. Veith).

Joseph von Sonnenfels, state councillor and reformer.

Opposite *Franz Joseph I in about 1860.*

Ferdinand Raimund.

Johann Nestroy.

Nikolaus Lenau (pseudonym for Franz
Niembsch Edler von Strehlenau).

Adalbert Stifter.

Franz Grillparzer.

divided afresh. Under a new heading the old order was re-established, Austria ceding its possessions in Belgium but gaining territories nearer home, such as the archbishopric of Salzburg, the whole of Lombardy, Venice, Istria, Dalmatia, Croatia, Slovenia and a large part of Poland. The crafty Prince Metternich, Franz's state chancellor, was to watch over a Europe stripped of Napoleon's reforms and threatened by growing nationalist tendencies, but kept stable by a system of political immobility – a constant balancing act designed to preserve the status quo and based, at least in Austria, on the existence of an ever watchful secret police.

All went well for the monarchs and their statesmen until revolutionary elements began to stir, first in small German towns, then in France, and finally, in the 'stormy year' of 1848, all over Europe. The new Austrian Empire, however, was blighted by two obsessions left over from the Holy Roman Empire of the German People, which were to endanger, or at least to delay, its entry into a more democratic age, and which further undermined its very existence once the forces of nationalism had begun to tear it apart. The first obsession was the emperor's belief, held by his ancestors and never abandoned by the House of Habsburg, in the divine right of kings. It was laid down in the historic 'great formula' used by His Apostolic Majesty on every decree and even now beginning with the words 'I, Franz I, by the grace of God Emperor of Austria and King of Bohemia', whereupon it went on to enumerate all his forty-three other titles, including, up to the days of his descendant Franz Joseph, those of Duke of Auschwitz and King of Jerusalem.

The second obsession was the 'Germanness' not only of the emperor but of his ruling class, his bureaucracy and even his liberal intellectual élite – though some of the aristocracy, while using German as their *lingua franca*, remained proud of their Slav or Magyár vernacular and ancestry. Austria, having not only joined but also presided over the 'German Federation' which lasted from 1815 to 1866, was now a separate, multi-ethnic state. Within its borders, many languages were spoken besides that softly accented German, laced with words or phrases originating in Italian, Hungarian or Czech, which was used in Vienna and in the surrounding provinces.

Yet, just as the Austrian emperor still considered himself to be a 'German prince', so those Austrians who were brought up to speak German insisted on this distinction from the rest of his subjects, though they were not necessarily even of German origin. Franz Grillparzer, one of the great writers now emerging in the country, saw himself literally as an 'Austrian subject' but a 'German poet'. From the outset, the Austrian Empire found it hard to establish its own multinational identity. Only in retrospect, long after its downfall, was it mourned nostalgically by the very peoples who had precipitated its doom.

The long reign of Franz I ended with his death in 1835, but his era seemed to continue under his kind-hearted but ineffectual son Ferdinand a further fifteen years, until the March rising of 1848. In these decades after the Vienna Congress, a tranquil, uneventful time later euphemistically called 'the era of good feelings', even the lower classes, thanks to the rise of industry, were able modestly to thrive. Yet men and women looking farther than their Sunday roast chicken felt sadly deprived of free speech and expression. Life seemed to withdraw into the idyllic ambience of the family hearth and of nature. While the body feasted, the mind starved.

And yet, in that period of Biedermeier, named after a fictional German schoolmaster embodying all the contemporary virtues of quietism, when liberalism had been purged and an absolute regime absolutely restored, the arts, within prescribed limits, enjoyed a first burgeoning. The great days of salon diplomacy, of splendid gatherings of wealth and wit such as had existed before and during the Vienna Congress, were over. A new middle class, rising from the lower ranks, began to assemble in small circles, societies and coteries, to play chamber music, sing in choirs or listen to piano recitals, to hear a writer read from works too daring to go into print or on the stage, and to walk through the Vienna woods to paint the autumn hues in watercolours.

If Schubert in his music probed the deepest emotions, not yet verbalized, of the truly sensitive, the introverted and often melancholy Viennese of his time, painters like Danhauser, Fendi and Daffinger portrayed the gay-hearted and contented among their contemporaries: those who helped form the image of the proverbially easy-going, fun-loving Viennese. Those writers, however, who appeared on the Austrian scene after Schubert's death – all at the same time, as if to make up for the many centuries lost to literature in their country – were bound, like him, to expose that misconception.

They were Franz Grillparzer, a dramatist first and foremost, but also the creator of poetry, epigrams and aphorisms in a wonderfully lucid prose; Ferdinand Raimund, heir to the tradition of early Viennese harlequinades and illusionist plays, but a moralist at heart; Johann Nestroy, author of great comedy, satire and even farce, who knew how to convey a great deal of philosophy and social criticism in a seemingly light-weight manner; Nikolaus Lenau, a romantic and elegiac poet, the Byron of his place and time; and Adalbert Stifter, the first great Austrian novelist.

Two of these five, Raimund and Stifter, took their own lives. Lenau in his later years fell into madness. Grillparzer, whose brother had committed suicide, died a morose bachelor. And even Nestroy, the eternal jester and lampooner, whose plays – in which he himself starred – night after night reduced his public to tears of laughter, fell victim, after many domestic crises and professional setbacks, to chronic depression. Many of these traits recurred in the second great wave of literary talent which arose during the *fin de siècle*, halfway through Franz Joseph's reign.

In 1848 the seeds were sown of Liberalism, Nationalism, Socialism, and whatever unholy alliance they would form in the distant future. Those students in Franconia and in the Rhineland who around 1820, in the name of their newly discovered patriotism, harassed the Jews and indulged in kinds of intolerance not practised since the days before the Enlightenment, had flourished the self-same black, red and gold-coloured flag which barely thirty years later was to become, in Austria too, a symbol of greater German unity. It was under this flag that the Liberals rose against the Habsburgs' black and yellow emblems in Vienna in March 1848, having taken their cue from the February revolution in Paris which had put an end to the reign of Louis Philippe.

Strange things happened in the Austrian capital during and after that stormy month. True democrats, mainly from the middle classes, among them prominent Jews such as Adolf Fischhof, Josef Goldmark and L.A. Frankl (who wrote their hymn), sided with fanatical pro-Germans in manning the barricades against the reactionary policies of Metternich and the absolute rule of the 'Kind Emperor Ferdinand'. At the same time, dissatisfaction within the ranks of the workers and artisans prompted them to join the bourgeois rising. Metternich, aided by the banker Salomon Rothschild, fled to England and was fêted there as the Grand Old Man of European politics. When London became too expensive for him, he settled in Brighton and calmly waited for the waters to subside and for an imperial call to return. As it happened, his exile was to last no more than two and a half years.

After Metternich's flight revolts had broken out all over the monarchy, from Prague and Budapest to Milan. For months, on and off, Vienna saw heavy street-fighting between the rebels and the military. On 15 May another concerted and even more radical rising than the one in March, bent on achieving a democratic constitution, forced the emperor to flee the capital and go to Innsbruck. A day after his departure, on the eighteenth, the first freely elected German National Assembly met at St Paul's church in Frankfurt-am-Main. One hundred and fifteen Austrian delegates had been invited to discuss the future relationship between the monarchy and a putative German empire. The empire took some time materializing.

Meanwhile Austria continued to be linked with the German states until Prussia decided to sever that age-old bond completely.

In August, some weeks after an 'All-Austrian' parliament or Reichstag had been called together to satisfy the people's wish, the emperor returned to Vienna. In that same month, Karl Marx visited the city and, invited to speak before the recently founded First Vienna Workers' Educational Union, attacked the dynastic principle itself. His attitude, however, was none too well received by his listeners, whose aim was not to topple the emperor, but to obtain better working conditions and more pay. In fact, the establishment of a more liberal government in the capital had led to a number of reforms and, to some extent, pacified the revolutionaries, when a violent rebellion broke out in Hungary. Just as in later years the proud Magyárs would play a crucial role in the disintegration of the empire, now they were instrumental in prolonging, and deepening, the conflict still simmering in the imperial residence.

The moderate prime minister of Ferdinand's kingdom of Hungary, Count Battyány, had been overruled by a new leader, Lájos Kossuth, who preached independence and social democracy but had little regard for the many minorities, mainly Slav, in his country. The rebel army he had formed first overcame the troops of an imperial field marshal sent to subdue it, then marched towards the Austrian border. Troops stationed in Vienna refused to go and meet the advancing Hungarians. At the same time a third outbreak of fighting, the so-called October rising, started up in the streets of the capital. An armed crowd stormed the Ministry of War, captured the minister, battered him to death and strung up his body on a street lamp – the worst outrage ever committed by the populace in Vienna, and especially brutal when compared with the bloodless revolution of 1918 that caused the downfall of the Habsburg dynasty.

The emperor hurriedly removed himself once again, this time to Moravia. During the following weeks the rising was quelled, totally and bloodily. Many insurgents and their supporters were shot, including the German Jew Robert Blum, a member of the Frankfurt Parliament. The recently established Reichstag had also left Vienna and, in the small town of Kremsier not far from the temporary seat of the court, Olmütz, was now supposed to go to work. The prime minister, Prince Schwarzenberg, however, though heading a fairly young and progressive cabinet, was determined not to upset the old absolutist order. And the *camarilla* or cabal surrounding Ferdinand, led by his sister-in-law the Archduchess Sophie and his field marshal Prince Windischgrätz, decided to get rid of an emperor all too willing to give in to popular demands. He was persuaded to resign in favour of Sophie's eldest son. On 2 December Ferdinand told his successor kneeling before him in gratitude for the imperial and royal crown: 'It was done gladly. Now be good.' Whereupon he retired to Prague, happy to be rid of his troubled throne.

It is against this turbulent background of his accession that we must view the early years of Franz Joseph I, who was to rule the Austrian Empire for most of the period with which we are here concerned. In almost all the territories of his reign he is now, seven decades after his death, revered both as a father figure and a symbol of the long-lost Danubian unity. A picture postcard portraying him as a kind yet forceful elderly man, and containing the first verse of the 'Emperor's Hymn' in Latin and Cyrillic letters, is currently sold in more than twenty languages of Slav, Magyár and Romanic origin. It strangely echoes an earlier one, printed in 1917, to be sent home by a soldier at the front, telling his family that he is 'well and in good health' in German, Hungarian, Czech, Slovak, Ruthenian, Polish, Croat, Romanian and Italian. Significantly, it is the citizens of Friuli and Trieste who buy up the postcard of Franz Joseph in such numbers that it is usually out of print. A great wave of nostalgia has welled up, not only in north-east Italy but – perhaps more under-standably – in several satellite states within the Moscow Pact, for the 'benevolent and democratic' government of the Habsburg monarchy.

Benevolent and democratic Franz Joseph may have become towards the end of his life, although he never abrogated his belief in the divine right of kings. But for a long time he hardly justified the name of his ancestor Joseph II, the 'Emperor of Reform'. (He had been given the additional name of Joseph at birth, but only started to use it in 1848, in an attempt to placate his unruly subjects.) Like his near-contempor-ary Queen Victoria, he dominated the destiny of his country for an almost unconscionable length of time. Yet, in contrast to her, he went through many phases and changing attitudes which only in later life softened to the stance of a dutiful, peace-loving, popular and well-meaning man, who after much personal tragedy had become if not wise at least very cautious. The real image, however, had by that time been replaced by an official one, an eidolon, a living legend representing the one and only unifying bond between nations in the grip of the centrifugal force of conflicting ideologies.

At the age of eighteen Franz Joseph had inherited from his uncle Ferdinand a not quite defeated revolution at home and a still virulent insurrection in Hungary. He now had to watch inept councillors like the princes Schwarzenberg and Windischgrätz burden his young reign with fatal mistakes. The inexperienced young man was advised to call on Tsar Nicholas I for help in the Magyár uprising and so, for the first time in history, caused a Russian army to wage war on central European soil. His lack of gratitude to the Tsar for having pulled his chestnuts from the fire was never forgotten, and was held against him in later days.

The second mistake was to allow a sadistic military commander of German birth, Baron Julius Haynau, to mete out bloody justice after the Hungarian defeat. With Franz Joseph's consent, thirteen of their generals were shot, as well as the moderate prime minister, Count Battyány. This act, too, had lasting consequences. Moreover, Countess Battyány was said to have put a curse on the emperor. If this was so, it certainly worked, for he was to lose his son through suicide, his brother through execution and both his wife and his second heir apparent by the hand of assassins. 'Truly, I am spared nothing in this world,' he exclaimed, when the news of the empress's death in Geneva reached the palace.

Brought up as a soldier, Franz Joseph wore uniform for the rest of his life, except when he went hunting, which was the only recreation he allowed himself. The first armed combat he took part in, however, cured him of any love of war he may have had. During the battle of Solferino in 1859, leading the high command in his campaign against Napoleon III for the retention of Lombardy, he was shaken by the slaughter he witnessed, lost his nerve and ordered a premature retreat. Solferino was only the first of two crucial military defeats suffered by Franz Joseph. But in its wake a pattern which had announced itself at the outset of his reign became clear. This was his granting of privileges when in a weak position, to be revoked, if possible, when his fortunes were high again. Though the Reichstag had been dissolved in March 1849, in May, as a result of the previous year's rebellion, Franz Joseph had sanctioned a new liberal constitution – only to cancel it, more in the spirit of Franz I than of Joseph II, in December 1851. A year after Solferino he issued a manifesto called the 'October Diploma' proposing many reforms – most of which were rescinded within four months.

Once the principle of showing more tolerance after a débâcle was established, it seemed to repeat itself. In this sense, the fruits of defeat – whether temporary or not – were a readiness to achieve compromise, even a measure of democratization in constitutional matters. In another sense, they helped create an atmosphere in which peaceful pursuits were thought preferable, even by the ruler and his entourage, to the dangers and uncertainties of war. During the fifties the emperor, having survived an attack on his life, concluded a love marriage with the Bavarian Princess Elisabeth, and welcomed the birth of a son and heir, began to learn his lesson. By the sixties he was mellowing.

Though the October Diploma had been replaced by the reactionary

February patent of 1861, four years later Franz Joseph, aware of the unrest caused in Bohemia, Hungary and Croatia by the present centralized government, himself proposed another new constitution. Far from wanting to challenge the recent claims for hegemony in Germany by a Prussia turned acquisitive after the advent of Bismarck, he tried at all costs to avoid a 'war between brothers'. The Prussians however, after leaving the German Federation, and thereby blasting it open, attacked Austria and defeated its army near Königgrätz in Bohemia on 3 July 1866.

It is now generally accepted that the eventual fate of central Europe, namely the fall of many dynasties and the disintegration of two empires in the course of the twentieth century, was decided then and there. Whatever far-reaching effect Königgrätz had upon multinational states, upon the unity of German-speaking peoples, and upon European stability as a whole, in Austria this utter defeat led to lasting reforms for the first time. Politically, these reforms were a mixed blessing. The Hungarians, who had clamoured loudest for governmental independence within the framework of the Habsburg realm and, in view of their bloody sub-jugation in 1848, indeed had the strongest claim, were granted 'equa-lization'. Henceforth, from February 1867 to its end, Franz Joseph's empire was known as the Austro-Hungarian or Dual Monarchy. The rapacious Magyárs were also given sovereignty over a number of Slav provinces as well as over Fiume, Austria's second port on the Adriatic. In every other way the liberalization was entirely beneficial. The long-overdue Parliament of Peoples, the Reichsrat, was at last established. And the new constitution laid down full civic rights for every subject, including the Jews, whose emancipation was now thought to be as secure as it was complete.

After Königgrätz came nearly six decades of comparative freedom from warfare and bloodshed. To the fruits of defeat were added the fruits of prosperity. Growing affluence, founded on steady industrial growth, was within many people's reach. The middle classes began to thrive. They were ready to support, as well as to bring forth, creative talent. And creative talent now came to the surface in profusion, in all the arts.

2

PRIVATE FACES
IN PUBLIC PLACES

During the early years of the Austrian Empire, after Napoleon Bonaparte had beaten its armies in 1805 and 1809, marching on both occasions into the capital and taking temporary residence in Castle Schönbrunn, the Viennese were compared to 'ants swarming in the head of a dead lion'. The lion presumably symbolized their own glorious past when their monarch was master, not servant, to the greater part of Europe. For a while the simile may have been apt, but it lost its meaning when, after Napoleon had been deposed, all the world assembled in the imperial city to redraw the European map for decades to come. It could be argued that in 1866 it became appropriate once more. Yet after that date Vienna and its citizens retained, even increased, their status until the empire met its doom. In the First Austrian Republic, which lasted but twenty years – and only fifteen as a democracy – the analogy gained at last a macabre truth.

At the time of writing the Second Austrian Republic has well overtaken the first, not only in its life-span but also in its health and wealth. To suggest that the pendulum has swung again, however, would be wrong. While the boundaries of the city, unreasonably expanded during the Hitler era and reduced after its end, now compare roughly with those of 1938, the population is steadily decreasing. Those spacious government buildings, designed to administer a far-flung realm, which were taken over by the bureaucracy administering the rump state left after the peace treaty of St Germain, are now filled to overflowing with civil servants increasing according to the principles of Parkinson's Law. The huge state theatres, monuments to Austria's former grandeur, are subsidized far more heavily than those of London, Paris or New York. But in the midst of all this splendour, the Viennese, busily bustling about like ants in their efforts to maintain their present political, social and economic stability, have to a great extent lost their former urban refinement and universal outlook. The lion is dead. And what was known as the *concordia discors* in the centre of a multinational state has been replaced by a uniform provincialism.

If this judgement sounds harsh, it is borne out by the number of petty family squabbles in public life, the general low standard of the press and the absence of stimulating intellectual controversy. While music is still played and performed, if not created, to perfection, and while the visual arts may be said to thrive moderately, neither the literature nor the philosophy nor the science in the Vienna of today can compare with those of the years before the Second World War. In the light of these facts, that uniquely fruitful period in Vienna's history, lasting more or less seventy years from its gestation to its decline, is thrown even more sharply into relief. An attempt to describe the characteristics of Vienna's inhabitants and its various districts must be confined to the period in question: its results are not applicable to present-day conditions. In the field of culture, at least, the Anschluss in 1938 was a greater watershed than the collapse of 1918.

It used to be said that a Viennese identity can be acquired. How else would it have been possible for members of all kinds of nations and mother tongues to assemble in this city over many centuries and, without shedding much of their outward and inner make-up, be integrated completely into a very specific community? Most of them were newcomers at one time or another. 'From the House of Starhemberg', claimed a chronicler in 1780, 'to the pauper swinging his rattle in the street there is hardly a family left among us able to trace its Austrian origin in unbroken line from its great-grandfather.' Fewer than five families could claim ancestors resident in Vienna before the second Turkish siege a century earlier. Those Romans, Huns, Slavs, Germans and Magyárs dwelling on Austrian soil in the first millennium AD were no more than a dim memory in the days of the dukes of Babenberg. To the Bavarians, Franconians and Swabians, who up to the time of the early Habsburgs had given Vienna the appearance of a truly German Gothic city, was soon added an influx of people from the south and east, who changed the indigenous habits of the place and added colour to a medieval conformity.

When in 1548 a schoolmaster from the Palatinate called Wolfgang Schmeltzl visited Vienna, strolling into the merchant quarter in the inner city he felt as though he had arrived at the tower of Babel: 'Hebrew, Greek and Latin, German, French, Turkish, Spanish, Bohemian, Wendish and Italian, Hungarian as well as Netherlandish, Syrian, of course, and also Croat, Arabic, Polish and Chaldean' were the languages he thought he heard. And though he did not attribute all of them correctly, it is true that dozens of tongues were spoken in a town which was a bridge to the East, rather than the last terminal before it. Once the newcomers from outlying parts of the empire had settled in Vienna, they began to adapt to its way of life. Even so, and in contrast to the rural population in the Austrian provinces, centuries later their descendants still displayed fiery Magyár eyes, a Venetian suppleness of limb or the high cheekbones of their Slav forefathers.

In Franz Joseph's early days a ditty was sung in the inns of Vienna praising the tolerance shown by his subjects towards one another:

> The Christians, the Turks, the Heathen and Jew
> Have dwelt here in ages old and new
> Harmoniously and without any strife
> For everyone's entitled to live his own life.

Their inherited qualities produced a singular blend. 'The Viennese are Germans, Czechs, Croats,' said the writer Hermann Bahr in the nineties, 'but they are illuminated by the other nations living with them, and in their light the German and Slav element looks different, grows more mobile, more liquid, loses its heaviness, is sublimated and reduced, as it were, to a reflection of itself. Hence the danger, which must not be ignored, of these people evaporating – they easily climb too high and are blown away by the wind, not at once, but in the second or third generation.'

Germans, it is true, made up most of the original stock, and until the early 1800s constituted the majority of the population. By 1880 every third inhabitant was of Czech origin, every tenth of Jewish. Yet Bohemians, Moravians and Slovaks had lived in Vienna as early as the thirteenth century, when their countryman Ottokar II Przemysl ruled the city for twenty-five years before the advent of the first Habsburgs. Their patron saint Nepomuk to this day protects the bridges of the city, as he does in Prague, and there are 627 statues of him within the precincts of Vienna. Their influence was much felt in the religious field, for the many northern Slavs who flooded the city in the early days of the Industrial Revolution, around the 1830s, brought with them their fervent Catholic faith. Like the Italians, they were often excellent musicians. Vienna's great school of medicine in the *fin de siècle* contained a number of Bohemian names. And the future president of Czechoslovakia, Thomas G. Masaryk, was a pupil and teacher at Viennese high schools. The majority of the Czechs and Slovaks in the capital, however, were cobblers, tailors and family servants. Their pastry-cooks dominated Austrian cuisine.

The Jews had come to the Danube with the Romans, as they had followed in their wake to the Rhine and the Main. Under the Babenbergs they were allotted their own streets and squares in Vienna, without however being confined to them. They were driven out repeatedly,

Above *Bosniaken: members of a
Bosnian regiment in the
Austrian army in about 1900.*

Opposite above *Servant girls
from the Slav provinces in
Vienna's amusement park, the
Prater.*

Opposite below *Slovakian
peddlers in about 1890.*

Right *A Bohemian child's nurse
in about 1908.*

mainly to Bohemia and Silesia, but always trickled back again. The attitude of the emperors towards them varied. In the early seventeenth century Ferdinand II had encouraged them to inhabit a quarter of their own, to the left of that branch of the river which was later to be regulated and known as the Danube Canal. At the end of that century they were evicted once more by Ferdinand's grandson Leopold, but were not prevented from settling down in other parts of the realm. Ostracized but not harmed by Maria Theresia, some of them began to rise in Viennese society under the benign rule of Joseph II. A family such as the Wertheimers, alias the Wertheimsteins, had lived uninterruptedly in Vienna for much longer than those who later contested their right to call themselves Austrian – in fact since 1679, when some of them had been readmitted by the Emperor Leopold. Their contribution to cultural life, like that of so many of their kin, will be dealt with in its proper context.

Gipsy music, rich and sharply seasoned food and deftly written boulevard comedies, as well as operettas, were the gifts from Budapest to its sister-capital in the Dual Monarchy. The linguistic border with Hungary, as that with Moravia, lay practically on Vienna's doorstep. Before 1918 a local train took an hour to Pressburg, now called Bratislava and incorporated into the state of Czechoslovakia. But even the endless grassy plain of the Hungarian Puszta began on today's Austrian soil, in the easternmost province of Burgenland, in whose small capital, Eisenstadt, the plaster heads of the Magyár royal dynasty of the Arpads look down from the Esterházy castle on the town that gave birth to Haydn. It was not the peasants or workers of Hungary, but its aristocrats and artists who swarmed to the imperial city, though they rarely made it their home. After 1867 members of great families such as the Andrássy, Zichy and Szécheny played a decisive part in the political life of the Dual Monarchy. Horses raised in the Puszta won many races in Vienna. The Magyár Honvéd regiment wore the most spectacular uniform in the Austrian army. And Hungarian writers and composers swamped the Viennese stage.

Nationals of countries outside the boundaries of the state, such as Turks, Greeks, Macedonians and Romanians, also felt drawn to the lively metropolis – to be added inevitably to the melting-pot. It was not surprising, therefore, that those Viennese who thought of themselves as Germans and thus superior to the rest, in their outward appearance rarely fitted the requirements of the Aryan cult as preached by the fanatically racist writer Lanz von Liebenfels around the turn of the century. Nòr were their names proof of their Teutonic origin. The archaeologist and orientalist Strzygowski, himself a native of Galicia, who in his theory of art was influenced by the racism of Houston Stewart Chamberlain; the influential historian Srbik, scion of Pan-Germanism; the deputies Pro-chazka and Skaret who stood for that creed in the Austrian Parliament – all of them, including Hitler's first Gauleiter in Vienna, Globocnik, obviously derived from northern or southern Slav stock.

What kind of people result from such an ethnic mixture? Certainly none of those single-minded, iron-willed empire-builders and exponents of a master race whose hands have lain heavily on the history of our globe. The Viennese, at least up to the Anschluss, were in themselves contradictory and inconsistent, their characteristics often cancelling each other out. Such inner conflicts are fruitful, yet also make for an inbuilt impediment. They can produce brilliant ideas, but at the same time hamper their being put into practice. Inside every Viennese, one might say, there is a critical adviser, a warner or preventer who robs him of his courage to act, or his power to finish what he has begun. When the dramatist Grillparzer talked of 'the half-trodden path and the half-finished act' as being the curse of the House of Habsburg, this applied equally to the Viennese.

Grillparzer himself was the best example of such a hesitant, dithering attitude, such a deep-rooted fear of making decisions. He never married the girl he loved, for instance, but allowed her to look after him from a safe distance until his death. The schizophrenic quality of so many Viennese may be illustrated by a quotation from the satirical playwright Nestroy, whose Holofernes is made to say: 'I'd like to drive myself against myself, only to see who is the stronger: I or me.' Later, Hofmannsthal explored the delicate ramifications of a Viennese soul in the 'passive hero' of his play *The Difficult Man*. And though all this may have applied merely to a particularly sensitive, introverted type of Viennese, the more robust among them showed similar traits: a constant inner strife and uncertainty as well as a lassitude caused by the awareness that nothing is permanent and death is forever lurking behind the door.

Even the simple folk sitting in the inns, given over to the enjoyment of good plain food and a very dry new wine, after a while fell prey to gloomy thoughts – exemplified by the songs and music played on these occasions. Was it the melancholy Slav element in their make-up, or the baroque heritage of their Catholic religion, with its stress on mortality and hope for a better life beyond, that motivated such flights from reality in the midst of sensual pursuits? In a way, by turning away from this world towards the next without abandoning its pleasures, they had the best of both. In the words of Hermann Bahr: 'They were able to indulge while renouncing, to be ascetically opulent and piously to sin.'

To the Italian influence might be ascribed the Viennese love of gossip, often personified in Goldoni's go-between characters whose only *raison d'être* is the carrying to and fro of scandalous news. Since the *commedia dell'arte*, seemingly despised by Goldoni yet the source of so many of his own plays, also inspired the early Austrian harlequin shows, the analogy cannot be denied. In the most Viennese of all comedies, Hofmannsthal's *Der Rosenkavalier*, it is Annina and Valzacchi who pull the strings and move the plot. In our day the conductor Lorin Maazel, having been ousted from his post as director of the State Opera through a finely spun web of reported hearsay, slander and wily stratagems, called intrigue a great form of art developed in the Austro-Hungarian Monarchy. He forgot to mention that the Venetian influence dates back much further, to well before 1797 when Venice first fell under Austrian rule.

To generalize and overstress national characteristics leads to racial prejudice. So it is better not to delve too deeply into the ethnic sources of the two most disagreeable attributes of the Viennese: their instinctive dislike of intelligence and their malice aforethought – often exercised without purpose, just for its own sake. The journalist Ferdinand Kürnberger, admittedly the harshest critic of his countrymen until Karl Kraus took up the torch, mocked their aversion to earnest thought. Not in two thousand years, he pointed out, in fact not since Marcus Aurelius wrote in Vienna his book *On Self-Knowledge*, had there been another philosopher in this town. The fact that a number of them appeared on the scene after Kürnberger's death in 1879 will find its explanation.

Grillparzer described his native city as a 'Capua of Minds'. Daniel Spitzer, another publicist of the last century, with one of those classical allusions typical of his time, talked of 'Pontine marshes of the spirit'. And Nestroy exposed the favourite ruse of his fellow Viennese, of evading too probing an intellect by feigning a comfortable ignorance, through the character of one Wendelin who declares:

> My superstition I'll yield never
> To the enlightened and clever.
> Nowadays it's a relief
> To have any kind of belief.

The cliché of the 'golden heart' in the breast of every Viennese, and that of their joviality, sociability, cosiness – or whichever inadequate translation may be attempted of the word *Gemütlichkeit* – is perpetuated despite all experiences suffered during the Anschluss and its aftermath. The Viennese themselves support it gladly, as is illustrated in the age-old dialogue: 'A: In Vienna everything is *gemütlich* except the wind. B: But the wind only comes here because of Vienna's *Gemütlichkeit*.' This short exchange has the same saccharine sweetness as those operettas or films that used to carry the cliché round the world. Even the doleful little grouser, usually played by the great actor Hans Moser, who found his way through the schmaltzy products of Wien-Film designed to bring light relief and self-esteem to the Viennese during the last war, only served to set off the general light-hearted merriment. Yet he was truer to type than all the others.

Grouching and grousing, moping and nagging – these are favourite pastimes in Vienna, for which a large number of synonyms exist in the local vocabulary. The emperor Franz, who more than any other Habsburg knew the inner soul of his people, since he could rely on his secret police to have a dossier on every citizen, did not take their complaints too seriously. 'While they are grumbling', he said, 'they are content. It's only when they fall silent that they are dangerous.' Again, the true Viennese prototype can be detected in Nestroy. The *tædium vitae* expressed by the cobbler Knieriem in one of his most famous plays, *Lumpazivagabundus*, may serve as a model: 'I look a merry fellow all right, but all that is just on the surface, inwardly it's strange with me. When I drink I believe every drop to be poison. When I eat, death eats with me. When I leap and dance, inwardly it seems to me as though I were walking with my corpse.'

Such inner poison often turns into outward malice – a desire to direct the sting in one's own heart against the rest of the world. This might be the case with public and civil servants, from the tram conductor to the income tax collector, and nowadays also with the man in the street who has noticed your car touching another car's bumper and is immediately ready to denounce you, or merely caution you, or simply stand and stare spitefully until you've driven off. The 'insolence of office', prevalent in the lower ranks of the Austrian bureaucracy, dominates some of the sinister allegories of Kafka, a citizen not of Vienna but of Prague. It may not, therefore, be an isolated phenomenon. Viennese maliciousness and *médisance*, however, take many shapes and forms. Hermann Bahr considers them a forgivable habit: 'The Viennese does not abuse anyone because he dislikes that person, neither does he abuse him because he wants to scare him off. He abuses him because it does himself good, and he even likes the person who affords him this pleasure.'

That is as may be. In accordance with their schizophrenic disposition, these grumblers, grousers and apparent harbourers of ill-will towards their fellow human beings have always shown the greatest respect for those who have made their way in life, who have acquired fame, or wealth, or titles whose status seemed to rub off on those who addressed them as 'Herr Doktor' or 'Herr Baron'. In short, it is truly difficult to pin down the

Viennese to a particular virtue or failing, since both are often inextricably tied. Their qualities come in opposed pairs: curiosity and gossiping with true empathy, malevolence with benevolence, rudeness with charm, envy with magnanimity and, most importantly, a sense of humour with chagrin.

The playful *Instruction of Carnival Children*, published in 1784, throws more light on the disposition of the Viennese than many a learned treatise. 'What is bliss for the Viennese? Coffee and a nice titbit. A little calumny of people. . . . What is a deathly sin to the Viennese? A reasoned discourse. A useful book. Drinking water. A bad meal. Economy.' It would seem that some characteristics of the people of Vienna have survived to this day. Yet most of the prototypes depicted in the *Cris de Vienne* of Maria Theresia's era and seen in public till the end of the empire or even a little beyond, such as the Croat peddler of kitchenware, the Moravian cheese-seller, the Slovak rug-vendor, the Jewish rag-and-bone man with his horse-drawn cart; all, except the lavender-woman, the organ-grinder, and the chestnut-roaster, have disappeared. So have the stock characters of Viennese society at the *fin de siècle* and up to 1918, as described, if not created, by the writer Arthur Schnitzler: the light-hearted and at the same time melancholic rake, or the sweet suburban seamstress destined to lose her upper-class lover to a *femme fatale* of the bourgeoisie.

While the social structure of Vienna was never as distinctly marked by linguistic niceties as that of London – another royal and imperial residence, though far less dominated by its successive dynasties – the various strata differed in the degree to which they used the local vernacular. Pure 'high German' was heard only on the stage of the Burgtheater, which was often administered by a director imported from Germany. Nearest to it came the slightly nasal but essentially dialect-free language of the high nobility. The emperor and his entourage, on the other hand, as well as upper civil servants, army officers and the educated part of the bourgeoisie, spoke – or affected to speak – the so-called 'Schönbrunn German', a soft idiom presumed to meet that of the people half-way. Genuine Viennese slang was current among a large section of the community, from the pleasant-sounding salesgirls in the inner city and surrounding quarters to the uniquely brutish-sounding ruffians in outer districts like Erdberg or Hernals.

In all class-ridden societies, such as Austria was up to the end of the monarchy, the right address is as important as the right accent. In Vienna this was more easily defined than elsewhere since the town had grown centrifugally from the start. If its spreading out could have been observed in time-lapse photography, like that of plants, in its development from a small bulwark of the Holy Roman Empire to its role as imperial city

Vienna would have resembled a rose unfolding. Well into the reign of Franz Joseph, its heart, the first district, lay in peaceful isolation from the rest, surrounded by built-up bastions, as in the days of the Turkish sieges and of Napoleon. Encircling the bastions was a stretch of open ground used for exercising troops and commonly known as the *Glacis*. In the old days a wall with twelve gates enclosed all that made up Vienna's identity: the Gothic cathedral, the houses of the aristocracy and middle classes, court life and popular life, hotels, restaurants, markets, dressmakers, milliners, hairdressers and coffee-houses, as well as the university, theatres, museums and concert halls.

Within that restricted space, while certain streets were inhabited by the grain-merchants, the venison-sellers, butchers or weavers – and still bear their names – no topographical hierarchy had developed. The beautiful baroque palace of a nobleman might adjoin more unassuming houses where tradesmen or craftsmen lived and worked. This microcosm stayed intact even when, beyond the ramparts and the Danube Canal, new districts sprang up and engulfed gardens, fields, vineyards and the green slopes of the Wienerwald. The Industrial Revolution had hastened the growth of Vienna and begun to change its social make-up. In time a second boundary line, called the *Gürtel* or belt, was reached and crossed. Then a third, the *Vorortelinie* or suburban line, brought nearer the villages surrounding the capital. But still the innermost part of the city, confined within its ancient ring, retained all the important landmarks of this historic town.

On Christmas Day 1857, however, the official Viennese journal published an imperial decree in which Franz Joseph expressed his wish to have the city walls removed, the bastions levelled and the Glacis turned into a built-up area. The dry manner of his proclamation hid the fact that he had made a far-reaching, even an epoch-making decision. To pull down the fortifications and hand over the Glacis to civilian rather than military use seemed an extraordinarily liberal measure – especially as Solferino had not yet deflected the emperor's mind from the glories of war. However, the reasoning that accompanied the decree contained the important sentence: 'The layout of the street [the new ring road] will have to pay special heed to military strategy.' In fact, at both ends where the Ringstrasse, resembling a bow, met the Danube Canal which formed its string, two enormous barracks which had existed for some time were to keep their parade grounds. Two more were planned at other points on the Ring, but were not built after the Italian defeat. A great step had been taken, however: the medieval aspect of Vienna was to be obliterated and a modern township created.

The emperor's decision had been prompted by the fast rise of industry and commerce, demanding rapid transportation of goods within the capital. Yet the historic heart of the city, the first district, was not to lose its distinctive features. Although the imperial castle forfeited its function after the end of the monarchy, part of it became the official suite of the president of the republic. The Chancellery and Foreign Office were opposite its entrance, in the building on Ballhausplatz where Metternich had conducted the country's affairs. The other ministries were also still located in that area. Thus the inner city has remained to this day the centre of government, as of gastronomy and fashion.

From the early sixties many of the *nouveaux riches* as well as longer-established financiers, factory owners and great businessmen began to build sumptuous private dwellings, flaunting their wealth, along the new Ringstrasse, generously designed and planted with trees. Not only local government and parliament, but also the arts were now to be splendidly housed in palaces of the most varied design. A neo-Gothic town hall, a neo-classical parliament, and several richly decorated, but chiefly neo-Renaissance palaces for the theatre, the opera, concert halls, museums of old and modern art and a science museum were put up during that decade. Historicism was rife – a style intended not so much to copy, as to incorporate elements of ancient architecture in new design; paraphrase rather than pastiche was the order of the day.

It was only after the ramparts fell and many people and institutions moved beyond the Ring for greater space and comfort, that the various Viennese districts acquired their modern characteristics. In the third, Landstrasse, many foreign embassies and legations were now established; the great town houses of Prince Metternich and the counts of Razumovsky and Salm, formerly considered to be on the outskirts, now seemed close to the centre of town. Yet the lower aristocracy settled mainly in the fourth district, Wieden, near the great palaces of the Schwarzenberg princes and the Belvedere, built in the days of Leopold I for his greatest general and victor over the Turks, Prince Eugene of Savoy.

While the affluent upper-middle classes now took up residence along and around the Ring, the comfortable merchants, professional classes and civil servants occupied the fifth to the eighth districts. The ninth became more and more the home of academics, especially medical scientists and practising physicians. Towards the Gürtel and beyond, the new industrial proletariat was shamelessly crowded into joyless and insanitary multi-storeyed living-quarters. Farther afield, in the elegant suburbia of Hietzing in the west and Döbling in the north, and at the foot or on the slopes of the Vienna woods, many villas rose during the last decade of the century to house prosperous artists and writers, higher government employees and the retired rich.

So lastly to the second district: situated on the left bank of the Danube Canal, the Leopoldstadt was the traditional home of the Jews, dating back to the reign of Ferdinand II, who opened it to the poor majority of them, while some Jewish court financiers were given special permission to live within the city gates. From the late eighteenth century wealthy, 'tolerated' and soon enough 'emancipated' Jews were allowed the same privilege. But it was in the Leopoldstadt that in the eighties, and again after 1918, many Jewish immigrants from the distant Carpathian provinces of Galicia and Bucovina, driven out first by pogroms, then by new rulers, joined their impecunious orthodox brethren. The progress of some of them, socially as well as topographically, from the Leopoldstadt to the ninth district, Alsergrund, and finally to the noble precincts of the inner city, will be traced later on. Since so much of Austrian cultural life up to 1938 was the product of Jewish talent, the part played by longer-established and – to a much smaller extent – newly arrived Jews in Vienna needs a very particular scrutiny.

3

THE RISE OF
THE BOURGEOISIE

Few accounts of Austria in the early years of the nineteenth century are as outspoken or as credible as that of Mme de Staël. In her book *De l'Allemagne*, describing her visit to Vienna in 1808, she remarks that the northern Germans accuse Austria of neglecting the sciences and letters. Although she agrees with that verdict, she is not inclined to attribute such failings to censorship alone. 'It is such a calm country,' she says, 'a country where everyday comforts are so tranquilly secured to all classes of citizens, that here one does not think much about intellectual pleasures.' While the principal interest of the monarchy seemed to lie in military exploits, in her view, the Austrian nation was devoted mainly to repose and to the *douceurs de la vie*. Genius does not emerge from such conditions, for 'in the midst of society genius is a pain and an interior fever'. Since there is little wish to suffer for greatness, 'in Austria many excellent things may be found, but very few really superior people'.

Coming from France, where the arts were much appreciated in aristocratic circles, Mme de Staël especially criticized the fact that in Vienna *les nobles* and the men of letters did not mix. Few books were read in the great houses to which she was invited and no writers were received. 'It results from that separation of classes that the literary people lack grace and the fashionable people rarely receive instruction.' In short: 'Society does not, as in France, serve to develop the *esprit* or to inspire it; it allows nothing in the head but vacuity and noise, so that the majority of the most spirited men in the country take good care to remove themselves from it: only the women shine here, and one is surprised at the *esprit* they possess, despite the kind of life they lead.'

It was in the salons of two women, then, that Mme de Staël encountered a measure of the intelligent discourse and literary interests she was used to at home, and craved abroad. For our purpose, the identity of these women is significant: they were a Jewish baroness and a suburban bourgeoise. Doubtless, of course, the 'most famous woman in Europe' at that time, 'Mistress to an Age', as a recent biographer called her, preferred to move in the highest Austrian circles – those of the princes of Ligne, Liechtenstein and Lubomirski or the counts Wrbna and Zamoiski, in some of whose private theatres she starred in her own plays. Nevertheless she found more congenial company and conversation in the palace of Fanny von Arnstein, soon to be hostess to most of the luminaries at the Vienna Congress. Far outside the city gates, at 27 Alserstrasse, the much more modest abode of the writer Caroline Pichler, she witnessed the emergence of a cultural patrician class hitherto unknown in Vienna.

Mme Pichler, though married to a commoner, had been born with a small handle to her name – her father was Franz von Greiner, a senior civil servant who was knighted by Joseph II for his help in preparing that emperor's Edict of Tolerance. This excellent man, a scion of humanism and the Enlightenment, may serve as an early example of the Austrian bureaucratic nobility which added another rung to the social ladder. At the same time he was the embodiment of those well-meaning and intelligent middle classes who now, in the 'bourgeois century', began to rise in the world. His daughter, too, was firmly middle-class in her life style and outlook. She wrote a great many books, among them the novel *Agathokles*, which led to a correspondence with Goethe; she was a friend of one of the most famous women of the German Romantic age, Dorothea Schlegel; and she had a sharp tongue. Of the statuesque Henriette Herz, another Berlin figure, she remarked that one had better look at her through a diminishing-glass, and of Napoleon I that he had the 'well-nourished face of a prelate'. When Germaine de Staël, in her turn, condescendingly called Mme Pichler *la muse du faubourg*, it was with the haughtiness of a royal banker's daughter come up in the *beau monde*.

The kind of literary salon this suburban muse established at Alserstrasse had few successors in the course of the nineteenth and indeed the twentieth centuries. Those families of higher civil servants and the ever-widening professional class who with growing wealth and influence applied them-selves to the arts, were mostly devoted to music. In the Biedermeier, gatherings like the *Schubertiades* were frequent, when a famous composer played from his work and amateur singers performed his songs to a circle of admiring friends, some of whom might be painters or graphic artists. The Viennese, given more to sensual than to intellectual pursuits, as we have seen, were similarly inclined in their aesthetic taste. On the whole, they fought shy of serious writing, finding it easier to peruse a visual masterpiece or to fall back on their inborn musicality. This enabled them, guided by a creative genius, to plumb the depths of their own emotions without having to verbalize them and thereby render them all too real.

It was left to the 'People of the Scripture' in their midst to revere writers and the written word. Having been forbidden by their God to make graven images, the Jews from ancient times had poured their pictorial fantasies into language, which they enriched with metaphors and tropological figures of speech. Karl Kraus, the satirist, was to call himself a dweller in the 'old house of language'. Thus, almost inevitably, literature and philosophical thought were often fostered in the homes of wealthy families, baptized or loyal to their faith, who since Joseph II's reign had begun to enter Viennese society. Many of those who had benefited from the Edict of Tolerance, 116 of them in fact, had been ennobled before March 1848, mostly for their services as suppliers to the army or as court financiers. Another 330 people of Jewish descent – industrialists, philanthropists or men of science – were created 'nobles', knights or even barons before the monarchy was out. Quite a few of them married into the old Austrian aristocracy and disappeared in that privileged crowd. Others, together with the rising Christian middle class, for a short but immensely productive time formed those theatre audiences, opera- and concert-goers, gallery visitors and constant readers of classical and contemporary writing who are indispensable to an active cultural life.

One of the first to stimulate that life – if indirectly – by assembling in her house men and women of talent and intelligence, was Fanny von Arnstein, who had befriended Mme de Staël in 1808. She was born in Berlin, the daughter of Friedrich II's Master of the Mint, Daniel Itzig, who headed a great and gifted Jewish dynasty. As a young girl, she had sat at the feet of the philosopher Moses Mendelssohn, harbinger of Jewish emancipation in Germany, and had admired Gotthold Ephraim Lessing, that country's most enlightened mind. When Fanny went to Vienna to marry the son of another court financier, she brought to the languidly elegant imperial residence some of the intellectual sharpness and vitality of her native city. As her husband rose socially, becoming in 1798 the first unconverted Jew in Austria to be granted the title of baron, Fanny's salon grew ever more splendid. Its reputation for being the foremost meeting place of eminent social, political and artistic figures soon attracted every distinguished visitor to Vienna, including, at the turn of the century, Lord Nelson and Lady Hamilton.

Keeping in touch with her family and early friends, Baroness Arnstein drew to her house great German writers such as the brothers Schlegel and August von Varnhagen, husband of the famous Rahel who had once herself united princes, scholars and romantic poets in her attic in Berlin. In Fanny's palace in Vienna at the time of the Vienna Congress, the Prussian statesmen Humboldt and Hardenberg met the Duke of Wellington, Prince Metternich, Cardinal Consalvi and the Counts Capo d'Istria and

Pozzo di Borgo. Much as she enjoyed these brilliant *assemblées,* Fanny still preferred smaller and more intimate occasions, such as when the Swedish diplomat Karl Gustav von Brinckmann, a less elevated but witty conversationalist, entertained her with recollections of his visits to Goethe, Schiller and Fichte or the Shakespeare translators Schlegel and Tieck.

No wonder that her only child Henriette, married to the Jewish Baron Pereira, with whom she adopted the Catholic faith, was to follow in her footsteps by founding her own salon in the quieter Biedermeier days. Courted in her youth by the gifted poet Theodor Körner, who fell in the war against Napoleon, as an elderly lady Henriette was hostess to the writers Grillparzer and Stifter, to Goethe's eccentric daughter-in-law Ottilie and to many actors, painters and composers, among them Franz Liszt. The informality of these gatherings has been stressed by Adalbert Stifter in a study of Vienna's artistic circles:

Everyone may come and go as they wish. There is no etiquette of sitting, standing, greeting. It is the law of this salon to have no law; one is by no means tortured there with literature; at no hour or day are there readings or recitals ... there is completely casual social freedom ... it is an honour to be invited – not for greatness of spirit alone, but for such fair behaviour and restraint that one may be sure the new member will be no alien element in the existing harmony.

It is a perfect picture of the bourgeois salon around the middle of the century. By that time, a number of Viennese families, formerly of modest means, had acquired wealth and high standing through the manufacture of or international trade in textiles, leather goods, glass, machinery, musical instruments and other typical Austrian industries. They too began to give larger receptions with cultural aims, and to become patrons of the arts. But the preferences of this new upper-middle class did not differ from those of the lower-middle class in pre-March days: if it had been chamber music then, now it was musical soirées. These people, often descended from simple workmen, like the piano-manufacturer Ludwig Bösendorfer, had music in their blood but little time for sophistication. Their intelligence was instinctive, and their feeling no less deep for remaining unexpressed. They were good, though not shrewd, businessmen and had been carried up on the wave of prosperity following the Industrial Revolution. To them the sixties were a decade of complete confidence and boundless enterprise, an era of founders and builders, known in retrospect as the *Gründerzeit.*

The new bourgeoisie was no isolated phenomenon in Europe, but it was unique in Vienna, which had known nothing like it before. Some of its sources of wealth went back to the days of Maria Theresia, when the first textile factories had been erected in Lower Austria, not far from the capital. Its true rise, however, was not set in motion until after the Napoleonic Wars. Then the Viennese district of Neubau became a centre for the urban silk industry and, because of its new affluence, acquired the nickname *Brillantengrund*, or 'field of diamonds'. One manufacturer, Johann Blümel, for instance, moved there from Upper Austria in 1814, setting up a production line of woollen shawls which he exported to as far away as Russia and the United States. Although the original factory collapsed in the mid-sixties when shawls went out of fashion, by then the sons of old Blümel had made their way in other professions and industries, one having become a banker, another a brewer and the third president of a railway company.

There were dozens of similar families who now formed the backbone of Viennese society, as the nobility slowly withdrew from public life into their own closed circles. Some worthies in the world of industry, trade and commerce were raised to the lower ranks of the aristocracy, as a number of Jewish financiers had been – the von Arthabers, the von Schoellers and the Barons Haas for example. But many of them held on to their bourgeois status, such as the brewer Dreher, the textile manufacturer Hutterstrasser, the braid- and lace-maker Lenneis, the art dealer and cartographer Artaria, the caterer of Lucullan groceries and wine-store-owner Stiebitz, and Fritz, the baker of fine bread and pastries. They were all highly respected, full of civic pride and contemptuous of feudalism, which in this new liberal age seemed to be played out.

For liberalism, as it was understood at the time, had at last come to Austria after Königgrätz and the subsequent reforms. It had been bitterly fought for in 1848, but now that it had arrived it had taken on a different, peaceful and tranquil face. After a while the ordinary citizen just took it for granted, accepting the easing of pressure from above, the loosening of governmental control, simply as part and parcel of the general improvement in his life style, never to be revoked. It was mostly the Jewish component of the new bourgeoisie which recognized in liberalism a precious and precarious gift to be watchfully guarded and, more than that, an ideology constantly to be strengthened by theory and argument. As the first potential victims of its loss, they were liberalism's fervent supporters. In view of the nationalist tendencies now threatening that multi-ethnic state which had finally given them full equality with the rest of its inhabitants, they were the empire's most loyal citizens.

'The liberal bourgeoisie, strongly interspersed with Jews, was indeed the last self-realization of a universal Austria, before it foundered on traditionalism on the one hand, national and social unrest on the other.'

Thus wrote Otto Schulmeister, a prominent Viennese journalist, in nostalgic retrospect twelve years ago. Yet it cannot be denied that it was the Jews themselves, integrated as they were into the German-speaking part of Austria's population, who sided with the Austrian 'Germans' in their arrogant claim to political and cultural hegemony in the Habsburg realm. There were many reasons for this paradoxical attitude. One was the symbiosis in which the central European Jews, the Ashkenazim, though periodically persecuted or evicted, had lived with the German people since the Middle Ages. The very names of Vienna's oldest Jewish families pointed to their places of origin along the Neckar and the Rhine: Wertheimer, Oppenheimer, Arnsteiner, Bamberger, Bacharach, Wetzlar – all indicating townships to which their ancestors could be traced, sometimes five centuries back and more.

Another reason was the deep regard, even reverence, in which they held German cultural achievements. Breaking the fetters of orthodoxy as Moses Mendelssohn had done during the Enlightenment, they instantly began to absorb German philosophy and literature. Their scholarship and bookishness, which they had hitherto applied to the single-minded and convoluted study of the Old Testament and the Talmud, was now turned outwards to the works of Kant, Lessing, Goethe, Schiller and, lastly, Heine. The brilliant writings of their own kinsman took their place, bound in leather and imprinted with gold, next to the German classics on the bookshelves in every cultured home.

If Caroline Pichler's literary salon was not succeeded by others of similar background, the emancipated Jewish families nevertheless took emergent Austrian writers to their hearts. Of the first wave in the Biedermeier not only Grillparzer and Stifter, but also lesser though amiable talents such as Baron Feuchtersleben or Karl von Holtei, on many Fridays graced Henriette Pereira-Arnstein's 'artists' soirées'. Musicians and painters were well looked after at the Arthabers', who not only invited Waldmüller, Danhauser, Kupelwieser and Fendi, but also bought their early works, and at the Miller von Aichholzes', great patrons of the Society of the Friends of Music and, in later years, of Brahms. Donizetti stayed with them on his visit to Vienna. Fewer such houses were open to 'scribblers', as men of letters were often known. When the second group of outstanding writers appeared on the scene in the eighties and nineties, they discovered the coffee-house as a place for informal and casual meetings. But at least one of them, Hugo von Hofmannsthal, was drawn into a circle of families (mostly interrelated) of literary bent, characteristic of a remarkable development.

From 1848, when most professions were thrown open to them, many

Above *Franziska (Fanny) Freiin von Arnstein (portrait by Guérin).*

Above right *The drawing-room of Gustav Pick, creator of the Fiakerlied.*

Right *Henriette Freiin von Pereira-Arnstein (portrait by Kriehuber).*

Above *Josephine von Wertheimstein*.

Left *Baroness Sophie Todesco*.

Above *Flower corso along the great alley of the Prater, 1900.*

Opposite above *Tableau vivant depicting 'The Alpine Song of our Homeland' at the Palais Todesco, early 1880s.*

Opposite below left and right *Two ladies of the bourgeoisie (the author's grandmothers Laura and Melanie) at their summer resort early this century.*

Right *An evening at a Prater restaurant.*

members of Jewish families whose wealth was founded on economic activities were now able and eager to devote themselves to intellectual pursuits. A typical example was Theodor Gomperz. His forefathers had lived in Nymwegen around 1600, then had become 'court Jews' in Vienna before moving on to Moravia in the service of the state tobacco monopoly. Theodor arrived in the capital the year after the March revolution to study at Vienna University. He became a disciple of John Stuart Mill whom he visited in England. Back home, he immersed himself in classical philology, wrote a book, *Greek Thinkers*, translated Mill's *System of Logic* and ended up, like his distant cousin Baron Josef Schey and others of his background and generation, as a highly respected teacher at the university which for so long had barred its doors to Jews. His son Heinrich was to follow in his footsteps by becoming a professor of philosophy.

Theodor's elder sisters had married the bankers Leopold von Wertheimstein and Baron Eduard Todesco. In both their houses, one the beautiful villa built by the Arthaber family in the suburb of Döbling, the other a splendid new building on the Ring, the tradition of Fanny von Arnstein's salon and of her daughter's was continued. In the Palais Todesco the young Hofmannsthal read from his poetry and lyrical drama. During Josephine von Wertheimstein's last years, he often stayed for days at the villa in Döbling. There, among other noteworthy company, he met the melancholic poet and novella writer Ferdinand von Saar, who spent long periods in the adjoining guest house. Old Eduard Bauernfeld, whose comedies were no longer in fashion, had recently departed this life there, having been dependent on the lady's generous hospitality like Saar. When she died, Hofmannsthal was heartbroken. It was his first 'grave and grievous experience', as he expressed it in his diary. And to her daughter he wrote: 'She dreamed more richly and beautifully than countless people, perhaps all of us.'

The days of the 'golden house', as Saar had called it, were over. He himself, a minor writer still renowned in Austria but otherwise unknown, later died by his own hand. The great salon of the Liberal age had ended some time after Liberalism itself. The Liberal era, comparable in its humanity to the short-lived central European Enlightenment a century earlier, had in fact lasted hardly more than two decades. Moreover, at its peak this epoch of economic *laissez-faire*, financial aggrandizement and political ease had been badly shaken in its complacency. On 9 May 1873, a week after Emperor Franz Joseph had inaugurated, in the presence of several crowned heads and foreign dignitaries, Vienna's World Exhibition – a glorious tribute to the wonders of industrial growth, which during that year attracted over seven million visitors to the Austrian capital – the stock exchange crashed. Supported by an all too optimistic Liberal party and press, speculation in real estate and banking had over-reached itself. On Black Friday shares dropped by up to seventy per cent; thousands lost their savings, and tens of thousands their jobs. Suicides abounded. The economy took years to recover. By 1883 Liberal Vienna seemed to be back in its stride, and in that year Crown Prince Rudolf, at the opening of the first 'Electric Exhibition', poetically predicted: 'A sea of light radiates from this city, and new progress will go forth from here.'

Yet the worm had entered into the fruits of prosperity. Within six years the crown prince – like so many of his seemingly light-hearted compatriots – had ended his own life, and soon after, Austrian politics became subject to that polarization the consequences of which would so bloodily erupt in the First Republic. If Liberalism had been anti-clerical and rationalistic, in accordance with a tolerant, undogmatic and secular-minded bourgeoisie, now the lower-middle classes were being indoctrinated in the name of religion or racial prejudice. At the same time the new industrial proletariat, made conscious of its social and legal disadvantages in this constitutional monarchy, decided to unite. Both these classes had been discriminated against by an electoral law based on voters' income. Most members of the lower-middle classes and all the workers were therefore disenfranchised owing to their small tax returns, and excluded from representation in local government.

In the name of Christian Socialism and the 'man in the street', Karl Lueger, a handsome and determined politician, now successfully fought the Liberal establishment in the town hall. In 1888 he and other organizers founded their party. Only nine years later, having in the meantime been elected mayor of Vienna five times, and indeed having run the city's affairs, Lueger received the emperor's confirmation of his appointment. These Christian Socialists, opposed to a bourgeoisie which was largely supported by, and to a considerable degree composed of, people of Jewish descent, were reverting to the old Maria-Theresian anti-Semitism based on religious grounds. On the other hand, a movement calling itself German Nationalism, and led by the fanatical Jew-baiter Georg von Schönerer, based its whole ideology on purity of race – thereby both forestalling and paving the way for twentieth-century National Socialism. In Vienna, melting-pot of so many peoples, this would seem a ludicrous undertaking. Yet so strong were the emotions aroused that adherents of that creed did not mind being represented, in public and later in parliament, by men whose origin and even whose names were undoubtedly Slav.

The Social Democrats had begun to form their cadres earlier on. A first demonstration of Viennese workers came about in 1869. After years of setbacks they were able to found their own party at Hainfeld not far from Vienna in 1889. A year later their first May Day procession took place, supported by the Socialist International, which had been created meanwhile. Before the century was out the Social Democrats passed a most important resolution at their party meeting in Brünn. They declared themselves in favour of a 'Programme of Nationalities', thereby stressing the multi-ethnic structure of the Habsburg monarchy and, paradoxically, remaining its fervent supporters. Again, as they had done during the March revolution, Jewish reformers played a decisive part. In 1848, the physician Adolf Fischhof had been among the leaders of the rebellion, and became a champion of liberal thought ever after, proving that Liberalism did not rest merely on the shoulders of capitalist Jews. Now the physician Victor Adler united the Socialists and founded their party paper. The ideologists of Austro-Marxism, as it developed in the next century, contained a large Jewish contingent.

Liberal Jews took a long time to realize that their admiration for 'Germanness' had backfired on them, and that they would be better off supporting a multi-national Austria with the new Social Democrats. Some never did. In 1934, Heinrich, son of Theodor Gomperz, signed a declaration of protest against the Christian Socialist authoritarian regime together with nationalist, soon to be National Socialist, professors at Vienna University. His father had been among those appalled when, in the last quarter of the century, their integration into Vienna's social fabric began to be threatened by an influx of eastern Jews. While their community had earned the respect of its fellow-citizens, first through its business acumen, then through its intellectual and artistic achievements, all the while practising more or less the same bourgeois virtues and conventions as the rest, these newcomers brought with them an alienness in life style and outlook long abandoned by Vienna's long-established and emancipated Jewish families.

Poorer Jews had always lived in the second district, the Leopoldstadt, holding on to their orthodox rites and disdaining any form of assimilation. However, as the generations went by, more and more of their sons looked for material and spiritual advancement in other districts of Vienna, moving to the ninth to be near the university and the company of academics, or to the first, where the well-to-do merchants occupied special quarters. Now the ranks of those remaining in the Leopoldstadt were swelled by thousands of immigrants from Polish and Russian *Shtetls* – mostly pathetic, haunted people fleeing from the Poles' growing hostility and the pogroms conducted periodically by the Russian soldiery. Many of their forebears had settled in Poland since the eleventh century, coming from Germany where the populace, at the instigation of fervent crusaders, had threatened their lives. As early as 1264 the Polish King Boleslav the Pious took them under his protection. Others had gone the same way centuries later, still safeguarded by tolerant Polish kings such as Sigismund I.

Most of them had remained in the pale within walls which, though they were imposed on them, were also welcomed by religious leaders anxious for their flock to refrain from too much contact with the outside world. Few of their progeny had ever been to central or western Europe. As in other places of refuge, after their arrival in Vienna they held on to their ancient traditions and rituals. When Adolf Hitler lived in poverty in the second district for a short time around 1907, the sight of these utterly foreign, archaic-looking figures in their caftans, felt hats, beards and ringlets seemed to confirm the race theories he had picked up from Schönerer and the even more odious Lanz von Liebenfels. The future Führer and mass murderer never entered the house of any of those Jews on the higher rung of the hierarchy, who by now were almost indistinguishable from their compatriot peers.

Left to themselves, the often uncouth but just as often highly imaginative and scholarly immigrants from the east would have followed the same path of slow but inevitable integration. In the little time left to them before Jew-baiting once more became the deadly scourge it had been in medieval times, they helped increase the hatred now being whipped up against anyone of their creed or origin. When a son of the enlightened Jewish bourgeoisie, dismayed by the growth of anti-Semitism, contemplated return to the Holy Land as the only remedy, he met with disbelief, even hostility, within his own class. Until the rise of National Socialism Theodor Herzl's followers were eastern Jews, and Israel's founding fathers were almost entirely refugees, or descendants of refugees, from Poland and Russia.

During the *fin de siècle*, while Austria's foreign affairs gave no particular cause for concern, conflicting forces inside the state were hardening their fronts against each other. Pan-Germanic, Pan-Slavistic and Italian Irredentist movements were preparing to tear the Dual Monarchy apart. In pursuing their different aims, parties of the right and left led the population in ever more diverging directions. On the surface, little of this was visible as yet. While the empire, at least outwardly, still seemed intact, while prosperity looked as though it might last, and the efforts of socialism, in this or that shape or form, were expected to improve the plight of the urban lower classes, conditions were right for much pent-up talent to erupt. Thus, in a deceptive atmosphere of calm, the 'Holy Spring' began.

4

IDYLL, PAGEANTRY AND THE GREAT INDOORS

Now that the historical and social pre-conditions for Vienna's most remarkable epoch have been set out, one last look must be cast back at some very diverse, even self-contradictory, propensities of its inhabitants, which found reflection in the arts. High-level political changes are known to transform the way of life of all strata within a community, to create new fashions, even radically to alter general taste. Thus, once the great drama of the Napoleonic Wars and their magnificent dénouement at the Vienna Congress was played out, the Austrian people, aware that they were no longer the focus of European politics, devoted themselves to the pleasures of nature and the intimacy of domestic life.

Idyll and introspection now suffused music and literature, painting and architectural design. Until the Period of the Founders, beginning in the late 1860s, small was beautiful, and cosiness – for want of a better word for *Gemütlichkeit* – seemed the most desirable climate and frame of mind. Picnics in the Vienna woods; a late afternoon spent in an inn among the sloping vineyards, watching the sun set and the lamps of the city below light up; a little piano-playing in one's own drawing-room before retiring early: these were the joys of the Biedermeier and for some time afterwards. Industrial growth led, as we have seen, to a sharp rise in population and the widening of the city boundaries, and also renewed the thirst of the Viennese for ostentation, pageantry and display.

To take part in a great spectacle, they were willing to put up even with the role of the vanquished watching a triumphant show of victory. When Napoleon had entered the emperor's city and temporarily usurped not only his castle but also the feast day of the Assumption of the Blessed Virgin to celebrate his own birthday, they streamed out of town to Schönbrunn to gather under his balcony. To the sound of church bells, the booming of big guns, banquets, illuminations and parades of French soldiery they cheered and shouted. Napoleon knew what to think of that. 'Ils crient toujours,' he commented drily, if not contemptuously. Thus they would shout their delirious welcome to Hitler in 1938, to the Second

Republic's democratic government, which had obtained a State Treaty for them in 1955, and to Pope John Paul II who came to visit them in 1983 – and all on the same spot, the vast Heldenplatz or 'Square of the Heroes', overlooked by the two enormous equestrian monuments erected to Prince Eugene and the Archduke Charles in about 1860. For heroism was a fluctuating concept, and civil courage a rare luxury.

It so happened that on 3 July 1866, the very day that saw Bismarck's army victorious in the bloody battle of Königgrätz, a great popular carousal took place in the Prater, the large amusement park on the fringe of town. When news of the disaster reached the capital, it filtered out to the revellers. Yet none of them thought of abandoning food or drink, and nobody rose to exhort them to do so in view of lost lives and national dishonour. In Schiller's trilogy on the Thirty Years' War, when someone mentions Wallenstein's generosity towards a beaten traitor, the general replies:

> In Vienna they had rented well before
> The windows and the balconies on the way
> To watch him on his cart go to the gallows.
> I could disgracefully have lost the battle
> But this the Viennese will not forgive me for,
> That I had cheated them out of a spectacle.

If Königgrätz had not managed to deprive the Viennese of an evening's merry-making, its aftermath provided for more glorious spectacles than had been seen in the city since the baroque age. Though by no means abandoned, pastoral pleasures were often interrupted or superseded by displays of pageantry based on both the sacred and the secular calendar. One of the regular ones up to the First World War was the annual procession through the streets of the inner city on Corpus Christi Day, when the emperor, bareheaded and on foot like everyone else, followed the high clergy with the Eucharist carried under a canopy. Priests in ornate vestments, students in their flashy attire, and regimental detachments in full fig blotted out the vision of a pale corpse being taken from the cross and laid in its grave. The Catholic ritual, while living out the horrors of divine and human martyrdom, makes up for it by unfolding all the terrestrial splendour which gilt, colour, candles and incense can afford.

The story of how Hans Makart, a small dark-haired and bearded painter with gigantic ambitions, aroused the *folie de grandeur* of the eighties will be told in a later chapter. Suffice it to say at this point that his evocation of the *Zeitgeist* of the Renaissance culminated in a masked parade round the Ring on the occasion of the imperial couple's silver wedding in 1879.

Makart himself headed the pageant, a minute figure on horseback, clad in a glowing red costume which recalled cinquecento Mantua or Florence. The painter died young only five years later. But in the new century, after Franz Joseph's manifold bereavements, another procession wended its way before him on the sixtieth jubilee of his accession. The old monarch, only just recovered from a serious illness, had to stand and watch for three hours the festivities that his loyal subjects inflicted on him.

Surrounded by eighty members of the imperial house, with the smallest archdukes and archduchesses kneeling in the first row, he was confronted by the historic rise of his dynasty. The first to ride past was his ancestor Rudolf of Habsburg, impersonated by the imposing Count August Eltz, and attended by nobles chosen from the oldest families in the realm, Liechtenstein and Fürstenberg, Auersperg and Trauttmansdorff, Hardegg, Harrach and Herberstein. A great-grandson of Field Marshal Radetzky represented Rudolf the Founder, that poet, visionary and forger of ancient documents about the Austrian dynasty, who among other things had invented the title *archidux* for everyone of Habsburg kin. The Emperor Maximilian I, Europe's 'last knight', appeared in the shape of Baron Georg Franckenstein, later to become Austrian Minister at the Court of St James and finally, when Hitler had annihilated his country's identity, a British knight by the grace of George VI. The pageant ended with floats of *tableaux vivants* showing the multinational aspect of the monarchy: 'Germans' and Poles, Ruthenians, Romanians, Magyárs and Italians in characteristic displays.

This apotheosis of Franz Joseph's reign in 1908 was the last flare-up in the evening glow. The next occasion for pomp and circumstance was a sombre one: the obsequies of the emperor on a foggy November day eight years after and in the midst of the war, when a long cortège, witnessed by the present writer as a small child, slowly moved along the Ring until it came to a halt at the Capuchin Vault where all Austrian monarchs are laid to rest. Gone was the memory of those rollicking days when Princess Pauline Metternich, *maîtresse de plaisir* of the declining empire and as ugly as she was fun-loving, as full of charitable feelings as she was of panache, organized events like the 'flower corso' on the great chestnut-lined avenue in the Prater. On each May Day the upper crust had driven by, up and down the road, in carriages bursting with floral decorations, while the populace lined the way, pointing out to each other members of the imperial family and the high nobility. When the Labour Movement began to claim the very same date for its annual demonstrations, one of the conflicting forces which tore the old fabric apart became evident.

There had been countless ballrooms in which, at carnival time, dances and masked entertainments were held on every social level – from the 'Washerwomen's Ball' and 'Cabmen's Ball' to the most exclusive entertainments at court. The Irish tenor O'Kelly, a friend of Mozart, had described, as early as 1786, the Bacchanalia of a Viennese *Fasching* – 'the waltzing from ten o'clock at night until seven in the morning, in a constant turmoil, tiring to see and hear'. And, waltzing to the sound of Lehár's *The Merry Widow* – Hitler's favourite piece of light music – the monarchy went to its doom. Yet, in the first hectic years after the Great War, as soon as the worst misery and starvation had ended, masked balls and *redoutes* were to flourish as never before, their participants trying to live down another more far-reaching defeat than that of 1866 to the loosening rhythms of the shimmy, the charleston and the tango.

A small and idyllic inn, a quiet walk along a stream between vineyards, might inspire an introverted composer to the most deep-felt piece of music. The splendid pageantry devised by Makart or Pauline Metternich might find its counterpart in the intoxicating colours of paintings by the master of ceremonies himself, as well as later in the golden, glowing visions of Klimt. A new generation of writers, emerging in the late eighties and nineties, had recourse to neither. Gathered around a slightly older man, the apostle of 'modern art' Hermann Bahr, they grew out of another fertile atmosphere, that of the Vienna coffee-house. Like the legendary Caffè Greco or the Rosati in Rome, the Deux Magots in Paris, the Café Royal in London, at least for a while, the Arco in Prague, the American in Amsterdam and the New York in Budapest, the Café Griensteidl harboured and fostered literary talent. It played a decisive part in the development of two of the most eminent Austrian writers, not only in their day but also in our own: Arthur Schnitzler and Hugo von Hofmannsthal.

The history of the Vienna coffee-house goes back to the second Turkish siege in 1683, when a Croat named Kulsczycki is said to have opened the first such establishment near St Stephen's Cathedral, using coffee beans left behind by the Turks. Under Joseph II an Italian named Milani had introduced in his café all the amenities later sought by habitués of that kind of 'home from home': billiard tables, playing-cards, chess-sets and draughts-boards as well as the official newspaper, *Vienna Diarium*. 'You may study there,' wrote a contemporary, 'you may play, chat, sleep, negotiate, blather about politics, haggle, canvass, devise plots, intrigues and entertainments, read papers and journals.' The Venetian coffee-houses lovingly described by Goldoni were the model. Milani, in white tails, a well-worn tricorne on his head, dusty pigtail dangling, was present all the time –

'vainly begging, pleading, cursing *corpo di Dio maledetto*, but to no avail; nobody thinks of leaving'. The habit of sitting over one or two cups of coffee from the early afternoon until closing-time, well after midnight, prevailed into the First Austrian Republic and beyond.

During the nineteenth century each coffee-house acquired a particular purpose and flavour, being frequented mainly by politicians or by writers, by painters or by merchants, by the idle and rich or by the luckless who, in the harsh eastern winters of the city, would otherwise have frozen in their homes. The main attraction, apart from congenial company, was the newspapers, local and foreign, which were usually piled on a large table or hung on bamboo racks, soon to pass from hand to hand. None of the local papers, not even the *Neue Freie Presse*, of which more later, was comparable in news, views or style to a truly cosmopolitan journal like the old *Figaro* or *Times*. But they satisfied the constant Viennese appetite for information and gossip, that unquenchable curiosity about their fellow beings which had prompted the emperor Franz I to have a dossier made on every one of his citizens, less for reasons of political surveillance than for him to browse through whenever he had time.

The 'Coffee Cave' of a man called Kramer, a dark hole in which newspapers from Hamburg, Frankfurt, Bayreuth, Cologne, and also from Hungary and even England could be perused, was the first of those *Cafés Megalomania* where budding writers encouraged each others' talents, even if nobody else did. During the Biedermeier period, it was followed by the famous Neuner's, habitual meeting place of Grillparzer, Raimund and their contemporaries. Before the March revolution, this was a hotbed of rebellious ideas where the fighting physician L.A. Frankl conspired with the liberal-minded Count Auersperg, who wrote satirical pieces and poetry under the pseudonym Anastasius Grün. Its most notable successor was the Griensteidl, founded on the ground floor of the Palais Herberstein, a stone's throw from the imperial castle, by a pharmacist in 1847. It came into its own during the next decades, when the first seeds of Socialism were planted there by Heinrich Oberwinder and Hermann Hartung, two friends and followers of Ferdinand Lassalle.

This coffee-house continued to play an important role as a place for ideological exchange, as when the initiator, or at least unifier, of the Social Democratic Party, Victor Adler, played tarot in the card-room with the politicians Hainisch and Pernerstorfer, until their views became too diametrically opposed for further social contact. In the same café sat Georg von Schönerer, precursor of Hitler and founder of the Greater German Party. Other rooms harboured theatre people, especially the director and main actors of the Burgtheater. Yet those who perpetuated the name of the Griensteidl were the writers who sat at the feet of Hermann Bahr. Born in Linz, provincial capital of Upper Austria, in 1863, this gifted journalist had been to Paris, picked up new trends and in a book published in 1890 proclaimed the end of naturalism, declaring Paul Bourget's neo-romanticism to be the order of the day.

In the name of *Die Moderne*, modernism pure and simple, he became the 'drummer and barker' of a group of gifted young people later known as *Jung-Wien*. Apart from several major figures, they included some lesser writers such as Felix Dörmann or Leopold von Andrian, who in a sense were more typical of the emerging *Zeitgeist* of an elegant decadence than those destined for world fame. At a separate table in the same front room sat a slightly deformed young man with beautiful blue eyes who contributed features to the Vienna press under the pseudonym *Crêpe de Chine*. When the old Palais Herberstein was torn down to make way for a new building, this young man, whose real name was Karl Kraus, wrote the first of his many witty and malicious attacks against one or a number of his contemporaries in an essay called 'The Demolished Literature'. There he lampooned the whole Griensteidl group by counting among their characteristics 'Lack of talent, precociousness, poses, megalomania, suburban girls, cravats, mannerisms, false datives, monocles and secret nerves.' Though far from demolishing Young Vienna, Kraus established himself in this attack as the greatest emerging satirist Austria had known since Nestroy.

The coffee-house existence, which many writers in the imperial city began to lead for some or even most of their lives, later prompted the blood-and-soil ideologues of the Third Reich to condemn them as *Kaffeehausliteraten*. One of the latter, Anton Kuh, may have provoked this contemptuous verdict in his wistful aphorism, 'A *Kaffeehausliterat* is a man who has time to contemplate in a coffee-house on what others do not experience outside.' By the time Anton Kuh, one of Karl Kraus's most effective adversaries, had appeared on the scene, some of the Griensteidl inhabitants, as well as a new generation of journalists and writers, were ensconced in another café, the Central. This was to remain, up to the First World War and slightly beyond, the meeting place of the most distinguished as well as the most eccentric men-of-letters. If the painters of Vienna sporadically gathered in the Café Museum, if the musicians preferred to stay at home at their pianofortes, the poets and scribes were unable to do without each other's company for long, fluctuating daily between the marble-topped tables in the three large rooms of the Central, especially the one with a high cupola known as the *Arkadenhof* or Court of Arcades.

The coffee-house literati, it is true, were mainly of Jewish descent, but, as has been pointed out before, so were most of Austria's considerable authors during the period with which we are here concerned. The collision or, to put it in a more positive way, the coupling of Jewish mind and Viennese soul, of the former's intellectual finesse and the latter's emotional subtlety, of an age-old capacity for suffering and a naïve *joie de vivre*, not least of wit and humour, produced a very singular and unrepeatable mixture. The sons and daughters of old-established Jewish families, and some of the newcomers who were willing to adapt themselves quickly to the Austrian way of life, became nature lovers, sportsmen, addicts of simple pleasures. On the other hand the Austrians who mixed and intermarried with them often became aware of their own natural artistic leanings, feeling able all of a sudden to verbalize their deep-down emotions. Owing to this new amalgam, extraverts and introverts on both sides found themselves communicating with each other. How the imagination can be kindled, how sparks of wit may be aroused by rubbing, as it were, one's spirit against someone else's, was discovered by those frequenting the coffee-house.

If neo-romanticism had been pursued in the Griensteidl, expressionism in Vienna was born in the Central. Among the literati could be seen all manner of cranks and parasites, apostles of healthy living breathing in tobacco fumes for hours, 'Viennese Schopenhauers', 'bank clerks with an ethical background', as the journalist and wit Anton Kuh dubbed them, and young men of the bourgeoisie who had been robbed of any hope in life by the pessimistic philosophy of young Otto Weininger. There were grubby vagrants and involuntary professional starvers who, as legends, entered into the novels of their more successful contemporaries, such as Franz Werfel's *Barbara or Piety*. Many epigrams coined in the Café Central concerned their place of origin. Thus the great critic and essayist Alfred Polgar: 'The Café Central lies on the Viennese degree of latitude at the meridian of loneliness. Its inhabitants are mostly people whose misanthropy is as violent as their need for other people, who want to be alone, but for this purpose need human company.'

Peter Altenberg, a genius of 'small prose', which became a fashion in the Vienna of the early twentieth century, thus described the panacea for any kind of worry or misfortune:

You have troubles, this or that – to the coffee-house!
She can't visit you, for some reason, however plausible – to the coffee-house!
Your boots are torn – coffee-house!
You earn 400 *Kronen* and spend 500 – coffee-house!

You're an employee and would have liked to be a doctor – coffee-house!
You can't find a woman to suit you – coffee-house!
You're inwardly ready for suicide – coffee-house!
You hate and disdain your fellow human beings yet cannot do without them –
    coffee-house!
You're no longer allowed credit anywhere – coffee-house!

In this great haven for escapists from reality and those weary of the world, occasional appearances were put in by men of deeds and action. Freud and the great surgeon Billroth are said to have looked in from time to time, as did the Socialist politicians Victor Adler, Otto Bauer and Karl Renner as well as their opponent Lueger. In pre-war days the Pan-Slavists used to gather in one corner, to plot, as Kuh called it, 'k.k. high treason' – the initials k.k. standing for *kaiserlich-königlich* or imperial-royal – among them the future creators of the republic of Czechoslovakia, Karel Kramár and Thomas Garrigue Masaryk. A Russian conspirator called Bronstein could be seen daily in the chess-room or near the table of the Austro-Marxists, before hurriedly leaving for Switzerland when war broke out. He was later to make world history under the name of Trotsky. When in 1917 Austria's foreign secretary, Count Czernin, was informed of the outbreak of the October Revolution, he put the famous question: 'But who would start a revolution in Russia? Perhaps Herr Bronstein from the Café Central?' To him it seemed no more credible that someone should rise from his chessboard to put an end to the Tsarist empire than that a dynasty should fall which had reigned in Europe for more than five hundred years.

Indeed, the overthrow of the Austrian monarchy began at the Café Central – if Anton Kuh is right. At least, its *habitués* joined the small crowd that started it in November 1918 by demonstrating before the gates of the Diet a little farther along the Herrengasse on the opposite side. A frequent visitor from Prague, the well-known reporter Egon Erwin Kisch, temporarily captured the editorial office of the *Neue Freie Presse*, the ever loyal newspaper read all over the empire from Leitmeritz to Novisad. The Court of Arcades, as Kisch would jokingly describe it later, had beleaguered the paper's building with soldiers and machineguns. And finally the Central itself fell victim to the upheaval, for in the course of events the Viennese intelligentsia moved out and into the newly opened Café Herrenhof.

Some, it is true, still preferred the Café Museum, which had been decorated by the architect Adolf Loos in 1899. Here caricaturists and artistic bohemians had made their home, as did the painters and sculptors of the nearby Secession building. Peter Altenberg, who once, in a literary handbook, had given his address as 'Vienna 1, Café Central', later chose the Museum for his new abode. Writers from abroad on short visits, such as Frank Wedekind, found the mixed company here more acceptable than that at the Herrenhof. And Karl Kraus, who had long before dropped his pen-name and become the scourge not only of sloppy and corrupt journalists but of most immoral or ineffective public figures, having poured scorn on the Café Central now settled down peacefully in the atmosphere created by his friend Loos. Still, it was the Herrenhof where literary history was made in the First Republic. In the midst of economic hardship and political strife, during those twenty short years between the end of the war and the advent of Hitler in Austria, plans doomed from the start were made for a better future, vain hopes were kindled, futile efforts undertaken, idealistic initiatives wasted. More than ever the coffee-house was a place to forget reality, or replace it with an illusory counterpart.

In the front room some of the better-placed civil servants, lawyers or working journalists spent their breaks between office hours or put in an hour's perusal of foreign journals before going home. It was the vast room at the back where a disinherited new generation, children of bourgeois parents deprived of their livelihood or their savings in the war, whiled away their afternoon and evening hours. Some of them were still studying at the university or had gained their much-coveted doctor's degrees, but no jobs were waiting for them, and one article going into print per month was the utmost they could expect to achieve. The small country whose capital Vienna had become no longer needed their brains and talent. There were more than enough of those about. What the First Austrian Republic lacked was not intelligence, but luck.

Even so, the Herrenhof generation behaved, according to the philosopher Vaihinger, 'as if'. They worked on a thesis, as if it were possible to 'habilitate' oneself as a lecturer at the university. They devised a monthly journal, as if a publisher were ready to support it. Action took place solely in their talk round the marble-topped tables. The suspended state of the interim existence in here was all that enabled them to bear the grim life outside the coffee-house doors. The fear of despair or boredom made them invent and tell each other jokes, often brilliant ones. Clowns and cranks were welcome. Many of them made the move from the Central to the Herrenhof without difficulty. Only one, a famous layabout and 'professional starver' by the name of Krzyzanowski, had not survived it. During the transition period he had fallen ill in his rented room. His friends in the Central believed him to be in the Herrenhof, those in the Herrenhof were sure he had stayed behind in the Central. Thus, bereft of any help, he starved to death, to be accompanied to his grave by mourners from both coffee-houses.

No successful author of the twenties or early thirties – and after all, there were quite a few – could afford not to show up at the Herrenhof once in a while. But mostly they remained at home at their desks, for they too had to go on working hard to keep their heads above water. Regulars at the café, however, knew that hard work could not get them much farther than they were. Two of them, neither by any means among the least privileged, might serve as examples. One was Ernst Polak, ex-husband of Kafka's Milena, a man of razor-sharp intelligence and a member of the Schlick-Seminar, the meeting place of the Vienna Circle of logical positivists. The other was Peter Hammerschlag, the most gifted of satirical poets and cabaret writers. When Austria fell to Hitler, Polak succeeded in emigrating to England. Hammerschlag stayed behind, hidden by a friend, until he was found and sent to his death in Poland.

The heroic and pathetic aftermath of Vienna's golden autumn will be considered in the final chapter. This glimpse into the future may have helped to throw into relief a great cultural period cut short by the follies of history.

5

ORNAMENT AND AUSTERITY

Whenever the period in cultural history summarized nowadays by the term 'Vienna around 1900' is analysed and described by learned scholars in Europe and the United States, it is first and foremost the visual arts that receive attention. This is only right and just. For although *art nouveau*, or *Jugendstil* as it was called in Munich and Vienna, made its first appearance in literature in the work of a group of young writers of the *fin de siècle*, its time of birth is usually connected with the 'secession', in March 1897, of nineteen painters and architects led by Gustav Klimt.

Their home until then had been the Künstlerhaus (art institute), founded in 1861, at the time of the beginning of Vienna's magnificent expansion and the building of its Ringstrasse, that tree-lined *via triumphalis* where edifices in the Greek, Gothic and Renaissance manner were being erected under the benign eye of the emperor, and with his generous funding. All those who designed the new layout of the city – not only the splendid houses going up everywhere and their interior decoration, but also the monuments raised in strategic positions to Maria Theresia, some valiant warlords and a few eminent writers – were members of the Künstlerhaus. But it was its sometime president, the painter Hans Makart, mentioned earlier as the originator of Vienna's great masked parade in celebration of the imperial silver wedding in 1879, who gave his imprint to the period.

The eighties, known in retrospect as the 'Makart decade', were concluded by his pageant. There appeared in sumptuous Renaissance costume not merely Austrian nobles, but also merchants and traders whose businesses still exist, conducted by their descendants, or at least bearing their names – among them the goldsmith Köchert, the art dealer Artaria, the purveyor of tea and delicacies Schönbichler and the two prime confectioners, Demel and Gerstner. Makart was a master of portraiture whose talent in that field has only recently been fully recognized. But mainly he composed gigantic canvases filled with likenesses of Viennese beauties in the guise of the Venetian Caterina Cornaro or of Flemish ladies hailing *The Entry of Charles v into Antwerp*. Most importantly, it was Makart's personal taste and life style which dominated those of Vienna's society at that time. Interiors overladen with carved and inlaid furniture, fringed plush tablecloths and heavy draperies, bibelots and bric-à-brac, thickly encrusted vases filled with the famous 'Makart bouquets' (composed of peacock feathers, sheaves of corn, palm leaves and quaking grass), and huge paintings richly framed were the rule in most wealthy middle-class households. Only the aristocracy held on to its simpler and more elegant heirlooms, even though, in an epoch of exuberance, these seemed temporarily out of date.

Until very recently, when the Secessionist movement in Vienna was under scrutiny, the great break with tradition was taken to have coincided with the departure of the Secessionists from the Künstlerhaus. The documentation and discussion of the period during the Vienna Festival weeks of 1985 has changed that view. While an exhibition arranged under the motto 'Dream and Reality' still displayed paintings by Klimt and Schiele, Kokoschka and Gerstl, and architectural designs by Olbrich, Hoffmann and Adolf Loos side by side, as though their basic concepts of style and expression had not been worlds apart, a symposium held concurrently brought out that very difference. Its title, suggested by the present author, was *Ornament und Askese*, best translated as 'Ornament and Austerity'. It took account, at last, of the fact that despite Klimt's influence both on early Schiele drawings and on Kokoschka's first important work, *The Dreaming Youths* (which was even dedicated to his master), a more radical change took place around 1908 when Adolf Loos proclaimed his polemic *Ornament and Crime*, condemning not only historicism but the decorative excesses of his own contemporaries.

Gustav Klimt, born in 1862, began as an academic painter. In his youth he designed innumerable adornments for playhouses, museums and other official buildings in Vienna and smaller cities in the Habsburg empire. A ceiling fresco for the great right-hand stairway of the new Burgtheater, called *Theatre at Taormina*, contained among the obligatory classicist elements, such as columns, carpets, winged statues and draped human figures, a gracefully contorted nude much resembling Frederic, Lord Leighton's *Bathing Psyche* – painted two years later in 1890 but probably copying the same early nineteenth-century model. Klimt's first portraits were also marked by a rather mediocre traditionalism pointing to anything but a glorious future. It was his painting of the society lady Sonia Knips, completed a year after the foundation of the new artists' union, the Secession, which established him not merely as the official head, but also one of the key figures of Vienna's 'Sacred Spring'.

It may have been the change in his private circumstances that brought about Klimt's new vision of opulent colour and emotional subtlety. Through the marriage of his brother Ernst to Helene Flöge, one of three daughters of a well-to-do manufacturer of meerschaum pipes who collectively ran a famous Viennese fashion house, he found entry into the cultured bourgeois circles of Vienna. His sister-in-law Emilie became his lifelong, much beloved and often painted but probably platonic friend. Also, through his elder colleague the painter Carl Moll, whose step-daughter Alma was to marry Gustav Mahler, in one salon or another Klimt met those young beauties of Jewish origin whom he soon began to portray, such as the proud Adele Bloch-Bauer or the young Margarete Wittgenstein, whose families had acquired not only wealth but also a progressive taste in art. Around 1923, a young Austrian artist, Anton Faistauer, would define the differing social interests and engagements of Klimt and Schiele in a significant way:

If Klimt may be thought of as the painter of high finance, decorating their drawing-rooms with panels gleaming in gold and silver as with cheerful silvery flowing landscapes, Schiele could be called the painter of the proletariat. These two painters, typically urban, divided between them the poles of social structure. Klimt attracted the lightweight, shallow and dissolute moneyed Jewry of the inner city [!], becoming their painter, while Schiele took on the suburbs with their tragic faces, their hunger, their hatred and their grimaces ... In detail, Klimt caught the blasé attitude, arrogance and vanity of his chosen type rather better than Schiele the features of his ... For neither of them did the human being appear significant, people were more or less figurines, for Klimt a refined, subtle play of nerves, for Schiele a dark and dreary drive.

This view from the twenties, showing the two artists as opposite sides of the same coin, survived the dark years when both were out of favour during Hitler's Fascist realism and, merely shorn of its anti-Semitic character, almost to the present day. A survey, necessarily condensed, of the development of what used to be lumped together under the heading of *Jugendstil* may help to put it right. So brief, in fact, had its various phases been, that it is difficult in retrospect to tell them apart. It was in the autumn of 1896 that, according to a contemporary witness in the salon of the art critic Berta Zuckerkandl, the three members of the Künstlerhaus, Gustav Klimt, Carl Moll and Josef Engelhart, decided to leave that institution. Their reasons had been outlined by the writer Hermann Bahr:

The Künstlerhaus is just a market, a bazaar; let the merchants there offer their wares ... Inevitably some friends of the arts will have to unite at last and rent a few well-lit halls in the city, in order to show the Viennese in the form of small, intimate exhibitions what is happening in European art.

In the following April the Vienna Secession was formally constituted, following similar foundations in Munich (1892) and Berlin (1893). Soon it was recognized as being the most fruitful and influential of the three. The first issue of the movement's monthly *Ver Sacrum* appeared in January 1898. Earlier, a plot had been acquired from the city council, and in April 1898 the foundation stone was laid for a building to house the Secessionist exhibitions. Its architect Joseph Maria Olbrich put it up within six months, and Hermann Bahr described it thus: 'It has been created like a good wheel: with the same precision devoted entirely to its purpose ... and seeking true beauty in the purest expression of its need.' These words contain the formula dominating the new love for the old ornament: subjecting what hitherto, in historicism, had been an end in itself, to the purpose and requirements of the object it was decorating.

Ver Sacrum folded in 1903. Two years later there was another split in the ranks of the Secessionists, and the most truly avantgardist (though by no means the youngest) of their members, headed by Klimt, Alfred Roller and Koloman Moser, parted company with the rest, grouped around Josef Engelhart. It was their famous art shows of 1908 and 1909 to which first Kokoschka then Schiele were admitted, thereby heralding a new age. What is known as Vienna *Jugendstil* may be said to have found its most characteristic expression during the first lustrum after the Secession. While in architecture and handicrafts this movement owed much to forerunners mainly from Britain, the painters developed more or less on their own – except for echoes of the symbolistic floral imagery and watery light used by the Belgian Fernand Khnopff and the Dutchman Jan Toorop, which may be detected in the new works of Klimt and some of his friends and followers.

These phases in both the form and the content of Secessionist art emerge more clearly when the progress of architectural and interior design as well as of the applied arts is traced. Here the programmatic changes of style and purpose in the work of Otto Wagner, one of the pioneers of what Hermann Bahr had simply called *Die Moderne*, may serve as a guideline. Born in 1841, Wagner had been one of the leading lights of the eighties, when historicist building was at its triumphant peak. In 1888, when he put up his first palatial villa outside town in what is now part of Vienna's fourteenth district, he was still wavering eclectically between free Renaissance, Louis XVI, Directoire and Empire. In the early nineties however, probably inspired by the American Louis Sullivan's dictum that decoration was 'a luxury, not a necessity', and by the Belgian Van de Velde's precept for ornament to be 'an organic part of what it adorned', Otto Wagner began to look around with new eyes. He discovered a dichotomy between art and everyday life, which manifested itself in the current disharmony of fashion and style. While furnishing his new billiard room in the villa with tables and chairs in the neo-classical manner that dated back to the imperial era of Napoleon I, this professor at the Academy of Arts began to write an epoch-making work, *Modern Architecture*, postulating and forestalling all the claims later made by the exponents of *Jugendstil*.

In his book, published in 1895, he laid down the rule that 'Nothing impractical can ever be beautiful.' As Wagner put it: *'Artis sola domina necessitas.'* He demanded that, as Oscar Wilde had earlier suggested, the new forms of art should penetrate every corner of life, adapting themselves to human needs. This meant the subjugation of an object's decorative elements to its function. In his first modernist phase, however, Wagner quite often followed the principle of what has been called 'metaphorical functionalism' – that is, inventing a need in order to satisfy it by adding attractive details to the basic design. The nails seemingly fastening the stone casings of his famous Postsparkasse, a building designed to house postal savings accounts, were its main ornamental distinction. And when he covered the armrests of its chairs with aluminium stripes, though this was ostensibly to serve as a protection against wear and tear, Wagner's real wish must have been to make them look so much the prettier.

The first examples of both practical and aesthetically satisfying interiors had been a bedroom and bathroom that he had installed in his own town apartment in 1898. There he introduced the light hues and floral textile patterns that were soon taken up by other interior designers. The glass bathtub and the colour scheme of 'hygienic white, noble silver and sanctified violet' were immensely admired when he exhibited these rooms at the Paris exhibition of 1902.

Curiously enough, though his work was the precursor of *Jugendstil* architecture, Wagner was not among the founding members of the Secession, although his ideas had inspired his younger colleagues J.M. Olbrich and Josef Hoffmann to leave the Künstlerhaus. In 1899 the teacher decided to join his pupils' movement. When a few years later, in around 1903, he dropped the floral opulence he had shared with the fluid imagery of French and Belgian *art nouveau*, before the turn of the century, this marked the end of the first phase. Some, but not all, of his younger colleagues followed his move towards a new and more austere aesthetic language, spare, relevant, not without ornament but with ever less of it. Adolf Loos had little to complain about by the time he uttered publicly his violent diatribe, which he subsequently published, against the criminal use of decorative elements. Around 1913 Wagner returned to his last historicist love, the neo-classicism of the Empire, and after that the Bieder-

meier. The interior and furnishings of his second, smaller villa at Hüt-
teldorf, built in that year at a lower level than his first palatial one, bore
witness to this. They are preserved only in photographs. The house stands
to this day, its façade bearing the traces of a purified *Jugendstil* that never
lost its charm, even during the many decades when this style was utterly
despised by the agents of functionalism.

The group of architects untainted by a historicist past who came into
their own on the Secessionist wave, foremost among them Olbrich and
Josef Hoffmann, had been initially motivated by Otto Wagner, but found
their kindred spirits in British artists and art reformers from Ruskin and
Morris to the 'Glasgow Boys'. This group of Scottish artists, who had
first exhibited their works at a London gallery in 1890, had been influenced
by James Whistler and the French Impressionists, but were later called
'natural Secessionists', owing to their modern, spontaneous painting and
their simple, spare, light-coloured furniture and interior decor designs.
Eighty of their works were shown first in Munich and later in Vienna in
the course of the nineties. Many painters from Glasgow were represented
at the first Secessionist exhibition in 1898, at the Gartenbau building, and
more at the fourth in 1899 in the new Olbrich house. The most decisive
contacts were forged with the Londoner Charles R. Ashbee and his Guild
of Handicrafts, and with the superb designers known as the 'Glasgow
Four': Charles Rennie Mackintosh, Herbert MacNair and Frances and
Margaret Macdonald. At the eighth exhibition of the Vienna Secession in
the autumn of 1900 they were invited to decorate and furnish an entire
room of their own.

When Vienna's arts and crafts workshop, the Wiener Werkstätte, was
created in 1903, the example of Glasgow helped to replace the floral motifs
with geometrical patterns. In architecture too, the square and the cube
were now used in large and small constructions. During a visit to Capri,
Josef Hoffmann had been stimulated by its whitewashed cubic dwellings,
and introduced these shapes as well as flat roofs and pillared loggias. Kolo
Moser, and to a lesser extent Olbrich, followed suit. The square began to
rule in Secessionist art, especially in its graphic work, its prints, textiles,
wallpaper and women's clothes. Even so, geometrical designs, often in a
black and white chessboard pattern, but also in coloured rhomboids or
regular wavy lines, were still combined with decorative elements based
on the flower motifs of *Jugendstil* – climbing plants, long-stemmed
intertwining lilies and snakes such as Klimt used in his famous *Medicine*
panel of the 'University paintings', commissioned and afterwards rejected
by Vienna University. While the applied arts now preferred technical and
tectonic forms in decoration, the archetypal painter of *Jugendstil* held on

to a vegetal abundance, and to outbursts of stylized florescence interspersed with jewelled or metallic insets – Klimt's 'golden phase'. Between the last group in his Beethoven frieze of 1902, *This Kiss to the Whole World*, and *The Kiss* of 1907–8 there appears to be no reduction but rather a proliferation of adornment.

Klimt's art has been called the expression of that sensuality which has always been prevalent in the inner make-up of the Viennese, though hidden or muffled by social conventions. This most masculine of painters was a master of feminine allure, whether in its veiled mystery or in its nude passivity. To a woman-hater such as the young philosopher Otto Weininger, or to prophets of the new, reformed woman such as the architect Adolf Loos, this view was an abomination. Karl Kraus made fun of Klimt's ladies by remarking: 'Whether their name is Hygeia or Judith, Mrs X or Mrs Y, all of his figures have the pallor of professionally misunderstood women.' In fact, apart from his beloved friend Emilie Flöge, Klimt found most of his sitters among the spouses of very wealthy men, and they were by no means misunderstood – as Ibsen's women had been a generation before – but often great hostesses, knowledgeable artlovers and happy creatures with minds of their own. Quite a few, as we have seen, came from a Jewish background. Their patronage or their husbands' played an important part in the cultural flowering of that period. When the industrialist August Lederer assembled the greatest collection of Klimt's works in private ownership and bought the Beethoven frieze, when Fritz Wärndorfer became the main financier and – with Josef Hoffmann, Koloman Moser and C.O. Czeschka – a co-founder of the Wiener Werkstätte, these were fruitful and lasting contributions to the furtherance of a branch of the arts in which Jewish talent was less directly involved.

By the time one outstanding painter of that origin entered the scene, it had reached its turning-point. Richard Gerstl, a passionate young man who burnt himself out emotionally and physically before shooting himself at the age of twenty-five, created his most important work in the last year of his life, 1908, which was also the crucial year of the Kunstschau arranged by Klimt's new group, of the appearance of Kokoschka's *The Dreaming Youths* and – most probably – of Adolf Loos's manifesto against ornament. Gerstl had studied painting at the Academy, and privately with a Hungarian artist, but his second love was music, the music of Gustav Mahler and soon that of Arnold Schönberg and Zemlinsky. It was his example which drove Schönberg to express himself in paint: he began his *Glances* and *Visions* six weeks after Gerstl's death and ceased three years later, when his personal crisis was over. To Gerstl we owe the most

penetrating portraits of this circle. His progress from an analytical naturalism to an almost abstract expressionism can be traced through the
Schönberg portrait painted in 1905 to the one created three years later of
the composer's family.

Some critics consider Gerstl to have been the first 'modern' Austrian
artist in Vienna. His last self-portrait, stark naked, painted in September
1908, a few months before his death, goes far beyond the portrait young
Kokoschka painted at that time of the actor Ernst Reinhold (*Trance Actor*)
as far as boldness of stroke and a grandiose contempt for accuracy are
concerned. Undoubtedly, had he survived, he would have proved most
royally. As it was, not only did his insane suicide after an unhappy love
affair with Schönberg's wife cut short this hope, it also prevented his work
from becoming as widely known in his day as it deserved. For Gerstl,
averse to the manner of Klimt, had refused to have his paintings exhibited
along with those of the *Jugendstil* master in 1907, and most of the fifty
then in existence were hidden from public view until the autumn of 1931.

Thus, heralded by the only notable Jewish painter of his time (Tina Blau,
although still alive, kept aloof from the Secession as from expressionism,
and Max Oppenheimer was still to emerge), the new age began. Kokoschka,
having at the age of twenty-two designed the poster for the Vienna Kunstschau in 1908, still belonged to the world of the Wiener Werkstätte where
he painted fans and postcards. His first important work, the illustrations
to his prose poem *The Dreaming Youths*, was still dominated by stylized
imagery, though the text of this highly erotic and mythological fairy-tale
already foreshadowed expressionist literature. Soon enough, in his painting
Still Life with Ewe and Hyacinth, he moved on from the decorative and
linear form to a visual expressionism – both in his landscapes and in his
early luminous portraits – said to have been created with X-ray eyes that
looked through the subject's exterior, exposing his innermost self.

In 1909, the year of Kokoschka's still life, the nineteen-year-old Egon
Schiele made his appearance at the second Kunstschau. By that time he
had produced over eighty-five works and, like Kokoschka, was about to
write prose poems as brilliantly frenzied as his paintings. Inevitably, Klimt
had been accused by his former comrades in the Secession of having
fostered these 'excesses'. In his opening speech at the Kunstschau, therefore,
he bravely declared that it was 'a totally futile undertaking by our adversaries to deny and fight this new artistic movement, for their fight is
directed against growing and evolving – against life itself'. Klimt's generosity in recognizing and patronizing a new movement in art diametrically opposed to his own was not ungratefully received by its two
young scions. In fact, Schiele's drawings of women, such as that of his

Carl Demel, confectioner.

Anton Gerstner and son, confectioners.

Johannes Köchert, jeweller.

Heinrich Artaria, art dealer.

Franz Joseph I opening the first exhibition of the Secession, 1898. From left to right: Gustav Klimt, Rudolf von Alt, Josef Engelhardt, Otto Friedrich, Carl Moll, Adolf Hölzel, Hans Tichy, Kolo Moser, J. M. Olbrich, Rudolf Jettmar.

Left J. Schönbichler, wholesale dealer, in the Renaissance costume he wore for Hans Makart's great pageant in celebration of the imperial silver wedding in 1879. Pictured opposite are some of Schönbichler's fellow merchants.

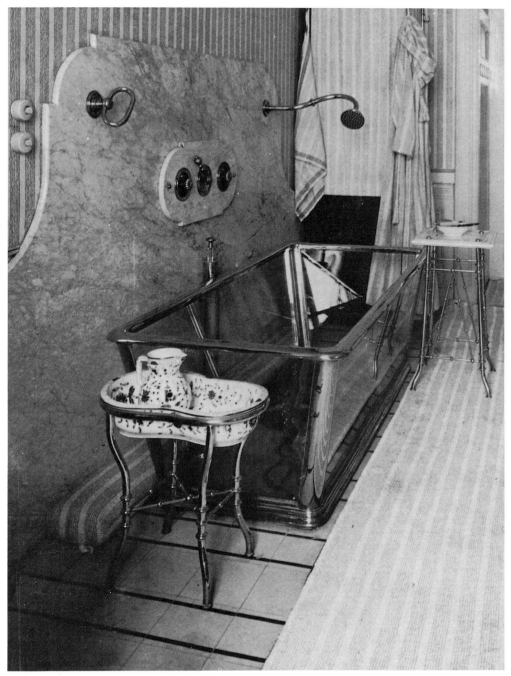

Above *Otto Wagner's glass bathtub.*

Opposite above *Otto Wagner's Postsparkasse (Post Office Savings Accounts building).*

Opposite below *The Otto Wagner house on Wienzeile.*

Architekt Adolf Loos und
Peter Altenberg! 1918
Zwei, die sich "Himmel-Trotzer".
Über dies, was bisher
unrichtig war!
Peter Altenberg

Above *Adolf Loos's American Bar.*

Right *Adolf Loos's 'House without Eyebrows'.*

Opposite *Adolf Loos and Peter Altenberg, 1918.*

Opposite *Secessionist artists preparing their Klinger exhibition of 1902.*

Above *A coffee-house in about 1908.*

sister Melanie (1909), or even more the *Portrait of a Lady* with an orange-coloured hat (1910), owe much to Klimt's example. Having himself contributed three postcard designs for the Wiener Werkstätte, he never quite denied, as Kokoschka did, his early allegiance to the stylized line.

Kokoschka, on the other hand, after dedicating *The Dreaming Youths* to 'Gustav Klimt in reverence', rapidly rose from being talented in arts and crafts to being the greatest painter of his place and time. This he owed to one man only – 'my real tutor, my real mentor, Adolf Loos, the great pioneer, architect and designer', as he told the art critic John Russell in 1962. 'For him', he added, 'England was everything. In fact the whole of Vienna, or the whole of my Vienna, was in love with England.' But it was Loos, above all, who preached its virtues. 'His lectures were so popular that he could fill the biggest concert-hall in Vienna. And they weren't all about architecture, either. He talked about walking, standing, lying down, eating, dressing and sleeping ... He told us how wrong it was to sit in chairs that were never meant to be sat in, and he showed us an English chair that was made to carry our weight and allowed us to relax our spine and spread out our legs.' Loos also preached the English way of cooking vegetables in steam, not with a roux, and of exposing children to the cold and the rain, so that 'they were tough and healthy and never sneezed'.

Some doubt has been cast recently on the date of Loos's epoch-making speech on 'Ornament and Crime', said by himself to have been delivered first in 1908. Since he repeated it frequently after the first documented occasion, January 1910, the claim that in later years he had pre-dated it in order to prove his seniority in the general move away from Secessionist opulence is not easy either to sustain or to disprove. In any case, two essays he had written before the turn of the century, one entitled 'The Luxury Vehicle', and especially his sparse interior and furnishings for the Café Museum, created in 1899, are ample proof that he was first in opposing from within *Jugendstil* the Secessionists' indulgence in decorative detail. Thus Loos was a better pupil of Otto Wagner than that architect's acknowledged followers Olbrich and Hoffmann, the latter becoming the main butt of his subsequent attacks. In his polemic against the sort of ornament considered by him to be an expression of exuberant sensuality, such as that of ripe womanhood or of savages, Loos called Hoffmann a 'Papua in the pay of the State'.

In his contention that exquisite material, well-processed, needed no addition – 'Even the most depraved person nowadays will shy from decorating a noble piece of wood with marquetry' – Loos was borne out by his own beautiful American Bar of 1908. Natural wood and marble dominated the design. His corner house on Michaelerplatz, however, built in the next year, provoked a public outcry and is said even to have annoyed the patient emperor – after all, Franz Joseph had opened the first Secessionist exhibition – whose own residence lay directly opposite. The mildest abuse it received was to be called the 'house without eyebrows', because its windows had no frames. Yet the plain upper part of the building, housing private tenants, was counterbalanced by an elegant marble-covered pillared façade to the ground and first floors, which were inhabited by a tailoring firm. The 'nakedness' of the Loos-Haus, its lack of eyebrows, has been likened to the leaning towards young and hairless adolescent females indulged in by some of the artists and writers at that time. 'The child-wife was in fashion,' as Loos wrote in retrospect, 'one thirsted for immaturity.' In fact, not only Schiele and the writer Peter Altenberg were noted for their preference for slender girls barely in their teens. Loos himself, though three times married, was at one time accused in court of paedophilia and barely escaped conviction.

Thus for at least ten years from about 1908, cultural life in Vienna was characterized by a dualism of abundance and restraint, an antinomy of aesthetic principles which ruled not only in painting and architecture, but also in literature, be it *belles-lettres*, satire or the utterances of a highly imaginative if sometimes absurd philosophy. More will be said about these ramifications in the appropriate place. In this context it will suffice to point to the tremendous support given to Adolf Loos in his rejection of 'abominable, if not perverse ornament' by Karl Kraus, the great fighter for truth in language, thought and emotion – in that order – and author of a long essay on 'Morality and Criminality' (1908). Although a self-confessed admirer of female charm and intermittent lover of an Austrian baroness, Kraus without doubt led an austere life – writing by night, sleeping in the daytime and holding court in the evening in some café before turning to his desk.

There is a significant contrast between this mode of existence and the voluptuous goings-on in Gustav Klimt's studio, which was always filled with beautiful models or ladies of society. As for the philosopher Otto Weininger, whose book *Sex and Character* had a long-term effect on Austrian intellectuals (he committed suicide at the age of twenty-three, soon after it was published in 1903), his misogynist views certainly implied an ascetic attitude. Yet the antithesis which has given this chapter its title has been questioned by the art historian Werner Hofmann in an essay he has called 'Recognizing the Flesh'. Here he argues that the self-sufficiency of an aesthetic pose untouched by real suffering, such as that of the *Jugendstil* artists, has its opposite not in austerity but in the unrepressed instinctive drive. 'To recognize the flesh instead of smoothing it down by ornament or stifling it by abstinence – this is the new radicalism around 1908, later to be called "Expressionism".' Quite possibly three instead of two leading principles may have to be distinguished when the *Zeitgeist* of the years up to 1918 is reviewed.

It was the last decade of the declining empire which gave rise to the most remarkably varied achievements, like a mighty river about to run into the sea and spreading out in a delta of rivulets, each beautiful in a different way. In that decisive year of 1908 Franz Joseph's sixty-year reign was celebrated by the great pageant already described. What had begun as a Sacred Spring and may be said rapidly to have passed, in Klimt's golden phase and Josef Hoffmann's heyday, into a blazing summer, now turned into an autumn iridescent with strong but morbid hues. Two years earlier, the most complete monument to Josef Hoffmann's idea of a *Gesamtkunstwerk* had been erected in Brussels. The Palais Stoclet, commissioned by the banker and art collector of that name, has been called a jewel case containing the most magnificent gems. M. Stoclet's dining room, where he was to entertain such fashionable geniuses as Stravinsky, Diaghilev and Cocteau, housed Klimt's famous marble mosaics *Expectation and Fulfilment*. Every piece of furniture, indeed every single thing within these walls, was planned to perfection, and taken as a whole it might be called the epitome of *Jugendstil* art.

This indeed was the last great glow of the Secessionist summer, though Hoffmann and his followers went on creating splendid dwellings for the wealthy Viennese middle class, embellishing the interiors and filling them with both exquisite adornments and immaculately finished everyday objects. Having built a number of such villas and a sanatorium near the capital, all designed in Viennese *art nouveau* style down to the last slop-basin or pail, Hoffmann moved into his own neo-classical phase after 1908. The private houses in the artists' colony he put up around 1913 on the Kaasgraben in the suburb of Döbling – later inhabited by the composer Egon Wellesz and his family among others – were simpler in line, as were his Austrian pavilions at the Paris World Exhibition in 1925 and the Venice Biennale in 1932.

While Hoffmann lived well into the fifties and was recently accused of lending his architectural services temporarily to the short-lived Nazi regime in Austria, J.M. Olbrich, his contemporary and co-rebel of 1897, had died in 1908, having left Vienna for Darmstadt before the turn of the century. It was in Koloman Moser that Hoffmann found his most prolific collaborator, both in his architectural work and at the Wiener Werkstätte, which he supervised until its end in 1932. Among the dozens of fields in which these Viennese manufacturers excelled were furniture, textiles and tapestries, ceramics and glassware, metal tableware and cutlery, tea-sets and coffee-pots, postcards, book-binding, posters, garden-design, and not least the most beautiful jewellery; and in 1911 a fashion workshop was founded, mainly inspired by the designer E.J. Wimmer-Wisgrill. All these accomplishments were taught by Hoffmann at the Vienna High School of Arts and Crafts, while being put into practice by him, Kolo Moser and many other gifted people such as C.O. Czeschka, Dagobert Peche, O. Prutscher, E. Loeffler, Gertrud Baudisch and Vally Wieselthier.

After having carried out a number of public commissions – first and foremost among them the metropolitan railway with its bridges and beautiful station buildings, some excitingly Secessionist blocks of flats along the new thoroughfare of Wienzeile, and the church of the mental hospital at Steinhof – Otto Wagner, now in his seventies, no longer dominated the scene. Of his one hundred and twelve often grandiose visions laid out in precise blueprints, among them a plan for a huge city museum, only thirty-two were translated into reality. Next to Wagner's pupil Hoffmann, younger architects such as Oskar Strnad were now in demand by private patrons. Yet in his own return to the purified form of Biedermeier he had not only influenced his own former pupils but also justified the – only slightly tempered – admiration Adolf Loos expressed for the grand old man of the Secession. The blocks of flats Wagner built in the suburb of Neustift in around 1910 had come very near to the 'house without eyebrows' in their bare and unadorned façades.

Like Klimt, Schiele and Koloman Moser, all much younger than he, Wagner was destined to die in the year 1918, which thus marked the end of an artistic as well as of a historic era. Though their paths diverged during that decisive decade, the two painters yet displayed affinities from time to time, as in their landscape paintings and some of their drawings. Their personal ties remained stronger than those with the group of artists who, under Engelhart's leadership, had stayed behind at the Secession when Klimt and his circle moved out in 1905. Many excellent artists were on the side of this former avant-garde, now set in their own tradition. But the more remarkable representatives of late *Jugendstil* painting, such as Carl Moll, Max Kurzweil, Emil Orlik, Rudolf Jettmar, Ludwig Jung-nickel, were friends and followers of Klimt. High above them towered one artist who, after his Wiener Werkstätte beginnings, had rapidly gone from strength to strength. In 1910 Oskar Kokoschka made his first forays abroad, to Switzerland and Berlin. He was to return to Vienna for another six years or so, during which time he taught for a year at the School for Arts and Crafts and then at the famous girls' college run by Eugenie Schwarzwald, suffered emotionally and gained artistically from his relationship with Gustav Mahler's widow, and was wounded in the war, but his ties with the city were broken in 1917 when he moved to Dresden. After that, despite occasional visits to Vienna, he went out into the world, which began to recognize his genius.

While the cultural scene in Vienna, as we have seen, came to be divided by conflicting aesthetic maxims, it is impossible to exaggerate its cross-currents and inter-relationships. In this metropolis, centre of a multinational realm, writers, artists and musicians lived within short distances of each other and were bound to meet, socially or officially, wherever they went. In the coffee-houses adherents of opposite ideological and artistic faiths rubbed shoulders. Yet the courtesy dictated to them by age-old conventions prevented clashes that might have been truer to their feelings than the polite nodding and hand-shaking practised between adversaries. A number of documents and letters bear witness to the mollifying atmosphere of this city, which made strange bed-fellows of antagonists and led them to simulate a nonexistent harmony. It is not surprising to read some laudatory lines by Gustav Mahler thanking Josef Hoffmann for a lovely piece of jewellery commissioned by him for his wife. But one wonders who betrayed whom when one discovers an enthusiastic letter written to Klimt in 1909 by the writer Altenberg, a dear friend of Karl Kraus and Adolf Loos, who at that very time were attacking all that Klimt stood for.

The subject of Altenberg's hymn of praise, among others of Klimt's pictures, was the portrait of 'the young Wittgenstein', as Altenberg called her – Margarete, sister of the philosopher and bride-to-be of the Englishman Stonborough. Three years earlier, Klimt had decorated the Palais Stoclet, built by the 'Papua of the State' in Loos's eyes, i.e. Hoffmann. But it was according to his own ascetic rules, very much akin to those of Loos, that Margarete's brother Ludwig, together with Loos's pupil Engelmann, was to design and build a house for her between 1926 and 1928 – only to see it filled by her with Klimt paintings, rich tapestries, glass-cases full of bibelots and decorative furniture. Thus a synthesis resulted from the dialectics of ornament and austerity. For despite the fact that according to the art historian Werner Hoffmann, Gerstl, Schiele and Kokoschka introduced a third component – the lust for naked flesh – into this polarity, here it found its supreme expression. After all, Margarete Stonborough stood for the ornate and opulent, 'golden' first phase of *Jugendstil*, while the most austere thinker of this century was none other than Ludwig Wittgenstein.

6

'QUITE FORGOTTEN PEOPLES' LASSITUDES'

It is, everyone agrees, as questionable and even dangerous to make general statements about countries or peoples as it is to search for so-called national or local characteristics in the inhabitants of a particular state or the citizens of a particular town. Yet few manage to avoid doing so, including the present author, as previous chapters have shown. If a trait common to many Viennese writers at the time under review is traced back to the city in the twelfth century AD, this will have to be taken with a large pinch of salt. The connection may be tenuous, but the poetry of Walther von der Vogelweide, who was brought up in Vienna eight hundred years ago, has found echoes in Viennese literature ever since.

In one of his elegies Walther mourns the vanished years of his life and queries their reality: 'Did I only dream it, or was it true?' This existential problem, which preoccupied Bishop Berkeley around 1710 no less than the Austrian philosopher Ernst Mach in the 1880s, underlies the writing of Austria's greatest neo-classicist, Grillparzer, as it does the plays and prose of his literary successors. When Franz Grillparzer died in 1873, Arthur Schnitzler was eleven and Hugo von Hofmannsthal not yet born. Yet both paraphrased the antinomy of *Schein und Sein* (Appearance and Real Being) which Grillparzer had used as the central theme of his 'dramatic fairy tale' *Der Traum ein Leben* (A Dream is Life) after Calderon – Schnitzler in many one-act plays and Hofmannsthal throughout his life, from his early poems and lyrical drama to his masterpiece *manqué Der Turm* (The Tower).

More than any of the other four great writers of the Biedermeier – of whom only Stifter was alive after 1866 – Grillparzer embodied what the Italian Claudio Magris has called the 'Habsburg myth in Austrian writing'. The myth encompasses the old and far-flung traditions of that dynasty, its link with Spain, its deep roots in the baroque age, a catholic as well as Catholic outlook which made emperors and subjects both worldly and ever conscious of the frailty of existence and inevitable death. It is this awareness of the long Habsburg past, and the feeling of continuity it seemed to impart, which may be found in Grillparzer's as in

Hofmannsthal's work. When the latter lectured on the former in May 1922 he maintained that in his last plays Grillparzer succeeded in achieving the well-nigh impossible: 'to render completely the historic content of a bygone but still effective epoch, and to render it with the help of characters conceived by himself'. Only an Austrian, Hofmannsthal said, would have been capable of this, and only with regard to that 'seventeenth century between which and us secret threads were still spun until yesterday' – that is, until the monarchy tumbled.

Even in the first republic, however, as we shall see, the myth stayed alive, buried for decades when it ended, but resuscitated and even glorified in retrospect whenever Vienna's cultural heyday is evoked. In Hofmannsthal it took shape most fruitfully. Like Grillparzer, but even more than his literary precursor, he was himself a character in the age-old Austrian drama through which its progress could be divined. If Spain was in his mind, the crownlands and Italian regions were in his blood. Among Hofmannsthal's forebears had been the Moravian Jew Isak Löw Hofmann, ennobled in 1835 with the affix of von Hofmannsthal, an aristocratic lady from Lombardy and members of a Viennese or Lower Austrian family of civil servants. When, as a very young man, in his poem 'Terzinen über Vergänglichkeit' (On Transience in Terza Rima), he wrote about his 'ancestors in their shrouds' being as near to him 'as my own hair', he probably meant all of them. Undoubtedly, though, he referred to the most ancient streak in his make-up in the last but one verse of another poem of that period, 'Manche freilich . . .' (Some however . . .):

> Quite forgotten peoples' lassitudes
> Can I not lift from my own eyelids
> Nor keep my frightened soul unaware of
> Distant planets silently falling.

It has been pointed out that Hermann Bahr, forerunner and spiritual head of what is now known as the group *Jung-Wien*, was also its only member not of Jewish descent. As to the 'percentage' of this controversial part in their ethnic compound – such as would have spoiled the 'ancestry pass' demanded from any Austrian during his seven years under Hitler's rule – little is known. Indeed little was known at all about these matters until Hitler's genealogists began to delve into everyone's 'Aryan' consanguinity. Had he lived later, Johann Strauss the waltz king, with his Jewish great-grandparents, Wolf and Theresia Strauss, would not have passed muster. And even Grillparzer, though he was probably ignorant of the fact (and would in any case not have minded), had a Jewish great-grandmother, Maria Ana Hönigh, 'servant to the widow of Count

Leopold Palffy, a baptized Jewess', who in 1728 had married Johann Michael Sonleuthner, quartermaster in the late count's regiment.

The lassitude, morbid fascination with death and decay, the eclecticism, preciousness and nervousness – in short the 'decadence' for which *Jung-Wien* was lampooned by its critics – did not however stem from the millennial burden of the biblical people, but came to Vienna from Paris, where Hermann Bahr had spent six months in 1889. He had been born twenty-six years before in Linz, capital of Upper Austria, the unruly but ambitious son of a local notary, and after finishing high school was thrown out of every university in Austria. Without completing his studies, he went to Berlin in the mid-eighties and became an apostle of naturalism, which, in the wake of Ibsen, had begun to dominate the German stage. Soon enough, he turned out to be the perfect example of the pushy, overbearing and at the same time fickle nature, the verbal exhibitionism, and the tendency to commercial exploitation of current trends, which have sometimes been ascribed to what Dr Goebbels called Jewish *Asphalt-literaten* – men of letters treading the city pavements. Bahr called himself a windbag, while the Berlin theatre director Brahm gave him the sobriquet of a 'perfumed horror'. Even so, this minor writer and journalist possessed an acute awareness of changes in the *Zeitgeist* as well as an unbounded enthusiasm for all the arts and was to become the leader and *spiritus rector* of his contemporaries.

In Paris he at once discovered his lodestar in Maurice Barrès, then merely the prophet of a decadent egotism, and not yet the unpleasant French chauvinist of later years. Two years later the seventeen-year-old Hugo von Hofmannsthal, having meanwhile met Bahr, was to write one of his early literary essays about Barrès. The very first piece young Loris, as the schoolboy author called himself, had published in a Berlin monthly, was about Paul Bourget, whom Bahr had also come to admire in Paris. Bourget's 'new idealism in art', his 'belief in the necessity of a synthesis of naturalism and romanticism', inspired Bahr to the theories of art he was about to develop. When he returned from Paris, not yet to Vienna but to Berlin, he set himself up as the 'surmounter of naturalism'. In the autumn of 1890, in the first of three volumes of collected essays entitled *Zur Kritik der Moderne* (On Criticism of Modernity), he preached the end of naturalism before Gerhart Hauptmann's first play, *Die Weber* (The Weavers), had even reached the German stage.

It was his second volume, *The Overcoming of Naturalism*, published in 1891, in which he defined 'the new psychology, the new romanticism, the new idealism designed to make up for the insufficiency of naturalistic art'. One searched for the last secrets lying dormant in the depths of man.

'But it was not enough. What was demanded was lyrical expression.' And so, said Bahr, the artist 'should no longer be a tool of reality in creating its reflection, but vice versa, reality becomes the artist's material in proclaiming his own nature ... I therefore believe that naturalism will be surmounted by a nervous romanticism, or I would rather say: by a mystique of nerves ... The fabric of the new idealism is nerves, nerves, nerves and – costume. Decadence takes over from the rococo and the Gothic masquerade.' In trying to formulate his idea of what art would henceforth be like he anticipated the imagery of early Secessionism: 'It will be something laughing, rushing, fleeting. The burden of logic and the heavy grief of the senses are gone ... It is something rosy, something rustling like green shoots, a dancing as of the spring sun in the first breeze of the morning.'

Among the many new terms that were to be applied to what Bahr helped to set in motion, such as idealism, symbolism, neo-romanticism and aestheticism, the definition 'impressionism of the soul' may seem the most appropriate. When, after a prolonged visit to Russia, the 'commercial traveller in literature' Hermann Bahr settled in Vienna for good, the Café Griensteidl had begun to serve as a meeting-place not only for politicians but also, and mainly, for journalists and writers. The young doctor of medicine Arthur Schnitzler, who besides publishing a tract on hypnosis had written poetry, prose sketches and some short one-act scenes later to be united in the play *Anatol*, was the eldest in a group of literati among whom Richard Beer-Hofmann, Felix Salten, Gustav Schwarzkopf and Paul Goldmann showed up most frequently at the Griensteidl. In the summer of 1890, at Bad Fusch, the actor and writer Schwarzkopf became acquainted with the enlightened pupil of Vienna's Akademisches Gymnasium, young Hugo von Hofmannsthal, then sixteen. Schwarzkopf introduced the schoolboy (who in June of that year had published his first poem, 'A Question', in a magazine entitled *On the Beautiful Blue Danube*) into the café circle, although at first young Hofmannsthal came accompanied by his father, an eminent banker and a cultured man.

It seems that from the outset Hofmannsthal senior harboured great plans for his son. Although he made him take up law at Vienna University – later dropped for Romanic studies – the banker quite obviously preferred his son to embark on a literary rather than on a commercial career. Yet the over-sensitive, fragile and sometimes even unbalanced disposition of the young genius came to worry him. In 1901, when his son underwent a crisis later described in his famous 'Letter of Lord Chandos', the father wrote to a friend about Hugo's depression: 'It is really sad that he so ruthlessly tortures everyone around him; to me especially, as the prototype of a simple bourgeois with normal inclinations, the whole thing is irksome. People envy us and we, with all these pinpricks, are unable to be happy about him.' Ten years earlier, when Hermann Bahr had met young Hofmannsthal at the Griensteidl and immediately came to adore him (calling him a 'Cherubino, Gontram or Guy, but translated into Maria-Theresian terms') the great advocate of 'nerves, nerves, nerves' fostered this precious *éducation sentimentale*. However, occasional bouts of melancholy may not have been too high a price to pay for one of the most exquisite talents that literature in the German language has ever possessed.

There are two distinct phases in Hofmannsthal's life and work. The first, at the beginning of which he used the pseudonyms Theophil Morren and Loris, lasted about a decade from his first schoolboy poems, and may be said to have ended with his fictional 'Letter of Lord Chandos' to Francis Bacon, which articulated his own sudden doubt in the possibility of the verbal expression of reality. The essays, poetry and verse plays he wrote during the Loris period were masterpieces of imagination, intuitive thought and polished form. He knew, without being able to prove it, that he and his generation were heirs to a great and irretrievable past.

> Thus do we wander through this city
> Crown guardians of a sunken realm
> Last of the knowing, last bearers of noble blood.

Not merely within his own circle in Vienna, but also in the France of Amiel, Barrès and de Banville, in the Italy of d'Annunzio and in the England of Swinburne and Walter Pater he found kindred spirits – witnesses to the fact that 'the whole work of this fine-grained eclectic century consists of instilling into things of the past an uncanny life of their own'.

The essence of Viennese decadence – which differs from its French model in the wealth and antiquity of the history by which it is weighed down – is contained in the confessions he made when commenting, in 1894, on the latest prose works of Gabriele d'Annunzio:

We have made idols of our dead, all they have they have from us ... we have equipped these shadows with a higher beauty and more wondrous strength than life can bear ... Yes, all our thoughts of beauty and happiness have run away from us and moved in with the fairer being of an artificial existence ... with us, there is nothing left but freezing life, stale and bleak reality, broken-winged resignation.

But he was also well aware that he belonged to an élite:

> I am talking of a few thousand people scattered in the big European cities ... among them need not be the geniuses, not even the great talents of the epoch, they are not necessarily the head or the heart of their generation: they are merely its conscience.

The modesty of this statement may seem in conflict both with the young writer's self-assurance and with the esteem, even awe, in which he was held by his contemporaries. As Arthur Rimbaud had been called *Shakespeare enfant*, so Hofmannsthal was deemed to be, and himself aspired to be, a kind of *Goethe enfant*. His poems, few but finely wrought, the lyrical drama of Loris, much of which first saw the light of day during his readings in the salons of Baroness Sophie Todesco and Josephine von Wertheimstein, together with the inspired and accomplished prose writings which appeared in the fashionable literary magazines of his day, resulted in an early fame that would have sufficed for a lifetime. Yet, after having mastered the German language to a high degree and endowed it with the melodiousness of Italian, the clarity of French, the metaphoric wealth of English and the grace and logic of Latin, Hofmannsthal one day – though perhaps briefly – lost confidence in the power of words. 'My case is, in short,' he wrote in the 'Letter of Lord Chandos' of 1902, 'I have completely lost the capacity to think or talk about anything in a coherent manner ... It was thus, for me, with people and their actions. I no longer succeeded in comprehending them with the simplifying look of habit. To me everything fell apart in bits, those bits again in bits, and nothing would any longer fit into a concept.'

Hofmannsthal's scepticism about language has been compared to that of the Vienna Circle of logical positivists and of Wittgenstein. There is also a theory that it was caused not so much by his own loss of faith in the writer's medium as by the silence of one of his friends after producing two or three dozen beautiful poems and one piece of epic prose before the age of twenty-one. This was Leopold von Andrian zu Werburg, whose father was the scion of an old and noble family and a scholarly anthropologist, and whose mother was the daughter of the Jewish composer Meyerbeer. 'Poldy' was young Hofmannsthal's dearest companion, born in the same year, and he appeared to him like a kinsman or even a mirror in which to view himself. When Andrian published his self-revealing novel *Der Garten der Erkenntnis* (The Garden of Cognition) under the motto 'Ego Narcissus', his friend Hugo told him in a letter: 'Your book is just like the young goddess Persephone, who in the company of other nymphs picks many daffodils on a meadow, though somewhat at a distance, and who is suddenly overcome by great fear and deep sadness.' And earlier he had told him, 'I believe as steadfastly in you as I do in myself.'

Thus when, after this subtle and poetic analysis of a mind troubled by the discrepancy between inner and outer experience, Andrian stopped writing altogether, Hofmannsthal told him he found it incredible 'that the power which has created this should fall to dust in interior cavities and lose its outward effect'. This would indeed point to a direct concern with the drying-up of Andrian's talent. Yet the point must not be laboured. For in a letter to his 'dear Poldy' soon after the publication of the Chandos letter there is no sign of its having been prompted by the fate of his friend. Andrian seems to have accused Hugo of hiding behind a historical mask when revealing 'these confessions and reflections'. 'But I really started from the opposite end,' replies Hofmannsthal:

Last August I browsed time and again through Bacon's essays, found the intimacy of that period attractive, dreamed myself into the manner in which *these* people of the sixteenth century felt about antiquity and had a mind to do something in *that tone of voice*, and the contents which I, in order not to seem coolly detached, had to borrow from some inner experience, some living experience, were *added* to this.

It may be taken, then, that this was another case of Ego Narcissus. But while the watershed in Hofmannsthal's life is assumed to have been the Chandos letter, this is true only to a degree. Certainly he suffered greatly, in the year of its publication and before, from an inner frustration. In December 1902 he told the German poet Richard Dehmel how he himself found it strange 'that in many months, and months of happy concentration, not even one single poem will emerge any more' – as indeed it never would from now on. Working feverishly on various projects, one of them an adaptation of the very same Calderon play, *La Vida es Sueño*, already used by Grillparzer, he applied for an academic post which did not materialize. 'Sometimes', he wrote in the following July, 'I feel younger, less mature, more helpless and isolated than three or five years ago.'

Meanwhile he had married, in church, a charming girl of Jewish extraction, Gerty Schlesinger, and they had settled in a small but lovely Maria-Theresian palais at Rodaun near Vienna. Their first child had been born. Ostensibly he was happy and very busy. Before the turn of the century he had published more verse plays, or at least plays in metrical prose, and had spent some time in Paris, where he visited Rodin and befriended Maeterlinck; but a change had set in which would slowly become apparent. The clear, straight river of his early Goethean genius began to branch out in many directions. Hofmannsthal's universal erudition, his wide-ranging interests, would open up for him countless paths, many of which led him astray. There was much to admire in his second, immensely fertile phase – the beautiful libretti he wrote for Richard Strauss, his stories, his comedies, even that questionable medieval pastiche, the everlasting *Jedermann* (Everyman). But if his novel *Andreas* remained incomplete, an enchanting fragment, the mere promise of a masterpiece, it was because there too he became entangled in too many intricacies.

What exists of this book is exquisite, a tale written in matchless prose, moving at a well-balanced, measured pace and containing descriptions unrivalled in Austrian fiction. But all of a sudden it trails off and vanishes, as it were, into thin air. When published posthumously it contained the author's notes, which make the most impressive and at the same time the most disturbing reading. There are drafts of sublime scenes that were never written. There are character sketches, sidelights, illuminations. But there are altogether too many of these, and they are too involved and too complex. In the end, one feels, Hofmannsthal was defeated by his own imagination. He saw too many possibilities and not one single certainty. Yet even in its incomplete form the novel is one of the finest prose works of this century. So might his intended *chef d'oeuvre*, his Faust, have been the finest drama. But though Hofmannsthal worked at *Der Turm* (The Tower) until his death, this adaptation of Calderon was not, apart from one attempt at Salzburg, to see the stage in any of its four versions.

So much has been said, and is still to be said, about Hofmannsthal's life and work, because undoubtedly he was in his own lifetime the Austrian writer *par excellence* – despite the fact that he considered himself to be part of German, not merely of German-language literature. Moreover, his example, and that of some of his friends, is likely to refute the theories about the place in Austrian culture of men and women of Jewish descent, and their contribution to it. When studies are made of these people, often by scholars based outside Europe, the true facts are obscured owing both to lack of information, and to lack of survivors from the deeply assimilated and mostly fully integrated Jewish families long-resident in Vienna before the days of awakening anti-Semitism. The great variety of their attitudes towards their Jewishness – whether they felt it to be of negligible significance or fundamental, whether they accepted or renounced it – is nowadays often ignored. Two of these approaches can be illustrated by the position of Austria's greatest writers during its sacred spring, or its golden autumn, as the case may be.

By the time he appeared on the scene, the grandson of the silk merchant Isak Löw Hofmann from Prostiebor in Bohemia found himself merged with Vienna's bourgeoisie and lower aristocracy – with friends like the Barons Franckenstein, Karg von Bebenburg and Bodenhausen-Degener, or Andrian zu Werburg and Oppenheimer. The antecedents of these last two were as immaterial to themselves and their circle as were young Hofmannsthal's. When he was stationed in far-away Galicia during his military service, he complained not only to his parents but also to his friend Baron Felix Oppenheimer, the grandson of Sophie Todesco, about being billeted with poor Jews whose caftans were grubby and whose houses stank. He would have written the same had he been put up in some desolate Slav working-class household. The stance of this twenty-two-year-old lieutenant in the Imperial and Royal Dragoons was certainly arrogant, but it was completely unselfconscious. His small though decisive Jewish heritage may have asserted itself in some of his writings, but in everyday life it did not concern him at all.

Not so with Arthur Schnitzler. Born in 1862 of unconverted parents – his father a Hungarian village carpenter's son who became a famous laryngologist, his mother a doctor's daughter belonging to a wealthy family related to the Barons Schey and long-established in the capital – he never forgot or denied his ancestry. To the faith of his forefathers he had, he confessed, 'as little inward relation as to any other'. But when he went to university in the early eighties, anti-Semitism had begun to infiltrate the student societies, and those of German nationalist leanings were expelling Jews from their midst – a fate that befell Theodor Herzl, who had been misguided enough to join one. Schnitzler had acquired the skill of fencing during his military service, but as a budding doctor he preferred the study of saving lives to risking his own in a duel, nor was he particularly interested in the heavy drinking that went on at student gatherings. All the same, he was aware even at that time that he might be rejected by some of his less tolerant fellow citizens, a danger that increased throughout the course of his life. Yet the thought never entered his head that his birthright in this city and this country might be seriously contested. He became, as it were, the Viennese writer *par excellence*, just as Hofmannsthal was the prototypical Austrian writer – a fact recognized in their time and even more so in retrospect.

Late in 1892, Schnitzler answered an enquiry by his 'most revered' friend Theodor Herzl as to the identity of Loris, who had written the rhymed introduction to his own play *Anatol*:

Unfortunately, he is not me. For one thing, I would have to be twelve years younger and, secondly, I would have written *Gestern* [Yesterday], the most beautiful one-act play in verse published in German for a long, long time. This strange eighteen-year-old will be much talked about. If you find the introductory verse to Anatol 'kissable', I would warn you of the indecent thoughts which the enjoyment of his other writings would cause you. In fact, the gentleman is called Hugo von Hofmannsthal, passed his high school exam in July and is studying law at Vienna University ... Besides, ask Goldmann [a critic and foreign correspondent of the main Vienna paper] about him – it was he who discovered him.

In his introduction, Loris had formulated, in a light-hearted way, the mood of his companions:

> Thus it is that we're play-acting
> Early ripened, delicate, wistful
> In the comedy of our soul
> Our feelings past and present
> Evil things in pretty formula
> Smoothly worded, many-coloured
> Secret and half-hearted feelings
> Agonies and episodes.

Any idea that *Jung-Wien* consisted of elegiac youngsters is dispelled by a faded photograph taken at an amusement fair of Bahr, Schnitzler, Beer-Hofmann and Hofmannsthal in the early nineties. These worthy males, all of them wearing hats – though with a rakish tilt – and beards, except for Loris who sports a thinnish moustache, in outward appearance are as far from the dandy of *The Yellow Book* as Klimt was from Beardsley at that time. Nor was it just a matter of a few years until the *fin de siècle* artists and literati began to look the part: the photograph showing members of the new Secessionist movement welcoming the Emperor Franz Joseph at the opening of their first exhibition reveals the rebels as portly gentlemen in morning coats, headed by the eighty-five-year-old painter Rudolf von Alt.

By about the turn of the century most beards had been shaved, but not that of Dr Arthur Schnitzler. Not yet forty, he had ended his medical career – rather than pursuing psychiatry, his favourite subject, he had reluctantly followed in his father's footsteps as a laryngologist – and written a number of plays, of which more will be said in the appropriate context. His first stories appear to have continued an epic tradition going back to Grillparzer in his *Der arme Spielmann* (The Poor Minstrel), to Stifter's essays on 'Vienna and the Viennese', to Ferdinand von Saar's *Novellas from Austria* and to Eduard Pötzl's *The People of Vienna* – sketches of the mores of his city and its inhabitants. Of these, as of his drama, Thomas Mann would one day say that 'the image of Vienna's soul, which he gave by giving himself, was rich in every kind of tenderness, and in half-tones, ironies, discrepancies'. Basically, however, Mann was to add, there was 'not grace and smiling beauty, doubt or goodness, but inexorability, something masculine and hard and bitter – the final seriousness of life, eye to eye with death, which had nothing of aestheticism, but rather the invulnerability of the knowing physician.'

It was in his story *Leutnant Gustl* (translated as *None but the Brave*), published in 1900, that Schnitzler hit on a new technique while probing, and exposing, the trivial thoughts of a young army officer. The 'monologue in thought', he wrote to a friend, was supposed to have been used by Dostoevsky in a novella, *Krotkaya*, which he had not read. His own impulse for availing himself of it had come from a story by Dujardin, *Les Lauriers sont coupés* (*We'll to the Woods No More*) – 'except that this author had not found the right theme for his form'. The *monologue intérieur*, a string of free associations (later turned into the 'stream of consciousness' by Dorothy Richardson, James Joyce and Virginia Woolf), was employed by Schnitzler with a distant, cold irony to expose the emptiness of the average military mind and the paltry pursuits of a feather-brained 'man about town'.

Leutnant Gustl is bored by the concert he has to attend, which happens to be an oratorio; indeed, he is bored by everything except idle chatter, girls and drink. Of course he is proud of the superiority his uniform seems to afford him, and is ever aggressively ready to pick a quarrel over any attack on his honour, no matter how slight, and even if unintentional. When in the crush at the cloakroom a mere baker touches his sabre and calls him a 'silly boy', he is obliged, unable as he is to challenge his social inferior to a duel, to prepare for suicide. After a night's anxious musings he is saved from his fate by the baker's unexpected death. The exquisite *décadent* whom Schnitzler had depicted in his play *Anatol*, probably modelled on someone like Poldy von Andrian, has his counterpart in this soulless, heartless type of young Viennese, who can easily be won over to and ruled by any kind of dogma, whether of the army code or of National Socialism, or any sort of racial prejudice or indifference to the suffering of his fellow men. Leutnant Gustl, who in his monologue rails against intellectuals, Slavs, Socialists, Jews, women and everyone in civvies, has been called a 'pre-Fascist' individual. It is not surprising, though it may go against the present tide of glorification of Emperor Franz Joseph's good old days, that six months after publishing this story in December 1900 Schnitzler was deprived of his (reserve) officer's rank for having damaged the army's reputation.

Very rarely, in fact only in his play *Professor Bernhardi* and in his long, somewhat rambling novel *Der Weg ins Freie* (The Path into the Open), did Schnitzler deal overtly with the problems of Jewishness in a gentile world. While the drama is among his most poignant pieces, the prose work, containing as it does too much ideological argument and too many characters who serve as standard bearers for their convictions, may have less artistic merit than historical value. Prompted by the Zionist movement recently founded by Herzl, Schnitzler uses two characters to discuss his own position and that of his 'revered friend'. 'My instinct', says the author's mouthpiece, 'tells me unfailingly that my home [*Heimat*] is here, precisely here and not in some country unknown to me which, as described, is not in the least to my liking and which some people now want to foist on me as my fatherland, for the reason that a few thousand years ago my ancestors were scattered from there into the world.' The Zionist replies that all this applies less to an assimilated Viennese artist than to the masses of eastern Jewry of whom that artist has not the slightest idea: 'You always think of yourself and the unimportant fact that you are a writer who, having been born in a German country, by chance writes in German and, living in Austria, writes about Austrian people and circumstances.'

This exchange of opposing views contains in a nutshell the basic difference between the poor, self-contained and unemancipated Jews of the east, whether within the Austrian Empire or without, and those who were the products of centuries of gradual integration into the fabric of Viennese society. It is as well to recall in this context the hostile contempt with which Franz Kafka was to judge Schnitzler's novel, as well as his play *Professor Bernhardi*, in a letter to his fiancée Felice Bauer in 1913. While Kafka had been attracted by Schnitzler's early writings, especially by *Leutnant Gustl*, whose technique was not without influence on his own prose, he saw the Viennese author's 'great plays and great prose works as filled with a wobbling mass of most repugnant scribbling'. The reason for this was Kafka's discovery of the Yiddish theatre and his belief that since the advent of racial anti-Semitism western Jewry was played out. This led him to condemn any attempt to prolong or justify what he thought was a hopeless symbiosis.

It was argued by another writer soon to gain fame in the literary world, Stefan Zweig, that the hierarchy erected within the Jewish families of Vienna was both snobbish and ridiculous. After all, he maintained, it was no more than a matter of 'having come from the same Jewish ghetto a mere fifty or a hundred years earlier'. But quite apart from the fact that many of their forefathers had never lived in a ghetto, the same sort of spectacular social rise within a generation or two can occur in virtually any country or any walk of life. If the grandson of a coal-miner could turn into Ronald Firbank, or the grandson of a rural blacksmith into Cecil Beaton, Schnitzler's own elevation from the status of his grandfather's village joinery to that of the imperial city's most important chronicler cannot be considered exceptional. In *Der Weg ins Freie*, however, Schnitzler did not confine the discussions to the Jewish problem. His novel sets out to prove that the general situation in Vienna around the turn of the century had become precarious in very many ways. The centrifugal forces in the empire find their expression in its capital. Among the nobility, Jews and artists alike, 'the centre does not hold'. The darker side of Schnitzler's love-hate for his native city and his compatriots manifests itself in a comment the only foreigner in his book, an English diplomat, is allowed to make: 'Austria is the country of social insincerity,' says Mr Skelton, where there is 'violent strife without a trace of hatred and a kind of tender love without the need for loyalty.'

Compared with these two outstanding writers, Schnitzler and Hofmannsthal, the other members of *Jung-Wien* appear as minor figures. Richard Beer-Hofmann, born in 1866 during that very month of July in which Königgrätz was fought and lost, entered the Café Griensteidl after finishing his law studies and failing to wound a Baron Seckendorf in a duel. During that same autumn of 1890 young Loris, clad in his schoolboy shorts, presented himself to Schnitzler at the café. With Hermann Bahr, these four formed the nucleus of the one literary Griensteidl group destined for fame. For at a different table, according to Richard Specht, a contemporary, sat another group – those 'truly German writers who without knowing it were already dead: Fritz Lemmermayer, Franz Christel, Hermann Hango, Joseph Kitir, all bright hopes of Viennese poetry where it was most Aryan'. Who remembers them now? asked Specht in his biography of Schnitzler, written in 1922. 'And yet it is an amusing fact that these poets refused to take part in a joint anthology with the explicit motivation that they found it repugnant to be represented in a volume together with dilettanti like Arthur Schnitzler and Hugo von Hofmannsthal.'

Beer-Hofmann must have been a very lovable man and his friends kept faith with him all their lives. There is less evidence that they considered him a truly great author. And though he wrote some novellas, a sensitive novel called *Der Tod Georgs* (Georg's Death) and a number of plays, he is best remembered for a very early poem, a lullaby dedicated to his new-born daughter, 'Schlaflied für Miriam'. He was the most conscious of his ancestry among all the members of *Jung-Wien*; for him there existed an unbroken continuity with the biblical people that he hoped to pass on to his child.

> Are you asleep, Miriam – Miriam, my child,
> We are but a shore, and deep in us flows
> Blood from those past – to those who will come
> All are within us! Who feels alone?
> You are their life – and their life is yours.
> Miriam, my life – my child, go to sleep.

Sentimental though the poem seems in translation, it has considerable impact in German, and found many admirers. Rilke, one of the most famous German poets after the turn of the century, asked permission of Beer-Hofmann to read the lullaby in public, which he did for many years.

Alone among his friends, Beer-Hofmann chose for his subject the fate and religious mission of Jewry. Felix Salten, the next to enter the café circle, fought that rising anti-Semitism in his journalistic work which was fostered for political purposes by Burgomaster Lueger, but he devoted himself mostly to exploring the mind and manners of the people in whose midst he lived. The only one apart from Hermann Bahr not to have been born in Vienna (though he left Budapest for the capital at the age of four weeks), he loved writing about the city's simple folk, among them the funny and pathetic creatures running the side-shows, working the merry-go-rounds and playing in the small musical bands of the *Wurstelprater*, the great fun-fair on the fringe of the town. Like his friends, he started by writing the delicate self-centred little novellas of the *fin de siècle*, and later even a novel or two, as well as theatre criticism. Among his best essays are those collected under the title *Das österreichische Antlitz* (The Austrian Visage), in which he showed considerable insight into the merits, follies and failings of his compatriots. But he became world-famous when he published *Bambi*, the story of a fawn. To the less high-minded the pornographic 'autobiography' of *Josephine Mutzenbacher* (ascribed to him though he never acknowledged it), may seem his crowning glory. It is certainly a masterpiece of its kind.

High-mindedness was clearly compatible with more trivial, or at least popular pursuits in the eyes of the members of *Jung-Wien*. A line by Felix Dörmann, whose first collection of poems was called *Neurotica* and his first volume of prose *Sensationen*, was often quoted as an expression of a *Jugendstil* motif: 'I love the slender and hectic/Narcissus with lips red as blood'. But he was also the author of the libretto to the operetta *Ein Walzertraum* by Oscar Straus, and Hofmannsthal is said to have helped with some of the others in putting together this charmingly primitive story. Schnitzler jotted down in his diary many more names who he said belonged to the Griensteidl clique, among them Richard Specht, C. Karlweis, Rudolf Lothar and that tragic young man from Brünn in Moravia, Eduard Michael Kafka, a well-to-do idealist who financed literary magazines in the capital, adored his creative colleagues and like his great namesake died of consumption at an early age.

The sharpest criticism of *Jung-Wien* came from within, of which more will be said later. A typical attack from without against these writers' mundane mannerisms has been quoted from a letter to a friend by the Moravian-born author O.F. Chalupka, who had adopted the Teutonic pseudonym of Ottokar Stauf von der March:

> What is he to us, temperaments aching for life and battle, this Bahr-Hecuba putting on different paints every day and flirting with a Dandy-Nirvana? Let him be, that semi-Gallic-Hispanic-Semitic [*sic!*] fool from Linz ... I hope you will visit me in my present digs. For I rarely frequent the Café Megalomania, *vulgo* Griensteidl – the crowd there is abhorrent to me in its blasé arrogance.

One of the two most eminent older writers still alive after 1900, the noble-minded Marie Ebner-Eschenbach, née Countess Dubsky, would have condemned Chalupka's racist and intolerant attitude. When the Dreyfus trial was re-opened in 1899 she wrote from Rome, where she happened to be, to Sigmund Freud's friend, the psychiatrist Breuer: 'If I were in Vienna now, I would buy only from Jewish shops and would especially draw attention to my doing so ... The brutalization and stultification dominating today seem to be necessary. People have to be prepared for the world war looming ahead. In order to gobble each other up, they must now sharpen their teeth.' The other, Ferdinand von Saar, was certainly well disposed towards a young writer like Hofmannsthal. Yet he did not hide his unease over this new kind of literature which threatened to replace his own:

> As far as your little piece goes [Hofmannsthal's first play, *Gestern*], I must confess I do not quite know what to say. For despite the ingenious dialogue, despite the accomplished verse, I have not received a deeper impression – nor have I found out *what* in fact these impressions of a mood, evoked as though by a strong stimulation of nerves, are meant to depict and express. Perhaps it is my fault, just as I openly confess that I am helpless when confronted with a good many creations of the 'newest writing', quite *sine ira*, yet *sine consilio*.

It was the recurrent reaction of one generation having to make way for the next. Saar was by no means played out, however, and soon published poems in the Secessionists' monthly *Ver Sacrum* that were as colourful and stylized as the paintings reproduced alongside them. And when he celebrated his seventieth birthday in 1903, a whole phalanx of young writers contributed to a congratulatory volume edited by Richard Specht. This was introduced by a letter from Marie Ebner-Eschenbach: 'Who do you think came and invited me to take part in a homage to our old Austrian writer! This was done by the young Viennese writers. Is this not beautiful and should it not please me in your soul and mine?' Among those represented in the Festschrift were Hermann Bahr, Schnitzler, Hofmannsthal, Salten, Theodor Herzl and Peter Altenberg, that lone genius who had frequented his own table at the Café Griensteidl before moving on to the Café Central.

Saar died in 1906. In the same year another new name had appeared in public and, after a brief manifestation, vanished again for two and a half decades. The name was that of Robert Musil, whose novel *Die Verwirrungen des Zöglings Törless* (*Young Törless*) impressed some of his contemporaries, notably the famous German critic Alfred Kerr, but led no one to prophesy that this writer would become the great chronicler of the Austro-Hungarian Empire after its end. *Der Mann ohne Eigenschaften* (*The Man without Qualities*) was not to be published until 1931, and then in an unfinished form. Its forerunner, the schoolboy story written by Musil between the ages of twenty-two and twenty-five, can be seen as a startling leap into the twentieth century – a century in which de Sade's exquisite pleasure in causing pain was to become the common pastime of large numbers of people. Young Törless, who watches and registers the outrageous acts of torture committed by some of his schoolmates against the most helpless among them, has been called only recently 'the first modern man in German literature'. Yet it is also true that his self-revealing reflections are not unconnected with those of Schnitzler's Leutnant Gustl. In both cases the workings of a young mind – or soul – are laid bare, in a manner akin to the way in which Sigmund Freud at that time was urging his patients to delve down into the unconscious in order to verbalize their buried drives and their hidden wishes and fears.

Schnitzler was not Leutnant Gustl, but Musil undoubtedly was Törless. His own experience at two military high schools, one in the Austrian province of Burgenland, the other in Moravia, where as 'Monsieur le Vivisecteur' (a name he gave himself at the age of nineteen) he must have witnessed the sadistic excesses of his fellow pupils with stoic lack of concern, had given rise to this first novel. Though Musil's own character did not suffer from such fatal practices in later life, and may indeed have been immunized by it once and for all against any further leaning towards what has been called 'the unholy alliance between aestheticism and terror', he had described the monster that was on its way. The aesthetic refinement of the nineties, the teachings of Mach and the model of Maeterlinck, as well as the analytical processes set in motion by Schnitzler in literature and by Freud in psychiatric medicine, had certainly influenced the young man from Carinthia when he dared write down what he had seen and not felt. Yet he could not know at the time, though he discovered later, that while doing so he had delineated the 'Instinctual Foundation (*Triebgrundlage*) of the Third Reich'. Thus, eight years before the edifice of the Austro-Hungarian Empire began to tremble, this young author led Austrian literature into a new but by no means better age.

7

THE WORLD IN A DEWDROP

Early in the new century the great scholar, wit, writer and actor Egon Friedell, Austria's only answer to Dr Johnson, described the new trend towards brevity in life and art:

We no longer settle down comfortably with the given things. Our whole civilization is dominated by the principle: *Le minimum d'effort et le maximum d'effet!* ... We travel not by leisurely mail-coach but in express trains, receiving hasty speed-pictures of the scenery we pass ... Books are surrogates for experience, a makeshift help for people who have no time. Brevity and stringency are thus the foremost need the modern book has to fulfil – not a skimpy or aphoristic brevity, but that substantial, compact kind which is a steady requirement especially of the most deeply thoughtful writer.

Friedell then added: 'This is the basic principle of Peter Altenberg.'

With Altenberg, the most eminent of those men of letters who perceived and rendered 'the world in a dewdrop', as it were, a new genre had entered literature. In journalism, or more precisely in those contributions to arts pages subsumed in the term *feuilleton*, the tradition of succinct, crisp and trenchant writing goes back to a much earlier time. As in the case of creative prose, a very distant ancestor can be discerned. Peter Suchenwirt, Vienna's first satirist, lived a mere hundred and fifty years after Walther von der Vogelweide, under the Habsburgs – still dukes at the time – in their city of residence. In his rhymed diatribes he lampooned the dandies of his age and attacked the gluttony, moral laxity and dissoluteness of his contemporaries, reserving special indignation for the decline of female virtue, high taxation and the venality of priests.

A good deal later, after Emperor Joseph II had waived or at least reduced censorship of publications, a flood of pamphlets, broadsheets, newsletters and satirical tracts swamped and usurped most of the literary space that fiction writing was unable to fill at that time. The *feuilleton*, which was to be developed into a fine art in Vienna, originated in France where Abbé de Geoffroy, editor of the *Journal des Débats*, wrote the first one on 18

January 1800. In Germany both Heinrich Heine and his adversary Ludwig Börne took up the new genre, which, hovering as it did between the literary form of the essay and pointed but ephemeral journalism (similar to the fourth leader of *The Times*), was looked down upon by purists. In his great attack on Heine Karl Kraus later observed vituperatively that Heine 'had loosened the bodice of language so that every *commis* was now able to finger her breasts'. Yet Kraus himself, as we shall see, started out as a writer of *feuilletons*, until he came to hate in others what he hated in himself.

The first true master of terse, pithy and often polemical prose in Vienna was Ferdinand Kürnberger, later to be revered by Kraus. The son of a lamplighter and a market-trader, he had worked his way through high school, taken part in the March revolution and gone into exile in Germany where he admired such *Jung-Deutschland* writers as Heine, Börne and Gutzkow. Back in Vienna, he tried to improve the morals of his fellow-citizens and, along with the small-town mayor Joseph Schöffel, helped save the Vienna woods from being cut down and sold to rapacious timber merchants. A bitter, solitary, incorruptible man, he was also a nature-lover and forerunner of today's Green movement. Though considered a virtuoso of the *feuilleton*, he saw himself merely as an 'infantryman of the literary low calibre'. He despised other representatives of this genre, devoting a whole piece to the mockery of those '*feuilletonistes* naturalized in coffee-houses' and describing them as 'misanthropes, egoists, *hommes blasés*, in short, Mephistos'.

In the seventies Kürnberger published collections of his short prose works in two volumes, one called *Siegelringe* (Signet Rings), the other *Literarische Herzenssachen* (Literary Matters of the Heart). In these, his brilliant command of language as well as his inconsistencies of judgement came to the surface. After his return from exile, for instance, he had been so full of praise for the Germans that he was accused in Vienna of preferring them to his own countrymen. His still reasonable answer had been: 'Just as I have an antipathy towards the Viennese as compared to the Germans, so I take little pleasure in the Germans as compared to other people.' But then he had gone on to call them 'coarse, boring, petty, opinionated, pig-headed, pedantic, without any serenity in their philosophy of life, without grace or courtesy'. His own Viennese, on the other hand, he criticized with an almost loving leniency: 'A Jeremiah or Demosthenes could talk until his lungs burst before finding an echo in Vienna. But crack a joke and at once you have an audience.'

In the light of these utterances, his ambivalent and at times wildly contradictory attitude towards his Jewish countrymen may not come as a complete surprise. In his youth he had many good friends among them, including the revolutionaries of 1848 Frankl and Fischhof, the writer Emil Kuh and his fellow student Samuel Engländer, who was for a while his closest companion. At the age of fifty-one he was still able to develop the following enthusiastic vision:

It is indeed one of the most beautiful mixtures – the Jew touched by the Greek spirit ... When I saw a personality like Moritz Hartmann, my fancy willingly and as of its own accord transported itself to those centuries – just as for me the ages do not pass and all being is constantly present – when the fine minds of the South, tolerant Moors and learned Jews, in the light-filled courtyards at Palermo or Granada, held symposia of a beautiful humanity with a Hohenstaufen or an Abercerragen. They enticed new blooms from the ruins of Greek erudition, and gave themselves up to taking a serene pleasure in life, pursuing refining arts, exploring nature and spreading knowledge while in pope-deranged barbarity the half-savage peoples of the Nordic lands of wood and mists worshipped the bones of saints and kindled their metaphysics with pyres. With their mild hearts and sensible minds those Hellenic Semites were the true early fathers of humanism, and gladly would I lend their features to their great-grandson and his to them.

One may concede Kürnberger the afterthought: 'When at last a Hellene also sprouted from the Northern soil, he was a Goethe towering over Palermo and Granada.'

This panegyric was written in May 1872. Yet a few months earlier, when Grillparzer was laid in his grave, its author had been capable of the most vicious attack on the writer's Jewish admirers who joined the mourners at his obsequies. Poor Baroness Todesco, who had sent a large wreath, was mocked along with her brothers-in-faith: 'Nothing but good society, as you see. Good old blood, there long before Christ. What comes to represent Vienna on such an occasion is a pure act of generosity stemming from Samaria and Jerusalem, and Vienna looks on approvingly. A true Viennese during the whole funeral was at most a small and hardly visible minor figure, namely Grillparzer.' Not content with this, Kürnberger enforced his argument by putting the rhetorical question: 'Where else but in Austria would we have stronger need for purer air?'

Thus even a declared friend of the Jews, coming – as his biographer Rudolf Holzer stressed – 'from the depths of the people', was able at the drop of a hat to change into a rabid anti-Semite when his fancy returned from Granada to his own latitudes. A year later, when the Vienna stock exchange collapsed and some Jewish financiers were among those who had wrongfully deprived small shareholders of their investments, Kürnberger's wrath was directed full blast not merely against them but against everyone of their creed or descent. His near-contemporary and successor in the mastery of the satirical *feuilleton*, Daniel Spitzer (born fourteen years after Kürnberger in 1835), was less prone to such sentiments – though not entirely guiltless of them – being himself of Jewish origin. In his 'Vienna Rambles', which he published for nearly thirty years in various journals and collected in books, he consciously followed the example of Dr Johnson's *Rambler* and Addison's and Steele's *Spectator*, but his declared favourite among English models was the *Letters of Junius*, which may or may not have been written by Sir Philip Francis – in Spitzer's day there seems to have been no doubt that they were.

It was Spitzer, not Kürnberger, of whom it was said that 'when everybody slept, he was Vienna's ever-waking conscience' – a description which would later fit the night-worker Karl Kraus in a literal as well as metaphorical sense. Spitzer wrote polemics against incompetent cabinet ministers, bribable deputies, corrupt journalists, fraudulent bankers, arrogant aristocrats, conceited scholars, insolent innkeepers, bad poets, voiceless tenors and, when the occasion demanded it and without heeding his own origins, against Jewish evil-doers. Nothing was sacred to him but the truth. Since he would not allow himself to be bought by anyone he was habitually poor, but still generous to those worse off than himself. According to his own confession, he aspired to what the French writer Rivarol, another of his leading lights, had described as the 'meilleure espèce d'homme: faisant une épigramme contre un sot et donnant un écu à un pauvre'. Indeed, Spitzer's epigrams and aphorisms survived his often too topical prose. In Richard Wagner, whose music he disliked no less than did the critic Hanslick – caricatured by Wagner in his Beckmesser – he saw the 'noisiest sufferer in Germany'. 'Without forgetfulness', he said, 'there would be no originality'. And like Bertolt Brecht, who saw simplicity in writing as the most difficult thing to achieve, Spitzer stressed that it took 'a lot of work for no one to notice the work of the work'.

Caustic wit, as was proved by Kürnberger, was no prerogative of the Jewish mind. Yet it is also true that a number of Viennese *feuilletonistes* living in Spitzer's time, among them Ludwig Speidel, Friedrich Schlögl and Vinzenz Chiavacci, preferred straightforward or inoffensively humorous attacks on public and political ailments to the often mordant, hurtful sarcasm as practised above all by Spitzer's forerunner in the Biedermeier, the critic Moritz Saphir. Speidel, who had come to Vienna from Swabia, was a mild and modest man, a critic who would rather remain on friendly terms with the actors of the Hofburgtheater than treat them harshly when they had failed in their parts. His dictum 'A *feuilleton* is the immortality of one day' did not prevent him from producing hundreds of them, or from editing those of others for more than thirty years.

Schlögl, on the other hand, did not shrink from castigating the dark and cruel side of the Viennese make-up, such as their revolting habit of torturing animals for amusement, yet hung his stories and anecdotes on a number of funny popular prototypes – folk singers, drunks, busybodies, concierges and so on. Chiavacci did likewise, inventing a wonderful character called Frau Sopherl, a market-trader with the same sly, pseudo-naïve drollery masking as great a measure of commonsense as was later attributed to his 'good soldier Schwejk' by the Czech writer Hašek. In the 1880s this lady greengrocer from Vienna's Naschmarkt, officially called Frau Sophie Pimpernuss, was made by Chiavacci to predict not only the air travel of the future, but even 'star wars', conceivable only in the 1980s.

When a new generation of satirists, critics and *feuilletonistes* appeared on the scene, all born in the seventies or shortly before, they came none the less – with the exception of Franz Blei – from the same background as the members of *Jung-Wien*. Two of them indeed, Felix Salten and Felix Dörmann, belonged to that group but, apart from their more ambitious undertakings, applied themselves to the sort of elevated journalism which eventually finds its way into a book. Leaving aside for the moment Egon Friedell, Karl Kraus and Peter Altenberg, three literary figures whose personality, interests and achievements went far beyond this genre, the most outstanding writer of short prose was undoubtedly Alfred Polgar, born in 1873. At the age of twenty-two he joined the staff of a newspaper, began to write criticism and published his first *feuilleton* under the title 'Hunger', obviously inspired by Knut Hamsun. In a book review of 1901 Polgar demanded of 'the modern writer a microscopic eye tracing the most subtle connections, and a similarly constructed ear'.

Soon enough he was praised by Karl Kraus, by then an oracle and the self-appointed judge of his own age-group, for an article he had written about Wedekind's 'Lulu' plays: 'But everything I could have wanted to say or said about the morals of *Erdgeist* I have found in a piece by a young critic', admits Kraus, the younger by a year, 'who has grasped the dramatist's meaning and the heroine's character better than his mature colleagues.' A little later, as he was wont to do, Kraus withdrew his esteem and praise for a fellow writer who by some minor lapse or unwelcome opinion had enraged the *arbiter moralis*. Meanwhile Polgar had been recognized as a theatre critic of acumen and *esprit*, and his reputation rose throughout his life, which was long and, until he was forced to emigrate from Europe, highly successful. The novellas that he, like his contemporaries, felt he had to write in his youth, had not found favour with them. On a volume called *Quell des Übels* (Source of Evil) Schnitzler had

Arthur Schnitzler and his family in 1910.

Opposite above left *Karl Kraus in about 1908.*

Opposite above right *Hugo (Edler) von Hofmannsthal.*

Opposite below left *Ernst (Árnost) Polak, married first to Milena Jesenská, then to Delphine, daughter of Sir James and Lady Leila Reynolds.*

Above *The Café Central before the First World War.*

Opposite below right *Anton Kuh.*

commented: 'Piercing intelligence but a total lack of creative power.' As soon as Polgar realized that brevity had better be the soul also of his own considerable wit, and began to perfect the art of 'condensing a hundred lines into ten', he had found his niche.

His rise – from birth as Alfred Pollak, son of a small-time piano teacher and nephew of a ritual butcher in the Leopoldstadt, not merely to fame and eminence wherever German was spoken and read, but also to being considered the prototype of an Austrian *grand seigneur* – was representative of that of many others of his background at that time. Once he had decided to leave the second district, much of which was inhabited by poor, mostly unassimilated Jews, and moved first to the ninth district, preferred by academics, then to the first, the *Innere Stadt*, changing his name on the way, the process of integration into Viennese bourgeois society and intellectual life took place with extraordinary speed. For many years he was respected mainly for his reviews and, during the time he spent in Berlin, earned equal fame in this theatre-mad city. Yet Polgar became increasingly important as a critic of his times whose rapier was as polished as it was sharp. The bulk of his work unconnected with the stage was written in the twenties and thirties, and comprises narrative or polemical pieces prompted by happenings in everyday life, in the courts of justice or in politics. A six-volume collection of these, together with his reviews, has appeared only recently, and puts into perspective a writer whose elegance of style ennobled even the shortest and most marginal piece of prose.

For a while around 1908 he seemed inseparable from Egon Friedell, who was five years his junior but already an eccentric at thirty, turning his massive appearance, ungainly features, ever-growing erudition and histrionic talent to good use by shaping himself into a 'character' and much-respected crank. The two cultural histories he was to write, one of antiquity, the other of the modern age, did not appear until the late twenties. Meanwhile Friedell, born into the wealthy Friedmann family, studied at Heidelberg University, wrote a thesis on the eighteenth-century German poet Novalis as a philosopher, gained his doctorate and returned to Vienna to help run the cabaret *Die Fledermaus* (The Bat), which had been founded and installed amidst Josef Hoffmann's perfect *Jugendstil* décor in 1907. There the young Kokoschka showed his first – Indian – fairy tale, *Das getupfte Ei* (The Dotted Egg), on slides. At the opening the first wife of Adolf Loos, Lina, delivered a prologue by Peter Altenberg. From Bahr to Blei, every writer of renown wrote contributions. Soon Polgar started to collaborate with Friedell on a series of sketches and short plays, the most famous of which showed Goethe, disguised as a schoolboy, failing an examination about his own life and work. Needless to say, Friedell himself played the pupil.

His main activities as a historian, dramatist – his play *Judastragödie* (The Judas Tragedy) was performed at the Burgtheater – and, after a spell as theatre critic, as an actor in Max Reinhardt's famous Vienna ensemble, took place in the twenties and early thirties. As a young man he had built up his reputation not only as a budding sage but also as a fellow of infinite jest and most excellent fancy. Another such, though in a more freakish way, was Franz Blei, whom Polgar called 'the well-known peripatetic professor of eroticism'. It is remarkable how, in the complex, cosmopolitan climate of Vienna, this son of a Silesian cobbler, educated in the school of the Benedictine abbey at Melk on the Danube, turned into a historian of manifold disciplines and frequently frivolous bent. Moreover, Blei became an extremely prolific writer of novels, plays, opera libretti, and essays in learned as well as juicy prose. He also translated the works of Lucan, Claudel, Chesterton and Wilde, whom he met in Paris, as well as those of Gide, who supported him in his exile later in life. In his youth, Blei had flirted with socialism and left the Catholic church. After the war he rejoined it and at the same time professed communist ideals. Yet he was able to maintain, in an autobiographical tale, that 'ecclesiastical Baal is jealous of communist Beelzebub because the latter is mightier in his godlessness than all European Christendom, which camouflages its worldly affairs with a spiritual manner'.

A crank and a crackpot, one might be tempted to say: yet Blei had his wits about him, especially when in 1920 he wrote *Das grosse Bestiarium der Literatur* (The Great Bestiary of Literature), in which he caricatured contemporary authors in zoological terms. Far less eccentric and much more in line with the tradition of fairly good-natured *feuilletons* was Raoul Auernheimer, who saw himself mainly as a playwright but for decades was on the staff of, and a contributor to, *Neue Freie Presse*. This leading Vienna daily, founded in 1864, was considered to be a link with the most far-flung outposts of the empire, second only to the Imperial and Royal Army. Of its two editors-in-chief Moritz Benedict, the main leader-writer, has been credited with having been for a lifetime one of the ten or twelve most powerfully influential people in Austria. To many of the literati mentioned so far the *Presse* gave space or regular employment. Its cultural page, edited up to 1896 by Ludwig Speidel, was taken over in that year by the paper's former Paris correspondent Theodor Herzl, who stayed at this post until his death in 1904. Of the founder of Zionism more will be said in later chapters. In his role as a journalist of *belles-lettres* he did not differ much from Auernheimer and his ilk – writers of a smooth and versatile, often graceful and even pointed, but hardly outstanding prose.

Were there no women writers yet? Just as Marie von Ebner-Eschenbach was almost the only eminent female author in Austria at that time, so Marie Herzfeld was the only truly gifted essayist and distinguished stylist of her sex. Next to Hermann Bahr, she was the main interpreter of *fin de siècle* literature, while the hostess and society lady Berta Zuckerkandl was for a number of years, next to the professional critic Ludwig Hevesi (who supplied the motto carved in stone on Olbrich's building for the Secessionists), the most fervent advocate of *Jugendstil* art. From the same social stratum as Ebner-Eschenbach came Enrica von Handel-Mazzetti, born in 1871, forty years after that great and noble lady, and destined to live well into the Second Austrian Republic. Less advanced in her views than her forerunner, but an accomplished novelist in the tradition of the colourful historical chronicle, she grew to become the doyenne of a number of respected Catholic women poets and prose writers yet to come.

If the good and courageous Rosa Mayreder, musician, painter, essayist and librettist, deserves mention in this context, it is less for her talents in all these fields than for her work as the pioneer of women's emancipation in Austria. Similarly Betty Paoli, who in her day was considered a great story-teller and essayist, is remembered in ours mainly as another distinguished social reformer. A year before Rosa Mayreder founded the first 'free-thinking and bourgeois' *Allgemeinen Österreichischen Frauenverein* (General Austrian Women's Union), the Socialist Adelheid Popp had brought out her *Women Workers' Paper*. Another woman who had a considerable impact on her own and future generations was Bertha von Suttner, née Countess Kinsky, who in 1889 published the epoch-making book *Die Waffen nieder* (Down with Arms). A trail-blazer of pacifism and leader of national and international peace movements, she received the Nobel Prize for Peace in 1905. The importance of these excellent women as harbingers of progress far outshines their achievement in literature and the arts.

And so at last to Karl Kraus, the man who over twenty years ago was called by the *Times Literary Supplement* the 'greatest satirist of the twentieth century and one of the supreme masters of German prose', then unknown to the British reader. Though the same anonymous critic dismissed Schnitzler and Hoffmannsthal (*sic*) as 'relatively minor litterateurs' who had 'more than their share of appreciation', he was right in deploring his countrymen's ignorance of Kraus. A selection of excerpts from the satirist's work, published first in Canada and more recently in Britain, may not alter much, owing to the famous 'untranslatability' of that author. In 1984 the TLS devoted a whole page to the Kraus volume *In these Great Times*, edited by Professor Harry Zohn, compared with little more than a column in 1962. Yet its reviewer, D.J. Enright, still maintained that the writings of Kraus 'are unamenable to translation'. One may ask whether this is the only known case in literary history, and if so, why.

Verbal quips, puns, cracks and especially allusions to topics unknown outside a particular region, are indeed difficult and sometimes impossible to render in any other idiom (as a contemporary translator of perhaps the wittiest modern dramatist, Tom Stoppard, would be sure to find). It has been tried, even so. Quite possibly the overruling significance, indeed the magic power with which Kraus invested language, in his day and even now far beyond his death in 1936 deters potential contenders, like Tutankhamun's curse. To that writer, obsessed with the 'purity of the word', bad grammar was the equivalent of messy thinking, just as it had been for Arthur Schopenhauer, the German philosopher.

For Kraus, born of Jewish parents in the Bohemian town of Jičin – in the shadow of Wallenstein's castle – and taken to Vienna at the age of three, earlier examples may have been influential. There is a saying in the Talmud that 'the omission or the addition of one letter might mean the destruction of the whole world'. And though Kraus probably did not even know it, for he referred instead to Confucius who had condemned verbal laxity for the same reasons and in much the same way, the religious awe in which language was held by the people of the Bible must have been in his veins.

A moral preceptor of his age, an uncompromising fighter against injustice, a rigorous adversary of everything and everybody in the arts, politics and social life that appeared to him false or corrupt, is not made overnight. As a budding writer supported by his wealthy father, Kraus began in much the same way as the aesthetes of *Jung-Wien*. An exact contemporary of Hugo von Hofmannsthal at the Akademisches Gymnasium – Grillparzer's former school – he too entered the Griensteidl. Like Peter Altenberg, however, he made a special point of sitting at a separate table. Even so, Richard Specht noted among the *habitués* of their circle 'Karl Kraus, a callow youth, *médisant*, full of civil malice, splendidly aping all actors, full of parody and satirical ideas, ever ready to review our first books favourably, still unsure as to where he was going'. In those days young Kraus published articles in a number of journals and offered his services to others. He did not shrink even from contributing, under his pseudonym *Crêpe de Chine*, to *Neue Freie Presse*. And though he rejected his friends' decadence, attacking Hermann Bahr in a Munich periodical as early as 1893 for having a 'devastating effect on our young literature', and warning 'youngest Germany against this Frenchie', he did indeed – on the whole – write approvingly though by no means uncritically about the works of Bahr's disciples, such as Hofmannsthal's play *Gestern* or Schnitzler's *Anatol*.

Small of stature, slender, gangling and slightly hunched, Kraus also had ambitions of becoming an actor. One evening in a Vienna suburb he was allowed to appear as an understudy in the part of Franz Moor in Schiller's *Die Räuber* (The Highwaymen). Max Reinhardt played Spiegelberg, another villain. Next day, after Kraus had been replaced, Theodor Herzl joined the cast as yet another highwayman, Kosinsky. All this goes to show how close, in their beginnings, ran the paths of people in Vienna who in due course were to become obdurate enemies. As Kraus still remembered in the year before his death, his Franz Moor was torn to pieces by an anti-Semitic critic. At the Griensteidl, not long after, the feud Kraus had started against Bahr began to alienate him too from the younger writers. Finally, with Peter Altenberg, he wandered off to the Café Central. From this safe bastion late in 1896, in a new periodical, *Wiener Rundschau* (Vienna Review), he launched his first satirical broadside. The demolition of the Griensteidl, to make way for a rebuilding of the Palais Herberstein where it was housed, was announced in November of that year, to the dismay of its guests. This inspired Kraus to write a diatribe, 'Die demolierte Literatur' (The Demolished Literature), in which, without giving names, he characterized all members of *Jung-Wien* with biting irony.

Of Leopold von Andrian he remarked: 'One of the most tender flowers of decadence blossomed at the Café Griensteidl in the shape of a young baron who, we are told, traces back his mannerisms to the Crusades.' Only when his text was published as a pamphlet in the following year did it include an outburst against his fellow pupil Hofmannsthal, who had been spared in the earlier version: 'The fact that one of them still attended the *Gymnasium* [high school] led his discoverer to exclaim enthusiastically: "Goethe on the school-bench!" There was a rush to acquire the youth for the coffee-house and his parents introduced him there themselves ... He went about writing a fragment, feeling he owed it to his own ripe age to prepare his manuscripts for his literary estate ... then he memorized his Last Words.' Thus and worse about the rest of the group, only one of whom responded to the mockery. This was Felix Salten. In his diary Arthur Schnitzler noted down in December 1896: 'Last evening in the Café, Salten boxed little Kraus's ears (having also been attacked by him) which was gladly welcomed by everyone.'

In judging this pasquinade directed against former companions, as well as his next vituperative onslaught in 1898 when under the title *Eine Krone für Zion* (A Crown for Zion) he savaged Theodor Herzl and his book *Der Judenstaat* (The Jewish State), it is only fair to remember that Kraus was not yet twenty-five. However, in these, the first of the satirical lampoons that Kraus was to produce throughout his life, he was not merely indulging in youthful pranks, but once and for all set the tone for his further comments on and interventions in public life. His purpose was made clear when, in the last year of the century, he launched his periodical *Die Fackel* (The Torch). The play on words with which in his introductory article he announced that '*kein tönendes "Was wir bringen", aber ein ehrliches "Was wir umbringen"*' (no high-sounding 'What we shall print', but an honest 'What we shall destroy') would be the tri-monthly's maxim, is indeed untranslatable. Kraus further promised that the 'wide-reaching bog of phrases' in Vienna would be drained and the 'shameless peddling of our literati, the connections between theatre and journalism' which he had not been allowed to expose in other journals would now be laid bare.

It is impossible to exaggerate the impact of this first issue of *Die Fackel*, a scarlet-bound paperback, or of the nine hundred and twenty-one numbers that followed over the next thirty-seven years, on the intellectual youth of Vienna. Modelled in some ways on Henri de Rochefort's *La Lanterne*, it developed into a unique instrument for an undoubted man of genius, with all the idiosyncrasies, foibles and failings the term implies. Not until it was written entirely by himself, after 1911, did *Die Fackel* represent exclusively his own views. But his choice of contributors, and the way in which he dropped them after some time because of some spiritual or linguistic misdemeanour, revealed almost as much of Kraus's aims and convictions as did his own writings. His political bent changed over the years: his *Weltanschauung*, his ethics and aesthetics did not. They sometimes seemed to be in conflict, as when his conservative tastes in drama, dictated by the old Hofburgtheater of his youth, clashed with the encouragement he gave to new forms of writing, especially to the new expressionist writers, the lyrical poets Albert Ehrenstein, Berthold Viertel, G.Ch. Kulka, the young Franz Werfel or the German poet Else Lasker-Schüler. In the theatre, one might say, he was still addicted to ornamental bathos. In literature and the visual arts he hated everything polished and purple, eclectic and decorative – in short, Klimt's paintings, Hoffmann's architecture and Hofmannsthal's prose.

The gist of his philosophy of language, as summed up succinctly by the British scholar J.P. Stern, was a belief in the 'prestabilized harmony between language and mortality'. This is pure metaphysics, of course, as Professor Stern does not deny, therefore diametrically opposed to the tenets of Wittgenstein, and even more so to those of the Vienna neopositivist circle. However, his theory served Kraus well whenever he attacked a stupid or corrupt politician, writer, journalist or other public figure. A mixed metaphor was enough to condemn a man, but since he usually chose as his butt people who had otherwise proved to be idiots or scoundrels, he could not go far wrong in pointing out their linguistic defects. Like Kürnberger, whom he chose to name as his lodestar – though Daniel Spitzer might have been nearer the mark – he was sometimes irrationally and unshakably opinionated in his likes and dislikes. In this respect he did a great deal of harm, because his ever-growing mass of disciples, mesmerized by his verbal command, his wit and his charm, ended up by swallowing uncritically all the admiration or contempt, every prejudice or partiality that Kraus harboured for or against his fellow human beings and never tired of expounding.

His charm, less evident in his writings, came to the fore in the many hundreds of public appearances he made in his life. He had begun quite early to mount one platform or another (later usually the Mozartsaal in Vienna's Konzerthaus) in order to read not only from his own writings but also from the works of Shakespeare, Nestroy and his beloved Offenbach – the music of whose operettas he would render in a high-pitched but well-modulated voice. As has been pointed out, Kraus was not a handsome man. But his features betrayed his sharp mind and sensitivity; when he took off his sparkling metal-rimmed glasses to stress a point, his eyes proved to be of a magnetic blue; and his hands, which he used extensively to support his punch lines, were beautiful. As his friends have testified, in private he was generous, lovable, mild. But he was merciless in his fight against what he considered to be evil, mainly the *journaille* (his portmanteau word denoting both journalist and *canaille*), and all those representatives of powerful institutions whom, when they erred in their conduct, Kürnberger, Spitzer and other satirists before him had exposed to ridicule.

To this day, fifty years after his death, such respected survivors of his age as the writer and Nobel prize winner Elias Canetti, the biochemist and near-Nobel prize winner Erwin Chargaff and the composer Ernst Krenek profess to having been under his spell and profiting from it all their lives. Many other less famous people in the German-speaking world or outside, wherever their exile took them, bear the traces, in their mental outlook and literary preferences or antipathies, of an early indoctrination by Karl Kraus. Having heard them mention his name, one can safely assume that they admire Shakespeare, Matthias Claudius, Goethe, Nestroy and Offenbach, but abhor Heine, George Bernard Shaw, Hofmannsthal, the later Werfel and Stefan Zweig – without in some cases even remembering the reasons. In politics they usually find it more difficult to follow his example. For around the turn of the century Kraus sympathized with the Socialists; then (spellbound by the attractive Baroness Sidonie Nádherný and her circle) turned conservative, in fact preferred Crown Prince Ferdinand to Franz Joseph; during the First World War showed himself to be a staunch pacifist; in the twenties renewed his friendship with the Left and afterwards, when democracy in Austria was ended by the Dollfuss regime, became an advocate of the 'pocket dictator' and his successor, Schuschnigg. This discerning, brilliant mind had not seen through the theory of the 'lesser evil' with all its fatal implications.

Despite his undoubted failings, Karl Kraus must be seen as one of the great moralists of this world, a man, who though he often overstepped the mark, did more than any other in his day to set standards of common decency and to expose hypocrites, frauds and scoundrels in every walk of life wherever he came across them. Early on he embraced the cause of women, protesting against the maltreatment or indignities inflicted on them and pleading for their sexual freedom, yet he could not have been called a feminist. Another issue with which he was deeply concerned, as we have shown, was the fight of Adolf Loos against the Secessionist conception of art. In around 1908, when he was still in his early thirties, Kraus threw himself into this controversy with youthful vigour: 'I sweep the streets, I loosen the beards, I shave the ornaments', was one of his slogans. And later he explained, 'All that Loos and I have done, he literally, I verbally, was to show that there is a difference between an urn and a chamber pot and that only in this difference does culture find room to play.' The hundreds of diatribes he published in *Die Fackel* were collected in books which up to the war included such titles as *Sittlichkeit und Kriminalität* (Morality and Criminality) and *Die chinesische Mauer* (The Chinese Wall), as well as three volumes of aphorisms. His greatest work, the drama *Die letzten Tage der Menschheit* (The Last Days of Mankind), was still to come, as was his growing obsession with a mysticism of language.

It has been said that Kraus induced in his contemporaries either complete devotion or abject enmity. In trying to do him justice *sine ira et studio*, one must be prepared for criticism from either side. One way of replying to his attacks at the time was simply to ignore him. The *Neue Freie Presse* did just that, according to the biblical curse, as Kraus himself put it, 'Let him not be named.' In the house of Hugo von Hofmannsthal, as the writer's daughter Christiane has disclosed, Kraus was never mentioned. The former schoolmate who with Hofmannsthal had celebrated their joint graduation in the small park outside the Akademisches Gymnasium, but who had begun to lampoon him a few years later, 'was not a topic of conversation' in the little baroque palais at Rodaun.

A devastatingly outspoken attack on Kraus was, however, made by Anton Kuh, youngest among the great wits, coffee-house *causeurs* and satirical authors during the period here described, having been born in 1891. He was also an outstanding orator with the ability to improvise, in front of gatherings much like the audiences at Kraus's readings or harangues, a sparkling discourse on any given or chosen subject. The most memorable of these, held in October 1925 (and sometimes repeated in the following years, when the present writer was old enough to attend one), consisted of an attempt not merely to ridicule, but seriously to undermine the authority Kraus enjoyed as the self-appointed preceptor of Vienna's intellectual youth. It was a feat of brilliant punch and spite, of penetrating observations and quite a few unanswerable arguments. Kuh himself came from a family originating in Bohemia like that of Kraus, yet nearer than the other's paper-bag-producing kin to the literary traditions of Prague. Kuh's uncle Emil had been Kürnberger's friend. His grandfather David was known as an 'ardent pioneer of Germanness in Bohemia', the first to doubt the authenticity of the *Königinhofer Handschrift* – a 'medieval' manuscript forged by a Czech to prove the six-hundred-year-old culture of the Slavs and finally exposed as a fraud by Thomas G. Masaryk, future first president of Czechoslovakia. A still earlier member of the Kuh family had been Ephraim Moses of Berlin, a soul mate of Moses Mendelssohn, who, in Germany's short era of enlightenment, had led the Jews into emancipation.

If during one of his many visits to Berlin and the Romanisches Café Anton Kuh earned himself the sobriquet *Hirnzigeuner* (gipsy of the brain), his braininess was probably inherited, and his gipsy life style a result of the easy-going, mellow atmosphere of the Vienna into which he was born. More than a thousand scattered prose pieces – mostly humorous sketches, anecdotes and aphorisms – and abundant proof of his rhetorical artistry may not yet entitle him to rank with contemporaries such as Friedell or Polgar. But Kuh also published some books of serious purpose, among them a long tract on *Juden und Deutsche* (Jews and Germans) and another on physiognomy, and he edited an anthology of the work of Ludwig Börne, with whom he felt an elective affinity. Like Peter Altenberg, he posed as a pauper and a scrounger, paying for his meal tickets and never-to-be-repaid loans with charm and wit. Yet he was quite able to support himself by writing. His most generous income, early in the First Republic, came from his contributions to a newspaper owned by the brilliant but allegedly corrupt Hungarian journalist, Imre Békessy. When that typical post-war figure (incidentally the father of a writer well known in our day under the pseudonym Hans Habe) was hounded out of Austria in 1926 by the rare common consent of *Neue Freie Presse*, the Socialist town council and Karl Kraus, Kuh lost the only regular livelihood he ever had.

Having been in Békessy's pay was not thought to be to Kuh's credit. Yet his great attack on Kraus, mounted about ten months before his employer's forced exit, should not be seen as part of the battle already raging between these two. Kuh earnestly considered the magnetic hold Kraus exercised on the city's youth – the writer Gina Kaus, who was a friend of them both, had called her near namesake the 'Pied Piper of Vienna' – as no less than pernicious. Before a mostly hostile crowd of Kraus's fans he dissected the idiosyncrasies and foibles of their idol, his mania for always being in the right, for having the last word in every debate, for laying down the law in all respects and for demanding blind conformity from his followers. 'The last word is nothing,' Kuh exclaimed, 'it is the first word that counts.' The 'intelligent plebeians' Kraus was breeding, he maintained, were taught to despise whatever and whomever their master hated, from Heinrich Heine to psychoanalysis. He conceded to Kraus the sharp 'stranger's eye' which looked past the graceful, elegant and attractive atmosphere of Vienna to its basic sloppiness, flippancy and triviality. But he warned his audience not to believe in the 'metaphysics of the comma' preached by Kraus, not to imitate the satirist's convoluted and 'preventive' style – designed to forestall every possible counter-argument – and not to paralyse their own powers of reasoning by simply accepting the ideas set before them.

Finally in his speech Kuh quoted from Friedrich Nietzsche's prose-poem *Thus spake Zarathustra*, likening Kraus to the fool called by Nietzsche 'Zarathustra's Ape'. The wise man asks the fool:

'Why did you dwell so long by the mire that you yourself had to turn into a
    frog and a toad?
Does not a foul foamy marsh-blood now flow through your own veins so that
    you also had to learn now to croak and scoff?
Why did you not go into the wood? Or plough the earth? Is the ocean not full
    of green islands?'

In a contemptuous peroration, Kuh then took leave of the subject of his polemic by asserting that he would not compete in a race with the 'foaming fool': 'Herewith I yield my place to him, the Lord of Speech to the Servant of the Word.' According to the printed version of 'Zarathustra's Ape', which contains audience reactions including derisive laughter and dissent, the evening ended with 'lively, sustained applause'. For once Kraus's faithful fans had been silenced by someone else's verbal mastery.

Even so, time has shown that Kuh's adversary did have the last word. The work of Karl Kraus, especially his masterpiece, the drama *The Last Days of Mankind*, has survived triumphantly and is now known outside central Europe, while that of Kuh enjoys no greater celebrity than some recent modest reprints in his native town. Posthumous global fame, except among some departments of Germanic languages and literature at American universities, was not achieved either by the only true poet and imaginative writer among those capturing 'the world in a dewdrop'. Peter Altenberg, strolling between the warring camps with both childlike trust and cunning, as we have seen, succeeded in keeping out of the internal feuds among Vienna's artists and intellectuals. It was Karl Kraus who in 1894 had sent a first collection of Altenberg's impressionist prose to the Berlin publisher Samuel Fischer. Around the turn of the century Arthur Schnitzler saw Altenberg in a Prater café 'with his repulsive disciples Pollak (Polgar) and Grossmann' – both soon to be equally disdained by Kraus. All his life Altenberg remained on friendly terms not only with Klimt as well as Loos, but also with some deadly enemies of his first helper and ever-devoted admirer, such as the Berlin critic Alfred Kerr.

Peter Altenberg came from a merchant family by the name of Engländer, and borrowed his pseudonym, which he liked to abbreviate to P.A., from a lovely small village on the Danube. In a short auto-biographical text published in 1901, he gave a simple explanation of his literary aims: 'Are my little pieces poetic works? Not at all. They are extracts! Extracts of life. The life of the soul and the random happenings of the day, boiled down to two or three pages, freed of the superfluous like the ox in the meat-cube.' It was not a pretty simile, as it happened. But Altenberg was never squeamish where his vocabulary or imagery were concerned. He wrote as the birds sing, as the saying went in Vienna, and mixed beautiful descriptions and evocative metaphors with sloppy idiomatic terms. About ten volumes of his collected sketches, verbal *moments musicaux*, remain in print. Many of their titles express the intensely personal, even egomaniacal way in which these prose pieces came to be written: 'The Way I See It' (*Wie ich es sehe*), 'What the Day Tells Me' (*Was der Tag mir zuträgt*), '*Vita Ipsa*', 'Harvest' (*Fechsung*) or 'The Evening of my Life' (*Mein Lebensabend*). To many great men of his age, among them Hofmannsthal, Kokoschka, Hermann Hesse and Thomas Mann, his word-paintings and musings were pure enchantment. Only Bertolt Brecht was unimpressed. 'Forgive me,' he said to Karl Kraus, 'but if I read that man, an iron curtain comes down for me.' This would seem to have been a premature but all the more prophetic expression, though neither Brecht nor Kraus foresaw the historic irony at the time.

What has remained of Altenberg, or rather what was resuscitated after decades of oblivion, is not so much his oeuvre but the legend of the man, and one of such luminosity that it continued to shine long after his death in 1919. The 'Holy Fool' in a Dostoievskian sense; the inveterate bohemian; the worshipper of very young girls and 'fallen' women, indeed the friend and protector of the somewhat innocently depraved, pretty and sentimental little whores of imperial Vienna; the first to proclaim that black was beautiful, after he had visited the Ashanti village set up for a while in the Prater and become the lover of an African girl called Akolé; the passive paedophile who plastered his room with photographs of scantily clad female children, in the manner of Lewis Carroll and with the same degree of sexual restraint – all these facets of Altenberg, though forgotten for a while, have now been disinterred for public examination.

His room was not to be found in a private house or apartment, of course, but in a hotel – in winter right in the middle of town, conveniently near the Café Central which was his only permanent address, in summer somewhere on the slopes of one of the nearest mountain ranges, the Rax or Semmering, or else by a lake in the Salzkammergut. Altenberg was an early apostle of nature, as Kürnberger had been. He adored alpine meadows as much as the parks of Vienna, especially the Volksgarten where, near the pseudo-classical Temple of Theseus, he watched pretty little girls at play. He wore loose garments and sandals, refused to sport the stiff hats that were *de rigueur* in his day, never wore a nightshirt and, as he liked to stress, left his windows wide open 'on the coldest of nights'. Yet, as the story went, when Friedell passed the Graben hotel one early winter morning he saw Altenberg's window tightly shut. Upon being challenged, the poet merely said with a twinkle: 'Well, Egon, it wasn't the coldest of nights.'

The manner of his death was all the more macabre: he had fallen asleep in his hotel bed one December night in a somewhat inebriated state, having first spilled on the sheets a full glass of wine which, as his eiderdown slipped off, turned to icy damp in the draught. Pneumonia killed him three weeks later. The self-styled pauper left a small fortune of 100,000 Austrian crowns, which he bequeathed to a society for the protection of children. All this is characteristic of a man in whose life truth and fantasy, fact and fiction, honesty and mendacity were curiously mixed. Altenberg was a hypochondriac, but he suffered from ill-health too. He feigned eccentricity, yet once had to be interned, diagnosed as paranoid, in the city's lunatic asylum. Hofmannsthal has told the story of how a crowd of friends gathered to confer on how Altenberg's present poverty could be relieved. The poet had sat in an armchair in a corner of the room, covering his face with his hands. 'I am a beggar and a dying man,' he moaned. 'Just let me depart in peace.' A pretty young woman got up and implored the others to let him have his will: 'Don't touch the beauty of his end!' Whereupon P.A. raised himself up and shouted: 'Damned silly goose! I don't want to die! I want to live! I want a warm room and a gas stove, and an American rocking chair, an income, orange marmalade, beef broth, filet mignon; I want to live!'

In view of these endearing if exasperating histrionics, it is sometimes amusing to find Altenberg elevated in modern interpretations to the status of a great cult figure of feminism, social justice, anti-racism, the pure and simple life. It is true that he preached all this and followed most of his own commandments. But he was also tempted now and again, in bouts of childlike egotism or boredom with his own convictions, to play the buffoon and the jester, happily breaking all the laws he had himself laid down. The Vienna of his day understood. Posterity, removed as it is from his time and place, is in danger of overlooking the self-mockery, frivolous antics and witty exaggerations to which P.A. and his fellow writers were prone. They fought, or at least ridiculed, even their best friends. But when one of them died, their grief was genuine and profound.

At Altenberg's grave, Karl Kraus, the great hater, gave a most loving and moving funeral oration. He praised P.A. as 'one of the great poets that have been merely loaned to their time'. But he also lamented 'the fool who set up norms', the artist who 'practised faith in inconstancy, ruthless self-preservation while spending all of himself. But I', he promised his dead friend, 'will accept you, as long as I can think of you, along with your rich work, in all your inscrutability.' If those nearest to Altenberg did not claim to have understood him, how can any of us now? His enigma is that of any true poet. His dewdrops shimmer to this day.

8

NOT LIFE
BUT APPARITION

In 1900 Vienna was one of the five largest cities in the world. Moreover, its inhabitants prided themselves on possessing not only the most majestic public buildings, such as its house of parliament, its town hall, its museums of natural history and the fine arts, its concert hall and its opera house, all of them gleaming with gold and marble and sumptuous frescoes as befitted the capital of a far-flung empire, but also the grandest and most venerated theatre in the German-speaking world: the Hofburgtheater.

Loath for the most part, until recent times, to entrust their thoughts and feelings to language and therefore late in developing a literature of their own, the Viennese had always loved play-acting and any kind of entertainment offered to them from a stage or rostrum. In this they were akin to the Italians, many of whom lived in their midst, and they were equally fond of harlequin shows containing stock characters like those of the *commedia dell'arte*. Indeed for centuries Kasperl and Hanswurst, the Austrian counterpart of Arlecchino and Punch, amused the simple folk, while the court and nobility attended splendid operatic spectacles or earnest Jesuit plays written and performed in Latin.

Enlightenment, worthy though it was in improving the morals and increasing the tolerance towards their fellows even of the easy-going and by no means unprejudiced Viennese, tried to rob them of the Kasperl so dear to their hearts. As we have seen, it was Joseph von Sonnenfels, Maria Theresia's adviser and a baptized Jew, who wanted to drive him out in favour of the classicist drama then emerging in Weimar, Jena, Hamburg and Berlin. In 1920 Hermann Bahr, the former head and protector of *Jung-Wien* but now in his old age reverting – though in a milder and more selective way – to the anti-Semitism of his student days, launched a posthumous attack against Sonnenfels. According to him only 'the grandson of a Berlin Rabbi and son of the Nikolsburg Jew Perlin Lippmann, an immigrant from Moravia', a man 'who personified resentment itself', could have mustered the 'heinous courage' to send to school 'a city in which every archway was then the monument to a living culture, with enlightened German tutors like Gottsched and Nicolai'. With Sonnenfels, said Bahr, 'there entered into Austria something which has since been called *Bildung* [higher education]'. Through this *Bildung*, Bahr maintained, the whole sensuous world would be deposed, in fact 'man himself, faded to an abstraction, had to be deposed and replaced by the word'.

Despite this belated sortie against the Maria–Theresian reformer, theatrical history had gone a different way. While the most primitive *Kasperl* plays disappeared, not merely thanks to Sonnenfels but of their own accord, the old Viennese folk comedy went on flourishing and coexisting with every kind of serious theatre. Two of the greatest playwrights on Austria's short list of dramatic genius, Johann Nestroy and Ferdinand Raimund, rose from its ranks. But the so-called *Bildungsdrama* (educative play) did indeed have to be imposed on the Viennese from above, if not by Maria Theresia and her adviser, then by her son and successor Joseph II. In 1776 he founded the Hof- und Nationaltheater – later Hofburgtheater – housed first in an annexe to his residence in the heart of the city and moved to the magnificent new Ringstrasse only in 1888, much to the initial dismay of the actors and their public.

Both in its former modest and its subsequent palatial abode, however, the Court and National Theatre by Imperial Command was taken to their hearts by the Viennese, especially since its directors soon added to their habitual repertoire of the great tragedies lighter fare such as Goldoni and Gozzi, or comedies by the German Kotzebue and the Parisian Scribe. In his edict concerning the theatre, His Majesty the Emperor had laid down 'that he would not have performed plays containing funerals, cemeteries, vaults and suchlike sombre scenes' – a formula parodied by Hofmannsthal's Majordomo in his opera *Ariadne*. Presumably *Romeo and Juliet* was not performed in Joseph II's day. What did go on at the Hofburgtheater were three Mozart operas, including *Seraglio* which contained, as he allegedly told the composer, 'too many notes' for the emperor's taste. Even if true, this anecdote should not blind us to the fact that Maria Theresia's eldest son was a man of erudition and some aesthetic refinement who, while not usually given to jesting, may on this occasion have meant to chide Mozart in a jocular way.

The Burgtheater, as it was known for short, was from the outset recognized as the foremost of all playhouses in the German-speaking world, and has never relinquished this claim up to the present day. For the Viennese it acquired an additional function, once more described (this time around 1906 and in a less polemical mood) by Hermann Bahr. In the theatre, he wrote, 'the Viennese wants to find out how to behave.

This goes for the common man as for the elevated. The one learns from Fichtner or Sonnenthal [two actors] how to move in a drawing-room, how to wear his hat and hold his cane; Vienna's elegance is always derived from the Burgtheater. The other listens to discover how to feel with distinction. The Viennese always needs an example. For this he visits the theatre. It is no image of life. Life is its image.' Not only the performers were being aped – certain moods, even in Viennese poetry, were not experienced but taken over, ready-made, from something seen on stage. Not many years after this was pointed out by Bahr, it was elaborated on by Felix Salten in an essay on two contemporary actors, the comedian Alexander Girardi and the tragedian Josef Kainz.

In a fictional letter to a friend in Berlin, Salten assumes that its recipient has heard of Girardi being the epitome of the Viennese character. And, says Salten, this is true, but only up to a point:

When Girardi speaks we hear in his voice primeval popular sounds, when he sings we hear in his gaiety the jubilant tones of drunken recruits reverberating in our streets in spring and autumn. When people talk of Girardi, they immediately compare with him all the Viennese types, the *Fiaker* coachman; the soldier in Vienna's home regiment, the *Deutschmeister*; the head waiter; the sporting baron. Yet in fact the Viennese character he portrays is not the real one, but one that he has invented all by himself.

Previously it had not existed:

Since he made it up it has been imitated. People have learned from him in the theatre how to be Viennese, and have gone on to copy it. Hundreds of his inventions, his new ideas of how to be Viennese, have now taken flesh and walk the streets . . . in the end every other young gentleman you met, every cab-driver, every postman, every philistine was playing a part by Girardi.

In Josef Kainz – an actor in whom he detected an 'Austro-Italian mixture of musical grace and suppleness' – Salten saw embodied 'a lasting, passionate urge to reach above oneself and, on a higher plane, find the way back to oneself'. Since Kainz was for more than a decade (1898 to 1910) the leading heroic and poetic young actor at the Burgtheater, his example can be assumed to have led its audiences towards the improvement of character envisaged by its founder, the enlightened monarch. Indeed before and after him generations of schoolchildren and other earnest theatre-goers have experienced, in this temple erected to dramatic art, spiritual uplift comparable only to a religious experience. As the twentieth century moved towards its more brutal phase, this function of a 'school of morals' – of which the present writer in her childhood was well aware – was bound to cease. Yet even now the Burgtheater, under various managements, has not quite lost its educative mission: a 'necessary yardstick' of traditional values, as the German leader of avant-garde aesthetics Bazon Brock has called it, against which to measure all progressive and experimental advancement on the modern stage. (The latest era, under the new director Claus Peymann, is about to introduce the Burgtheater and its smaller house, the Akademietheater, to these very innovations.)

During the period described here the ultimate aim of every Viennese playwright was to have his work performed at the Burgtheater. Earlier on this institution born from the imperial wish to create a home for neo-classical drama in the German language had found its one and only Austrian classical writer in Franz Grillparzer, director of the treasury archive. Even after achieving fame he held on to his post until due for retirement from the civil service at sixty-five, when he left with the most coveted Austrian title of *Hofrat*, Court Counsellor. His early plays, mostly in iambic verse, delved into both Greek and Austrian history. But he also tried his hand at one light-hearted comedy at least, *Weh dem der lügt* (Woe to the Liar), which, ill-received at its first performance in 1838, caused him to withdraw from public life and to bury his subsequent work in a drawer. Two years before that failure he had praised the merits of solitude in his dramatic poem after Calderon's *La Vida es Sueño*. Since *Der Traum ein Leben* (A Dream is Life) offers a key not only to Grillparzer's own soul, but to the inner make-up of a small though significant number of his compatriots, it had better be touched upon briefly.

In the course of one night a young man goes through the experiences of a lifetime. He falls in love with a beautiful princess, fights a glorious battle and becomes involved in intrigues which end in his being convicted for murder. At the right moment, however, he awakens, cured for ever of his longing to enter the great world and content to remain in the idyllic seclusion of his home. 'For', it is said in this play, 'there is danger in greatness, and fame is but an idle game.' This sentence might serve as a motto for Grillparzer's own existence, which was beset by fears and anxieties, and by a definite reluctance to commit himself in any way. The best of his histories was no doubt *Ein Bruderzwist in Habsburg* (Family Strife in Habsburg), built around the lives of the emperors Rudolf II and Matthias. Yet, though he would not have realized it, his own life and career were as much of an Austrian tragedy as his drama of the two hostile Habsburg brothers. For he was himself the model of a peculiar kind of Austrian – not the familiar, easy-going, voluble, extravert type, but one made of finer stuff and therefore all the more defenceless. He might have

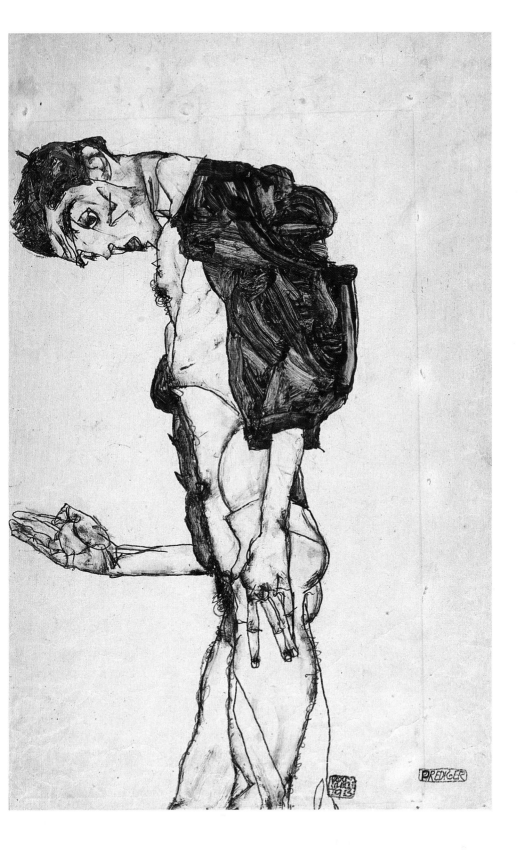

1926

Opposite: 2 *Marie Louise Motesiczky,
Self-portrait with Comb, 1926.*
(*Marie Louise Motesiczky, London*)

Previous page: 1 *Egon Schiele,*
Prediger (The Preacher), 1913.
(*Archiv Brandstätter, Vienna*)

Above: 3 *Oskar Kokoschka,* Die
Windsbraut (The Tempest), *1914.*
(*Kunstmuseum, Basle/Bridgeman Art
Library*)

4 *Maximilien Lenz*, Sirk-Ecke, *the social meeting place opposite the opera house,
1900.* (*Historisches Museum der Stadt Wien, Vienna*)

5 *Gustav Klimt*, Adele Bloch–
Bauer I, *1907* (*detail*).
(*Osterreichische Galerie*,
Vienna)

Opposite: 6 *Karl Marx-Hof, the largest workers' tenement building in Vienna.*

The Secession building.

Above: 7 *Historicism and the Secessionist style as typified by the Musikverein and Otto Wagner's underground station, Karlsplatz.*
(Photos on this page, Hubmann Archiv, Vienna)

Above: 9 *Georg Merkel,* Italian Landscape, *1923.*
(*Dr Merkel, Vienna*)

Left: 10 *Richard Gerstl,* Self-portrait, *September 1908.*
(*Dr Rudolf Leopold, Vienna*)

been the first in a long line of characters created by later writers such as Hofmannsthal and Musil – men of talent, of genius even, who are unable to face reality, unable to declare themselves to a woman, unable to stand up to their superiors, and unable to utter the right word at the right time, even though they have hit on it sooner than anyone else.

In Hofmannsthal's play *Der Schwierige* (The Difficult Man) this prototype found its most lovable literary expression. Count Bühl, a man of forty, constantly ties himself up in knots as he tries to clear up the tangle of his emotions. Though he goes through life wishing to hurt no one, he leaves a trail of broken hearts and misunderstandings behind him. He is convinced that one cannot open one's mouth without causing unholy confusion. Everything one utters is indecent. At certain moments 'it may be impudent even to live'. All this, as his nephew tells him, may be a *bizarrerie*, but it very nearly leads to his undoing. Still, this is a comedy, so all ends well. Astonishingly, this graceful work, seemingly unburdened by outside political events, was published three years after the end of the conflagration and the downfall of the monarchy. It is set not in a no-man's-land but in a never-never time, since the aristocratic hierarchy and way of life remain intact, while the war seems to be over and Count Bühl speaks of his experiences in the trenches. At the same time *Der Schwierige* is a perfect example of that autonomy of Austrian literature within the sphere of German writing which was so often denied, on occasion by Hofmannsthal himself. No wonder the prominent Berlin critic Alfred Kerr – whose appreciation of Viennese whims and fancies did not stop short even of Peter Altenberg – found himself helpless before this exquisite masterpiece: 'Oh dear, three acts, social comedy. In the ultra-refined Austrian air. Aristocracy. So what? Where everyone calls everyone else by their first name, you know.'

Written at the beginning of a period which, in our context, can only be treated summarily as the aftermath of Vienna's greatest cultural era, *Der Schwierige* must be considered a late crowning of Hofmannsthal's dramatic invention. When he began to write verse plays at the age of sixteen – the first, *Gestern* (Yesterday), published under the pseudonym Theophil Morren – he depicted himself in many guises. In *Gestern* he was Andrea, the young Renaissance man, drunk with words, yet doubting their ability to convey the fullness of his emotions. In *Der Tod des Tizian* (The Death of Titian) he may have been Gianino, of whom he says that he is 'sixteen years old and very beautiful'. In his most famous early work, *Der Tor und der Tod* (Death and the Fool), his Claudio – another image of himself, as Werther had been Goethe's – became a role model for his generation no less than Werther had been for an earlier one.

In all these plays the mood of the nineties prevailed. Though 'deeds are powerless' and 'true feeling cannot be uttered', as Andrea asserts, he goes on verbally to paint the fleeting expressions of today – for 'yesterday is a lie and only today is real' – in glowing colours. Gianino, pupil of the dying Titian, is so gripped on a warm Venetian night by his own visions of women's hair and scented aloe, that their 'overwhelming heavy splendour renders the senses mute and robs words of their meaning'. For 'life, the living and omnipotent – / You may have it but still forget it'. And Claudio, called away by Death before he has known how to feel, to love, to pray, becomes aware only in his last hour that he exists:

> When someone dreams, he may by a full measure
> Of dreamed emotion from his sleep be roused.
> So now in overflowing feeling
> I wake from life's dream to the consciousness of death.

Even though they expressed or influenced the mental and sentimental attitudes of his contemporaries, the early dramatic works of Hofmannsthal were never publicly performed. He read them to a selected circle in the salons of the Gomperz sisters – at the Palais Todesco and at the Villa Wertheimstein – or they were read and even performed by others in private. It was not until 1899 that two later one-act plays of his, *Der Abenteurer und die Sängerin* (The Adventurer and the Singer) and *Die Hochzeit der Sobeide* (The Marriage of Sobeide), reached the Burgtheater. Despite – or because of – the poetic beauty of these works, their formal grace and polish and their elevated thoughts, neither these nor his subsequent works in similar style appealed to a wider audience. Apart from his pastiches of old mysteries – *Jedermann*, after the middle English *Everyman*, or the *Salzburger Grosse Welttheater* (The Great Salzburg Theatre of the World), after Calderon – Hofmannsthal's writings for the stage did not gain popularity until he decided to use the idiom of his own day and social environment, as in his *Der Schwierige* and *Der Unbestechliche* (The Incorruptible). These loveliest of all Austrian comedies had been preceded, in 1911, by *Der Rosenkavalier*. But by then, in fact five years earlier, he had found in Richard Strauss a congenial if more than forceful partner whose music supplied the dramatic power lacking in Hofmannsthal's fastidious texts.

Of the two greatest writers in Vienna during the period covered here, it was Schnitzler who became its foremost playwright. Of him Egon Friedell said that he had 'captured *fin de siècle* Vienna and conserved it for later generations; through him, a whole city ... became resounding and luminous ... His works are costume dramas of the soul which can never be lost.' This, however, was due to the fact that after Schnitzler's first verse play, *Alkandi's Lied* (Alkandi's Song), much in the vein of Hofmannsthal's poetic scenarios and like these never staged, he began to mirror the world around him, or rather that part of it which he knew and moved in. The nineties, after all, were not exclusively the decade of Parisian and Viennese decadence but also of naturalism, which had entered prose and dramatic writing in the eighties. While in 1891 Bahr wanted to 'overcome' it, this literary school persisted and, as in the works of Hauptmann, survived the short-lived neo-romantic, symbolist phase. By the turn of the century contemporary metrical, lyrical drama was more or less played out. In the six years before Strauss set it to music, Hofmannsthal's *Elektra*, though a poetic *tour de force*, had little success.

In his *Anatol* cycle, written between 1888 and 1891, Schnitzler depicted in a number of short and poignant sketches typical characters and situations among the light-hearted and loose-living but modishly melancholic youth of Vienna's bourgeois society. In doing this he created new legends – among them that of the lazy, charming, sensitive, self-absorbed and gently ruthless young man-about-town, as personified by his hero Anatol; the *süsse Mädel*, a sweet and unselfish, tender-hearted girl who in the end is always deserted; and the *femme fatale*, a lovely and well-married but usually scheming and utterly faithless creature, a much more fitting partner for the passionate but heartless Anatol. These playlets (nowadays invariably shown in one evening) quickly found their way one by one onto one stage or another, the most charming of them, *Abschiedssouper* (The Farewell Supper), being first performed at the small theatre of Ischl in July 1893, during the emperor's sojourn in that town.

Two years later, in a double bill with a one-act play by the Italian Giacosa, Schnitzler's *Liebelei* (Playing with Love) reached the Burgtheater. And though he did not, or was not asked to, entrust all his premieres to that venerable playhouse, the fact that most of his works sooner or later reached its stage led to his being regarded as the most outstanding though by no means the least controversial dramatist in Vienna. One play which had no hope of being mounted on the august boards but nearly ruined his reputation instead, was *Reigen* (1921) – usually known in English productions as *La Ronde* after the French film version – a sexual merry-go-round described with as much cynical wit as compassion. After running for more than three hundred performances in Berlin, yet causing a scandal at its Viennese first night on a minor stage, it was withdrawn by the author during his lifetime and banned for decades after. From Schnitzler's large dramatic output two works must be singled out. One, *Professor Bernhardi*, a study of clerical narrow-mindedness and nationalist anti-Semitism in the realm of medicine, as experienced by the author's own father, has been mentioned before. Its characters and their attitudes are still relevant today.

The other, rather more dated since its dénouement, caused by a duel, would no longer be possible, yet still valid in its psychological insight, is *Das weite Land* – revived comparatively recently in both London (*Undiscovered Country*) and Paris (*Terre Etrangère*). Schnitzler's sceptical view of human loyalty, constancy and reliability, based as much as Hofmannsthal's elegiac poetry on the theories of Ernst Mach, manifests itself here in the relations between his protagonists. The soul is a large and unexplored field: marital tragedies are caused by flippant flirtations, and a young man is killed in a duel by his lover's husband not from jealousy but because his opponent, an older man, is outraged by his provocatively youthful looks. Egotism, if not sheer egoism, rules every character's moves. In the course of 1911 this play was staged in seven major German cities as well as in Vienna and Prague. Six years earlier Sigmund Freud had written to Schnitzler telling him of his own long awareness of 'a wide-ranging consensus' between his and the author's 'views on psychological and erotic problems'. Yet Schnitzler's pessimism went deeper than Freud's. In some notes on psychoanalysis jotted down in 1922 he doubted the overriding importance of libido: 'The opposite of a longing for sensual fulfilment does not seem to be a longing for pain, but a longing to do someone else harm.'

One famous and often-quoted line, in which Schnitzler paid tribute to the prevalent ideas of his time, is not contained in these works. It comes at the end of *Paracelsus*, a rhyming curtain-raiser performed in 1899 at the Burgtheater before two other one-act plays of his. Here the great quack doctor and philosopher Theophrastus Bombastus von Hohenheim, alias Paracelsus (a historical figure, by the way, much revered now in Germany as a forerunner of pharmacology and psychosomatic medicine) takes leave of Basle, where he has caused much commotion through miracle healings of body and soul, with the words:

> ... A meaning
> Is found alone by him who seeks it out.
> Thus melt into each other dream and waking,
> Thus truth and lie. Assurance there is nowhere,
> We know naught of the others, naught of us;
> We always act, and wise is he who knows it.

Not life but apparition: this is undoubtedly one of the polarities that can be detected in Schnitzler's plays and prose. Another is that of *Eros* and *Thanatos*, a contraposition also employed by Freud. Whether Schnitzler was directly motivated by them or was paying his due to the *Zeitgeist* is a moot point, but probably irrelevant.

Despite his sombre view of life and humanity, he was quite capable of irony and at times even caricature, as is shown in the middle act of *Das weite Land* or in a comedy such as *Fink und Fliederbusch*, a piece mocking journalism. As a craftsman Schnitzler was unsurpassed by his contemporaries, especially those of his own circle who now and again also received the accolade of being performed at the Burgtheater. Paradoxically it was an East Prussian, Paul Schlenther, who during his time as director of the imperial playhouse paid special attention to Austrian dramatists. Thus, beside works by Saar and Ebner-Eschenbach, Schnitzler and Hofmannsthal, he staged lesser efforts such as Hermann Bahr's *Apostel* or, in 1900, a comedy by Theodor Herzl called *I love you*. The much more earnest writer, Richard Beer-Hofmann, had to wait until 1919, however, for his play *Jaakobs Traum* (Jacob's Dream) to be performed at the Burg. Resolved to break with the fastidious traditions of his theatre, which up till then had promoted Shakespeare and German classicist drama, tolerated French conversation pieces and reluctantly accepted the naturalism of Ibsen and Hauptmann, but had drawn the line at native comedy writers, Schlenther now admitted Raimund and Nestroy to its stage. In their wake came later playwrights concerned with urban and rural simple folk, such as the moral reformer Ludwig Anzengruber – by then ten years dead – and Karl Schönherr, creator of passionate peasant tragedies, still young and very much alive.

It cannot be said that the actors of the Hofburgtheater, royalty in their profession, took to all this gladly. We know that neither Stella Hohenfels, the foremost sentimental heroine in the ensemble, nor any of her colleagues had been willing to accept the part of Christine in Schnitzler's *Liebelei* – that poor girl who in the end runs off to commit suicide because her lover has fallen in a duel fought for another woman. An actress from the Volkstheater was finally brought in to play the role. Indeed, a strong sense of dignity had first to be overcome before these proud thespians, spoilt by their adoring Viennese public, deigned to doff their buskins to impersonate ordinary people. After all one of them, Katharina Schratt, from 1886 until his death conducted an *amitié amoureuse* with the emperor himself. Among those who looked up to them as gods was, strange to say, Karl Kraus. To his dying day he cherished the memory of actors such as Zerline Gabillon, Charlotte Wolter, Friedrich Mitterwurzer and Adolf von Sonnenthal, writing poems about them and comparing unfavourably with the often high-flown and stilted style of the 'old Hofburgtheater' every kind of acting or actor deviating from its path.

In the eighties a new and self-assured bourgeoisie had considered the time ripe for the foundation of a playhouse of its own. A year after the Burg had moved to the Ringstrasse, the Deutsches Volkstheater, financed by private patrons, opened on the second peripheral road with a popular Anzengruber play. The new house constituted a real alternative to the imperial temple of dramatic art. Though decorated nearly as sumptuously as the other building and offering almost as much space to the actors and audience, it refrained from overawing its public, and was ready not merely to educate but also to entertain. Education here meant a far more deliberate introduction of modern playwrights – many of those works of Schnitzler's that did not find favour with the Burg were first performed at its less censorious and more progressive counterpart. Entertainment meant not only constant and loving care for the old Viennese comedy writers, but the formation of an ensemble of great comic and character actors, among whom Alexander Girardi was the foremost until called to the Burg in 1918, a few months before his death. Most of the Volkstheater's outstanding players were sooner or later enticed away to the house on the Ring, a process still active today.

Since Professor Anton Bettelheim, the initiator of the move to build a new theatre 'for the Viennese burghers and craftsmen', belonged to one of the enlightened families of Jewish descent so often to be encountered in these pages, the Volkstheater's tradition for many decades remained liberal. It also followed those circles' admiration for German culture: hence the adjective *Deutsches* preceding its name. Before the century was out, however, a similar undertaking was launched in a then outlying district, Mariahilf. Well into the First Republic the Raimundtheater attempted an even more advanced dramatic programme. Pirandello, Hofmannsthal's *Der Unbestechliche*, later even Brecht, were performed there. But the distance from Vienna's inner city proved too great to attract serious-minded theatre-goers and the Raimundtheater gradually fell back on the very lightweight fare it is still offering in the present day.

The playhouse where in the Biedermeier period Nestroy and Raimund themselves had stood on stage, a charming small house called simply Theater in der Josefstadt, had a much older history still. Founded in 1788, two years after Joseph II's Hof- und Nationaltheater, it supplied whatever its suburban audience demanded in the way of *Kasperl* plays, musical comedy and even popular opera. In the early years of this century a highly gifted impresario from Budapest, Josef Jarno, took over the pretty theatre and for more than two decades put on both French farces – 'for the box-office' – and the plays of Strindberg and Wedekind – 'for any ambition and heart's need'. His wife, Hansi Niese, was one of the great and unforgotten popular actresses of Vienna: an eminent example, but by no means last in the line, of the *chanteuses, diseuses* and comediennes who seem constantly to spring from the soil of this city. She it was who in 1913 played young Julie in *Liliom* by the Hungarian Ferenc Molnár, set by its author in Budapest's amusement park and by his translator Alfred Polgar in that of Vienna. Jarno himself was Liliom, the brutal bouncer with the sentimental heart.

For a while, Jarno also rented two other playhouses in Vienna and, after going bankrupt in the first post-war years of inflation, tried running a third, which also failed. During the monarchy, with Austrian subjects flocking from everywhere to the capital to see its sights and visit its shows, there was no crisis in the world of entertainment. After 1918, reduced to poverty amid a population of about ten million as compared to five times that number in the last decades of the Habsburg reign, the former centre of an empire had to adjust itself to being the capital of one small and comparatively insignificant state. It was due to the extraordinary passion the Viennese bore for the theatre that there were still a great many playhouses left, and that new ones were founded while others collapsed. Dozens of them had thrived before the war, but it was the actors not the authors who attracted audiences and bound a particular public to each playhouse.

Authors there had to be all the same, and not only those belonging to the past. A number of minor writers were needed to provide what all these theatres required besides classical and foreign plays, that is, drawing-room comedies set against a local background – sub-Schnitzler or even sub-Bahr, as it were. Most notable among them were Raoul Auernheimer and Otto Soyka. In his early days even the master of small prose, Alfred Polgar, was not above producing the kind of light fare that later, as a critic, he would mock or condemn. Serious dramatists in Vienna were few, and they were not particularly encouraged. An early effort of Felix Salten's failed, after which he turned exclusively to prose. When, before trying his hand at comedy, Theodor Herzl produced a play of ideas called *Das neue Ghetto* (The New Ghetto) it did not reach the stage for three years, and when it did was torn to pieces by the press. Beer-Hofmann's first and best drama, *Der Graf von Charolais* (The Count of Charolais), had been rejected by the Burgtheater and found its way to Vienna, following a triumphant reception in Germany, only after the war.

Writers who concerned themselves with the plight of the poor and underprivileged (as Anzengruber had done up to his death in 1899, mainly on the stage of yet another beautiful playhouse, the Theater an der Wien), were few and far between in the last two decades of the monarchy. Yet social conditions in these years, as we shall see later, offered many examples of injustice and misery. It was a former magistrate (or 'investigating judge' in German and Austrian law), Anton Wildgans, who, after witnessing much hardship among and ill-treatment of those who did not benefit from the empire's prosperity, decided to expose such abuses in dramatic form. His play *Armut* (Poverty) went straight to the heart of the matter. In *Dies irae* he castigated the moral shortcomings that follow in the wake of destitution. And in his tragedy *Liebe* (Love) he devoted himself to the shaky ethics of a hypocritical age. Though Wildgans considered himself first and foremost a lyrical poet, in retrospect his true merit seems to lie in those dramatic exploration of the failings and pressures of his time which he published in three volumes in 1920 under the title *Die bürgerlichen Dramen* (Bourgeois Plays).

The comparative paucity of stage writers in Austria up to 1918 and even beyond cannot be glossed over. As has been said before, and stressed by, among others, the future chronicler of the declining Austro-Hungarian Empire, Robert Musil, Vienna was 'a city not of stagecraft, but of actors'. To this day the names of great performers are remembered, while many of those who provided them with parts in which to shine have been condemned to oblivion. One last fact must be mentioned which added to the difficulty of being a playwright. This was censorship, which had existed since the days of Maria Theresia, and which had been only gradually and never completely relaxed. There were instances when the displeasure of some archduchess or other who happened to be sitting in the imperial box when a new play was performed immediately led to it being banned. A case in point is that of the comedy *Der Feldherrnhügel* (The Generals' Vantage Point) by the excellent humorist writing under the pseudonym Roda Roda and his co-author Carl Rössler. When this amusing skit on military life, having been banned soon after its Vienna premier, later once again failed to pass the censor, the authors were told categorically that it would not see the stage as long as the monarchy lasted. He replied with a smile: 'All right, let us wait those few weeks.' His prediction, as it happened, was not far out. Whether in the end this pleased the former artillery officer – born Rosenfeld – and enthusiastic raconteur of the old imperial army is another matter, not easily resolved.

9

THINKERS
AND DREAMERS

Many studies have been written in recent years aiming to present a history of the ideas that sprang up during our period in Vienna. This book is not an attempt to do the same. It sets out merely to offer a guide, for those not conversant with it, through a territory which has been much explored in detail but seldom surveyed as a whole, by a native inhabitant born well within the time here covered. While suitably impressed by the extensive researches of foreign or indigenous scholars, and by some of their profound analyses of past events, creative feats and artistic achievements, as well as of the motivation of the people connected with them, I neither wish nor hope to emulate them. All I can offer is a primer – more easily readable, at best, than some elaborations of deeper intent.

Even so, we must probe briefly into the thoughts and concepts of the epoch. As has been mentioned, around the turn of the century Vienna gave birth to or developed every innovative theory of art and science, except – though it made a great contribution to it soon enough – modern physics. The self-imposed rule of this survey being the famous precept of E.M. Forster, 'Only connect', it cannot but explore the interrelation between ideology and cultural activity on every level. Admittedly, it would be a churlish simplification to suggest that had Theodor Herzl been as successful a playwright as Schnitzler he might not have initiated Zionism, or at least would not have devoted the later years of his short life to this cause. All the same there may be a grain of truth in it. On the other hand, the direct connection between Wittgenstein's philosophy and the house he built for his sister – referred to earlier – cannot be overstressed.

No account of the influence exercised by thinkers on creators in *fin de siècle* Vienna can fail to begin with Ernst Mach. Even before this great Moravian-born physicist and epistemologist came to the Austrian capital from Prague in 1895, his ideas had spread among its young intelligentsia. When he began to teach at Vienna University, Hofmannsthal – in the last years of his studies – attended his lectures. The work which had the greatest influence on *Jung-Wien* was a book first published by Mach in

1886 under the title *Die Analyse der Empfindungen und das Verhältnis des Physischen zum Psychischen* (The Analysis of Sensations and the Relations between the Physical and Psychical).

In that book, which was re-issued with still greater impact in 1900, Mach maintained that the ego is not a substantial entity but a complex of sensory perceptions. Since its thoughts, sentiments, moods and memories are structured differently every day, the self has a merely relative continuity. In fact, it exists solely as a perpetually changing bundle of feelings. Also, for that reason, it cannot be held responsible for its actions. According to Mach an attempt is made by physics, with the help of mathematics, to organize what is perceived through the senses. His own dismissal of metaphysics – derived from his philosophical ancestor, Bishop Berkeley – led Mach equally to dismiss the stable and consistent self as a necessary concept and to classify it as a 'useless hypothesis'.

His theory was bound to appeal to the Viennese mind which, since early days, had been imbued with the idea that reality might be no more than a delusion. The fact that Mach's *Empiriokritizismus* later gave rise to such divergent schools of thought as those of positivism, materialism and even phenomenology, has little bearing on its influence on *fin de siècle* writers. To them, only Mach's notion of an uncertain and fluctuating identity mattered – a notion that tallied with the destruction of an undivided and authoritative self in the teachings of Sigmund Freud. Just as Mach denied the existence of a uniform conscience, an inner world – to quote Shakespeare – 'of one entire and perfect chrysolite', so Freud split the soul into segments. His discovery that human beings are motivated not merely by their conscious thoughts and feelings but also by their unconscious ones, and that their use of reason is more often than not subject to instinctual drives over which they have little control, revolutionized psychology and had more impact on the arts for generations to come than any other theory of the time.

In the first year of the new century Freud's *The Interpretation of Dreams* was published. So were Schnitzler's *Leutnant Gustl* – the story in which the interior monologue was first employed as a deliberate literary technique – and his *Reigen*, in which the sexual drive was shown to be the prime mover of human relationships. In 1906, we may remember, Freud had told Schnitzler that he had long been aware of a far-reaching correspondence between their views on psychological and erotic problems. He admitted that he had often asked himself with astonishment where Schnitzler had obtained 'this or that secret knowledge which I have reached through laborious exploration of the object', and that he had ended up by 'envying the writer whom I had otherwise admired'. In 1922, on Schnitzler's sixtieth birthday, Freud wrote again, telling him that he had avoided him 'from a kind of awe of meeting my double'.

'I have plagued myself over the question of how it happens that in all these years I have never sought your company and enjoyed a conversation with you.' After explaining this as *Doppelgänger-Scheu*, Freud goes on to say:

whenever I get deeply interested in your beautiful creations I always seem to find behind their poetic sheen the same presuppositions, interests and conclusions as those familiar to me as my own. Your determinism and your scepticism – what people call pessimism – your deep grasp of the truths of the unconscious and of the biological nature of man, the way you take to pieces the social conventions of your society, and the extent to which your thoughts are preoccupied with the polarity of love and death: all that moves me with an uncanny feeling of familiarity. So the impression has been borne in on me that you know through intuition – really from a delicate self-observation – everything that I have discovered in other people by laborious work.

In these words (quoted here in the translation by Freud's Welsh disciple and biographer Ernest Jones) he reiterated not only what he himself had written twenty years before, but also what he had expressed time and again in one context or another about the advantage of spontaneous insight over scientific discovery.

Thus, in a passage in his analysis of Wilhelm Jensen's book *Gradiva* – published in 1907 – which had been inspired by a bas-relief in the Vatican Museum of a lovely Grecian girl, also admired by Freud, he stated:

Imaginative writers are valuable colleagues and their testimony is to be rated very highly, because they have a way of knowing many of the things between heaven and earth which are not dreamed of in our philosophy. In the knowledge of the human heart they are far ahead of us common folk, because they draw on sources that we have not yet made accessible to science.

Twenty years later, writing about the 'wonderful people' who achieve insights that cost him much labour, he admitted: 'One may heave a sigh at the thought that it is vouchsafed to a few with hardly an effort to salvage from the whirlpool of their emotions the deepest truths, to which we others have to force our way, ceaselessly groping amid torturing uncertainties.' He even went as far as to say, 'Unfortunately psychoanalysis has to lay down its arms before the problem of the imaginative writer' – meaning that like all artists they possessed some mysterious gift which he could admire from a distance, but the secret of which he could not divine.

If Ernest Jones is to be believed, the founder of psychoanalysis, who has often been described as an authoritative, self-assured and rigorous believer in his own theory, was in fact a very modest man. With regard to *The Interpretation of Dreams* and his *Three Essays on the Theory of Sexuality*, his own two favourite works, Freud told his biographer, 'It seems to be my fate to discover only the obvious: that children have sexual feelings, which every nursemaid knows; and that night dreams are just as much a wish fulfilment as daydreams.' Nor was he in any way serious when he wrote on the publication of *The Interpretation of Dreams* to his then friend Wilhelm Fliess, asking him whether it was likely that the spot where he had devised its main tenets five years earlier (the Bellevue restaurant in the Vienna woods) would ever display a marble tablet bearing the inscription 'Here the secret of dreams was revealed to Dr Sigm. Freud on July 24, 1895.' Indeed, there was little ground for assuming, at that time or for many decades to come, that anything of that sort would happen – as in fact it did in February 1955 when a memorial stone so inscribed was erected on the site of the demolished restaurant.

Six hundred copies of *The Interpretation of Dreams* were printed, and they took eight years to sell. When Hofmannsthal wrote to Bahr in 1904 in order to borrow from him 'the book by Freud and Breuer about the healing of hysteria through the release of a suppressed recollection' (*Studien über Hysterie*, 1895, translated as *Studies in Hysteria*), he was not aware of its title nor of the fact that he would sooner find in *The Interpretation of Dreams* what he looked forward to finding in the earlier publication: 'Things which will assist me greatly in *Life is a Dream*.' This book, deemed by Ernest Jones to be Freud's most original work, contained not only the basic idea that dreams are the masked fulfilment of an unconscious wish, but also a first model of the psychic apparatus as later developed by its author. Here, too, the Oedipus complex is first described (with a famous footnote on Hamlet), and many incidental discoveries are made that subsequently led to more detailed investigations. Of all his writings it was to exercise the strongest influence on artists and authors. When Freud stated in his writings on *Gradiva* that 'the true writer ... has always been the forerunner of science, and thus of scientific psychology too,' he meant this flow of knowledge to be mutual. 'The writer', he said in the same context, 'can no more shun the psychiatrist than the psychiatrist the writer.' And since these words were put on paper a year after Freud's first letter to Arthur Schnitzler, one may assume that he had this particular author in mind.

Obviously no attempt can be made in such a limited space to trace the life and set out the doctrines of Sigmund Freud, reputedly the best-known Austrian throughout the world after Johann Strauss. Towards the end of his days, in July 1938, he himself began to sum up his discoveries and teachings in his brief *Abriss der Psychoanalyse* (Outlines of Psychoanalysis) which, unfortunately, he was not able to finish. In its short chapters it does however contain the main aspects of his theory. They deal with the psychical apparatus, with its divisions into id, ego and super-ego; with Freud's concept of the instinctual drives and their vicissitudes; with repression and sublimation; with the development of the sexual functions; the quality of the psyche; and lastly the interpretation of dreams. Two chapters are then devoted to the practical role of the analyst, and two more to the theoretical yield of Freud's findings with regard to people's exterior and interior worlds. Although the manuscript breaks off at this point without an indication of how its author meant to complete it, a reader intimidated by the collected works of the founder of psychoanalysis will find in it most of what is relevant to its understanding.

Although Freudianism has been and is being vigorously challenged, in whole or in part, by present-day opponents, only contemporary schisms from Freud's theory are discussed here. The leading figure among those of his Viennese followers who dissented in and after 1911 was Alfred Adler. This desertion of a member of the earliest group that had formed around Freud in 1902, the Psychological Wednesday Circle, was a hard blow to him. Yet it was more in sorrow than in anger that he saw him go, and Adler was never struck by such verbal thunderbolts as was Carl Gustav Jung, Freud's quondam crown prince, after his subsequent breakaway: 'Now we are rid of the brutal sanctimonious Jung and his disciples.' This Swiss adherent, who had joined him in 1906 and withdrew from the Psycho-Analytical Association in 1914, went on to establish a school of his own which at times had as great an impact as that of Freud. But it is Adler's *Individualpsychologie* (Psychology of the Ego), which, though it was less universally acclaimed than Jung's theory of the collective unconscious and archetypal determinants of the mind, we must deal with here as the second great movement in psychology to have emerged from Vienna.

Adler, Freud's junior by fourteen years, had been born in Vienna and graduated in medicine. His English biographer Phyllis Bottome has suggested that he was for a while Freud's family doctor, but no proof of this has emerged. When he began to attend the Wednesday Circle he was one of five. He took part in the steady progress made by the small fellowship which turned into a psychoanalytical society, soon to arrange international meetings; and he was editor, with the other 'oldest follower' of Freud, Wilhelm Stekel, of its periodical the *Zentralblatt*, founded in 1910. The 'most forceful member of the group', as Jones has called him, he worked out a new approach to the nature of neuroses, a psychology of the ego alone, based far less on the recognition of sexual factors than on his own new motive of aggression, which he attributed to 'masculine protest'.

Freud took his ideas very seriously indeed, but was not willing to accept them in place of his own. In fact, he stressed that Adler's theory was not psychoanalysis but 'something else', and reproached him for possessing an 'antisexual tendency'. Instead of the psychology of the unconscious, said Freud, Adler expounded a 'surface- and ego-psychology', instead of the psychology of the libido merely general psychology. However, he predicted that Adler's ideas would have a great impact. When in 1911 two evenings of the association were devoted to these heresies, Freud stated outright that 'the Adlerian teachings are incorrect and therefore dangerous for the future development of psychoanalysis.' While insisting that they were 'scientific errors due to false methods', however, he stressed that they were none the less 'honourable errors'.

So Adler left the fold, taking six other renegades with him. He called his own new group the 'Society for Free Psycho-Analysis', which was particularly galling to Freud. Even worse, he had the American Stanley Hall on his side, which meant that his theories reached the United States as soon, if not sooner, than those of Freud. His own followers, now as passionate in their adherence to him as they had been towards the movement's founder, considered that Freud had done great injustice to Adler during the split. This view was still being given expression sixty years later in the autobiography of the writer Manès Sperber who in 1921, at the age of sixteen, had become Adler's youngest devotee. Although the movement gave itself the title 'Psychology of the Individual' (this being the correct translation), it concentrated on the sociological aspects of consciousness rather than on the repressed unconscious – preferring the study of the relationship between the individual and the collective to that of the individual *per se*. Adler himself was a Socialist, married to a Russian who was a friend of Trotsky, and he drew his followers more easily and logically than Freud from among the more moderate Marxist left.

Among his lasting concepts was the idea of the 'feeling of inferiority', the compensation for which can be a motive for wrong behaviour in society. Another was a pan-sexualist view of the human mind, based on the assumption (previously expressed by Freud's early friend Wilhelm Fliess and by Otto Weininger) that it is composed in every case of both masculine and feminine components. The former, Adler held, do not assert themselves merely through aggression, but are also motivated by the 'will to power' – a Nietzschean concept. The young Manès Sperber, in an essay on Adler written in 1927 which he later partly disowned, called his teacher 'the social genius of our time' who 'gave every one of his followers a task for life: to bring about a reduction of the lust for power and an education towards a true community spirit.' Adler paraphrased Marx's dictum that material existence determines consciousness (and not the other way round as Hegel thought) in his own maxim '*Das gesellschaftliche Sein bestimmt das Bewusstsein*' (social existence determines consciousness). His theory could therefore more easily be endorsed by Marxists who rejected Freud's concept of an overriding libido.

By the time Adler was fifty he was firmly established as the founder and head of *Individualpsychologie*. Around him were gathered a number of adherents who by now had their own periodical and treated neuroses according to his principles. One of his friends and supporters was a forceful member of the feminist and socialist movement of the twenties, Sophie Lazarsfeld. At her and her husband's house labour leaders such as Victor Adler and Otto Bauer met Alfred Adler, and also the Freudian Siegfried Bernfeld. It was on the advice of Victor Adler's son Friedrich, a scientist by profession, that Sophie's son Paul F. Lazarsfeld took up the study of physics and mathematics. And it was Bernfeld who introduced the young graduate and schoolmaster to the Psychological Institute of Vienna University, headed by Karl Bühler, where Lazarsfeld was able to combine his interests in mathematics, psychology and sociology with astonishing and far-reaching results.

In pre-war Austria, as in most other central European countries at the time, there existed no chairs of psychology. However when in 1922 Karl Bühler, a native of Meckesheim near Heidelberg, received a call from Vienna University it was to teach that subject in the philosophy faculty. In due course he built up a Psychological Institute, which was to grow into one of the most advanced institutions of this kind. Bühler and his work deserve attention, not least because they represented accepted academic psychology in Austria at the time when Sigmund Freud was further developing and practising psychoanalysis outside the world of university life. Dr Charlotte Bühler, his close collaborator as lecturer at the institute and a prolific scholar in her own right, has classified her husband as a 'pre-Freudian thinker' who later created 'new concepts partly opposed to, and reaching beyond, the tenets of psychoanalysis'.

Bühler saw himself in the tradition of 'experimental psychology' which had prevailed in whichever context the science of the soul had been academically pursued in Vienna. This meant that he was bound, as Ernst Mach and the Swiss Richard Avenarius had been, to explore the functioning of the mind in relation to the functioning of the body. This was done partly with the help of technical apparatus such as he had himself developed before the First World War at the Munich 'psychological laboratory'. From his Austrian chair, assisted by young collaborators such as Count Egon Brunswik, Else Frenkel and Käthe Wolf, Bühler also encouraged all manner of forays into aesthetics, among them an attempt at devising a theory of presentation in the new art of film. His whole scientific work was dominated by two main inquiries: one into the, for him, supreme role of biology in the understanding of the human mind, the other into the nature of creative thought. Simultaneously with Freud, his daughter Anna and his pupil Melanie Klein, Bühler and his wife delved into the formative years of human beings, in their case again mainly from a biological starting-point.

Besides his book *The Mental Development of the Child* and a critical appreciation of the three contemporary forms of psychological theory – behaviourism, psychoanalysis and his own experimental psychology – under the title *Die Krise der Psychologie* (The Crisis of Psychology), Bühler also published long treatises on his own theories of language and expression, which found much favour among his colleagues in German-speaking countries and in the Anglo-Saxon world. His lectures and seminars were also attended by students and scholars who were or became eminent exponents of psychoanalysis, such as Heinz Hartmann, Rudolf Ekstein, Siegfried Bernfeld and René Spitz. Indeed the figure of Freud, the grand old sage and prophet enthroned in his large but modestly middle-class apartment in Berggasse, constantly loomed in the distance. The lectures he had delivered between 1915 and 1917, as *ausserordentlicher* (external) professor at Vienna University (subsequently published as *Vorlesungen zur Einführung in die Psychoanalyse*, A General Introduction to Psychoanalysis), had not been resumed after the war. His home and practice had become the temple to which flocked all those for whom the study of Freud's theory seemed indispensable to an attempt at understanding the human soul.

There is an element of tragedy in the fact that Karl Bühler, an imaginative thinker, a stimulating teacher and a thoroughly decent man (in 1938 he was temporarily imprisoned by the Nazis and forced to emigrate not merely because of his wife's Jewish descent but also for his courageous stand against them), inspired hardly any of his students to carry his studies further, let alone leaving behind a school of thought. Some of his assistants, unbeknown to Bühler, underwent training analyses while working for him at the Psychological Institute. Others, who had to emigrate to the United States when Hitler marched into Austria, converted to Freudianism before they could take up teaching posts in psychology at American universities. Bühler's main argument against psychoanalysis had been that its method of treating neuroses did not suffice for the under-standing of the fundamental processes of life. While Freud, he suggested in *Die Krise der Psychologie*, saw human beings in terms of a constant effort to overcome psychic disorders and re-establish their balance of mind, Bühler preferred to consider them under the aspect of their desire to function satisfactorily and to fulfil their creative urge. However, this approach did not appear to all of his pupils as fruitful as that of Freud. It is as a theorist of language that Bühler is still respected and remembered. Recent editions of *Bühler-Studien* (Bühler Studies) by scholars who picked up the threads of his teachings after his death show that modern linguistics and semiotics have profited greatly from them.

Is it ungracious to see his greatest merit in the help and encouragement he gave to Paul F. Lazarsfeld, one of the pioneers of modern social psychology and scientific market research both in Austria and in the United States? It was Lazarsfeld's mathematical knowledge which first caused Charlotte Bühler to employ him at the institute as a lecturer on statistics and the analysis of data. When the young man wished to found an institute of his own devoted to social and economic research on a psychological basis, both Bühlers pledged their support. Karl Bühler became president of *Wirtschaftspsychologische Forschungsstelle* (Institute for Economic-Psychological Studies), but also on the board were some eminent industrialists and chairmen of the chambers of commerce and agriculture, as well as other university professors.

The institute's real purpose was to look into the grave problems of the world slump in that troubled inter-war period. But it helped finance itself by undertaking market research for important businesses in Austria and Switzerland. Significantly, most employees at the institute, mainly stu-dents of the Bühlers, were at the same time active young Socialists. The greatest achievement of Paul F. Lazarsfeld, his then wife Marie Jahoda and their co-worker Hans Zeisel was the enquiry into the unemployed of Marienthal, *Die Arbeitslosen von Marienthal*, a sociological masterpiece and one of the most moving documents of life in an industrial village after its one and only factory has closed down. Lazarsfeld himself left Vienna for the States in the autumn of 1933, on a Rockefeller grant. A few months later, after the Socialist movement had been crushed by the Austro-Fascists, his institute was raided, some of its staff were imprisoned, and it was finally forced to disband. Lazarsfeld did not return to his homeland. As a matter of course his politics became more moderate in America: he supported the Liberal Democrats while distinguishing himself in many fields of empirical social research. As in most similar cases, Austria's loss was another country's gain.

In this chapter it is no more possible to distinguish thought and dream, visionary theory and therapeutic or social practice, than it is to adhere to the chronological order of events. So far it has seemed apt to treat the time up to the outbreak of the Great War more or less separately from that of the First Republic. But for the flow of ideas this watershed is unimportant. What happened around the turn of the century in the fields of philosophy, psychology and pure ideology had its ramifications up to the Anschluss, when most of the surviving originators were swept out of Austria, together with their theories. Thus we had to pursue the impact of Freud's revolutionary discoveries on disciples, dissidents and scholars of different persuasions right up to the twenties and beyond. Even if the life and work of all his Viennese collaborators cannot be discussed here, mention should at least be made of the great advances achieved by his daughter Anna in the study of defence mechanisms and in child psychology (which she continued during her exile in London). Nor must we forget her great rival Melanie Klein, whose successful treatment of child neuroses received as much attention and influenced as many English and American analysts as that of Anna Freud. However, the most controversial of Freud's followers turned out to be Wilhelm Reich.

This extraordinary man, like Adler very young when he joined the movement, at the age of twenty-five was put in charge of the Seminar for Psychoanalytic Therapy in Vienna. Freud thought highly of him until Reich's involvement in politics began to annoy him. By defining man as a social if not a totally material being, Alfred Adler had paved the way for an understanding with Marxists. Unwavering adherents of Freud, when trying to reconcile his theory with that of dialectical materialism, were faced with an impossible task. During a debate held in 1928 in Berlin, some analysts such as Siegfried Bernfeld wanted to prove not merely that Freudianism was compatible with Marxism, but also that the two systems were mutually complementary. Much later Bertrand Russell, after looking into the question, concluded authoritatively that there was no hope of combining them: 'Even when we are only considering large communities, the exclusively economic view is an oversimplification, and a more psychological outlook is essential to political wisdom.'

Freud did not think otherwise and repeatedly argued against attempts to fuse his teachings with those of Marxism, a theory 'founded on an untenable illusion'. He was therefore far from pleased when Reich prepared an article for the official journal of psychoanalysis, aimed at the odious amalgamation and stating – nonsensically, Freud thought – that 'what we have called the death instinct is a product of the capitalist system'. After much discussion the paper was published, followed by a full critique written by the same Siegfried Bernfeld who four years earlier had spoken up for the *rapprochement*. In 1934, by which time the estrangement between him and Freud was irrevocable, Reich resigned from the association. Not content with inciting the founder's wrath through his 'political fanaticism', he went on to carry the psychoanalytical concept of the dominant libido to an extreme equally unacceptable to Freud. Reich's concept of the libido, in the eyes of the first user of this term, was 'purely anal', and his preaching of the healing quality of the orgasm showed 'a simple, mechanistic view'.

In the United States, from 1939, Reich propounded his theory of 'orgone energy' – a health-giving force which, he maintained, could be tapped by means of his orgone accumulators. However, the brilliant mind that had produced a number of excellent books, notably *Mass Psychology and Fascism* (1933) and *The Sexual Revolution* (1945), gradually went astray. Reich's stubbornness in wanting to cure even serious diseases by means of his 'orgone boxes' or 'blankets' – condemned as fraud by American law – led to his undoing. He was convicted of criminal contempt in 1954 and sent to a penitentiary, where he died aged sixty, a broken man.

The account of Reich's strange pursuits has led us far from the early 1900s until almost into our own day. As the most excessive offshoot from the mainstream of psychological and philosophical theory during our period he was rivalled by a precursor. The reputation of Otto Weininger, who took his own life at twenty-three shortly after his fundamental work *Geschlecht und Charakter* (Sex and Character) was published in 1903, is now undergoing a remarkable resurrection. This outrageous book, an elaboration of his doctoral thesis running to nearly six hundred pages including appendices, had been acclaimed by such eminent contemporaries of its author as Strindberg, Wittgenstein and Karl Kraus. Later it is known to have impressed and even influenced Arnold Schönberg, Italo Svevo, Giorgio de Chirico and D.H. Lawrence, as well as Leo and Gertrude Stein. With the renewed and by now inordinate interest in every whim and vagary which sprouted in the hothouse of talent that was *fin de siècle* Vienna, a more or less favourable reappraisal of Weininger is under way from Scandinavia to Israel.

Deservedly, the many prodigious ideas, reflections and fantasies to be found in *Geschlecht und Charakter* are singled out for interpretation and comment. Yet few of the belated admirers of Weininger are prepared to state clearly that the two main theses of his book, supporting anti-feminism and anti-Semitism, are blatant and dangerous nonsense. To call his writings a 'grandiose error', as Wittgenstein has done, or even a 'valuable error' according to the recent generous judgement of Roberto Calasso, is to perpetuate the same contradiction in terms that Weininger perceived in the words 'female genius'. While most intelligent and erudite, this young son of an educated Jewish goldsmith was also deeply neurotic. Undoubtedly he had leanings towards a hidden and guilt-ridden homosexuality, and tried to justify his aversion to women with every scientifically masked falsehood and philosophical casuistry he could muster. And when he castigated the Jewish character it was with all the self-hatred of an ungainly youth – so described by Stefan Zweig, who put his whole attitude down to an 'irritated inferiority feeling'.

In Weininger one may observe driven *à l'outrance* the uncertainty of a Viennese Jew halfway between orthodoxy and complete assimilation. Having left behind the haven of a solid Jewish identity (as his free-thinking, Wagner-loving father had already done) yet far from being integrated into Christian society like Hofmannsthal and his friends, Weininger suffered all the ills of a man in transition. When he asserted in his diatribe against his own ilk that there never could be such a thing as a 'Jewish gentleman', he could not foresee that his own brother Richard, seven years his junior, would turn into a perfect example of that 'impossibility'.

Born in 1880, Otto Weininger had the great advantage of entering university at the point when academic life in Vienna was at its peak and scholars like Ernst Mach, Richard Avenarius and Friedrich Jodl were expounding an enlightened empiricism in the realms of science and philosophy. Thirsting for knowledge, he began to explore whichever disciplines were within their range. The *curriculum vitae* accompanying his doctoral thesis throws light not merely on the precociousness but also the early megalomania of Weininger's mind. It states that he began to 'ponder over philosophical and cosmological matters at the age of thirteen'. He also reports that besides his main subjects he has studied mathematics, physics and chemistry, zoology and botany, as well as attending lectures on branches of medicine including anatomy, physiology, histology, embryology, neurology, psychiatry and pathology.

Inevitably one is reminded not so much of Goethe's Faust who complains that his various studies left him the poor fool he was before, but of the pupil who turns up to consult him as to the courses he should take. In the guise of Faust, Mephistopheles asks the boy which faculty he wants to choose. The pupil cannot decide: he wants to become very learned and 'to grasp whatever there is on earth and in heaven' both in science and nature. But when the devil warns him of the intricacies of a 'thought factory' with its thousands of threads shuttling back and forth as on a loom, the pupil feels lost, 'as though a mill-wheel were going round and round' in his head.

Otto Weininger would not have admitted that in his case too much learning was a dangerous thing, nor was he saved from mental aberrations by 'drinking deeply of the Pierian spring'. His dissertation, submitted to Professors Jodl and Lorenz Müllner of the philosophical faculty in June 1902, was shot through with fabulous ideas and flashes of psychological insight which suitably impressed his teachers. Yet Jodl, though appreciating some 'fine observations', deplored Weininger's 'fantasies', such as his 'denial of a soul, in the transcendental sense, in the female type'. He wondered whether the applicant's 'subjective and comparative method' was able successfully to compete with that of experimental psychology, and whether it would 'keep clear of dangerously arbitrary assumptions and of that fantastic speculation which has done so much damage to the prestige of German psychology in the age of speculative idealism'. Müllner went even farther: 'Weininger's hypothesis, ingenious though it is, ... leads in fact to groundless and bottomless metaphysics ... it gives the impression of a rhapsody, rendered effective by the strength of his private motives, rather than of a scientific train of thought.'

Despite these reservations both professors accepted Weininger's thesis – then called *Eros und Psyche* and not yet containing the last chapters of *Geschlecht und Charakter* on the perniciousness of Jews and the 'substance of woman and her meaning in the universe'. When its author tried to publish the work after gaining his degree, he encountered unexpected difficulties. Sigmund Freud, to whom he had respectfully sent the manuscript, did not like it at all and refused to recommend it. Professor Jodl demanded 'important alterations' which Weininger was not prepared to make. After his suicide, Jodl informed the Munich psychiatrist Löwenfeld that he had found Weininger, who was 'indisputably highly gifted', also 'highly unappealing'. 'I cannot claim directly to have influenced his thinking. He came to me as a convinced supporter of the empiricism of Avenarius and underwent in the course of a few years the metamorphosis which turned him into a complete mystic. His soul is a mystery to me.' Perhaps, he suggested, Weininger got caught in his own trap. Yet while others thought that the young doctor had shot himself because he hated the Jew in himself, or because he had recognized the error, even the criminal falseness, of his theories, Jodl declined to pronounce on the possible reasons.

The scintillating hotch-potch of ideas that makes up Weininger's book is derived from such conflicting sources as Kant's ethics, Schopenhauer's misogyny, Nietzsche's metaphysical concept of genius, Kierkegaard's 'tension' between the temporal and the eternal, Richard Wagner's aesthetic mysticism, Houston Stewart Chamberlain's anti-Semitism, and many more. Tempting though it would be to look more closely at this fabric of theories (as mesmerizing as the Medusa but easily defeated once one begins methodically to dispose of one snake's head after another), in our context it cannot be done. Weininger's most fascinating and acceptable notion was that of the permanent bisexuality of all human beings. To him there is no such thing as a man or a woman, only a masculine and a feminine substance – M and W for short – which are dealt out to each individual in uneven portions. Though Weininger quotes in his tome every conceivable scholar or writer who has stimulated his thoughts, here he makes no mention of the fact that he owes the notion of bisexuality to Freud's early friend, the ear, nose and throat doctor Wilhelm Fliess.

The 'Fliess affair', which led to an open controversy over Weininger's 'plagiarism' and to the break between the Berlin physician and Freud, has its unsavoury side. Without doubt it was an indiscretion of Freud's, committed during his treatment of Weininger's closest companion, Hermann Swoboda, which brought the as yet unpublished theory of Fliess to Weininger's knowledge. The polemics got under way only after the suicide, when Karl Kraus took Weininger's side in his *Fackel* and refrained from replying to five letters from Freud trying to clear up the matter. Kraus, though a professed 'admirer of women', enthusiastically approved of 'Weininger's arguments for his contempt of women' and had told him so. He also appreciated – and was not shaken in this by the Fliess affair – the young man's Kantian morality and generally austere attitude, especially in sexual matters. As has been shown before, this austerity was also endorsed by Ludwig Wittgenstein – most probably another crypto-homosexual who suppressed and sublimated his leanings as Weininger had done.

The period of transition in which many Jewish Viennese on the way to assimilation found themselves around 1900 bore witness to the most conflicting attempts to solve their problem. Richard Weininger may serve as an example of a method diametrically opposed to that of his elder brother, triumphantly victorious where his poor pathological sibling had failed. In the memoirs he dictated in his ninetieth year Richard – named after Wagner – confessed that he never understood 'how one man could have so much knowledge, so much wisdom, as my brother'. Yet, quite apart from the fact that Richard achieved command of at least as many languages as Otto – though not Sanskrit – he came to master practical life more consummately than Otto was able to master existential theory.

After a pleasant childhood – 'infinitely happier than my brother's' – Richard was sent by his father to the United States at the age of eighteen. During a stay of three years he was introduced to big business by Otto

H. Kahn, bought shares on his advice, made a million dollars and lost it again. Back in Vienna he pursued a more sober commercial career, married, moved to Munich, studied economics and political science, and indulged in cultural pursuits. He spent the war comfortably in Austria-Hungary's War Ministry, wearing the uniform of a mounted artillery officer, and afterwards, rather than finish his studies at Munich, pulled off a number of successful financial coups characteristic of the inflationary post-war period.

After entering into a second marriage with a millionaire's daughter from Prague, he adopted the habits of a true *grand seigneur*. Though at some point he had become a Quaker his life style was far from frugal. Both in Europe and, after 1947, in the United States, Richard Weininger – a tall, well-made, impressive man – mixed with the aristocratic, political and cultural élite. He patronized Berthold Viertel's avant-garde theatre troupe during the hectic twenties in Berlin. He played polo with King Alfonso of Spain, Lord Louis Mountbatten, the German Prince Fugger and the Maharaja of Kashmir. He became involved in a scandal together with the MP Robert Boothby, and secured the support of Harold Macmillan and Lloyd George. In America he did business with Howard Hughes, became the owner of several steamship companies and was appointed to some highly selective industrial boards. His last decades he spent looking after his interests from an office in Madison Avenue, returning home to a mansion surrounded by over a hundred acres of parkland near New York. There the Weiningers mostly went about in traditional Austrian costume, Richard in a Styrian suit and his wife Gertrude in a dirndl.

The donning of native peasant dress by Viennese Jews before 1938 was not a demonstrative act, but rather a mark of conformity with general bourgeois habits. Urban Austrians wore these garments when they were in the country, in their gardens, or at a *Heurigen* inn, and children often wore them all the time. A photograph of Theodor Herzl, now in the Museum of the City of New York, shows him in his study surrounded by his offspring, Hans, Trude and Pauline, who are all so attired. Herzl himself has been described as an 'extremely assimilated Jewish dandy', but in fact never reached a very high degree of integration into Austrian society. It is true that in Budapest, where he was born in 1860, his parents had acquired wealth and shed the rigid religious beliefs of their forebears. But the 'elegance' attributed to young Herzl by his fellow pupils at high school had a Hungarian flair, and was presumably a shade too flashy compared with that of the capital. His father's move to Vienna (after he had been somewhat impoverished by the stock exchange crash of 1873) when

Theodor was eighteen, led first to the second district of Leopoldstadt – never a very good address, though it was in or near its main street, the wide and occasionally ornate Praterstrasse, that the ascent of the Freud and Schnitzler families also began.

This chapter devoted to Viennese thinkers and dreamers cannot pass over – even at the risk of not doing him justice in an inevitably potted account of his tremendous achievement – the only great man of the period whose utopian vision came true. The pattern of Herzl's tragically short life is not the least extraordinary thing about him. Having spent the first seventeen years of his adult existence carving out a career which would satisfy his compulsive ambition, effecting as rapid a social rise as possible, and occasionally thinking up all sorts of childish ways of defeating anti-Semitism (such as a mass baptism of all his co-religionists in St Stephen's Cathedral, from which he, the last proud Jew in Austria, would however abstain), he devoted the last nine to untiring efforts in the Zionist cause. It is common knowledge by now how, having conquered the two cultural bastions of Vienna, the Burgtheater and the *Neue Freie Presse*, as well as becoming a haughty cosmopolitan who was at home in all Europe but most admired German culture, Germanic looks and the music of Wagner, he swung round 180 degrees and became the saviour of the hitherto despised eastern Jewry. A more unlikely choice for the saviour who would lead his people back to Palestine could not – up to 1895 and the Dreyfus trial – be imagined. Yet with all the refinement of manners, all the dignified stance and all the theatricality Herzl possessed, he turned out to be the only person likely to be able to prepare the way for this grandiose aim.

Herzl's position as a former correspondent and present cultural editor of central Europe's most influential paper opened doors to him that would have been shut to anyone else. The Turkish Sultan, a daily reader of the *Neue Freie Presse*, on this account received the petitioner for a Jewish influx into the Holy Land, then under Ottoman rule. (At one point it was Sultan Izzet's hope that with Herzl's help the editor of the paper, Moritz Benedict, could be persuaded to turn it into a clandestine organ for Turkish propaganda.) It can also be assumed that neither Kaiser Wilhelm II nor Pope Pius X would have listened to Herzl's plea for support but for his international standing as a journalist. Though neither these two nor the Sultan in the end lifted a finger to help the Jews, the Zionist leader's protracted negotiations with the high and mighty at least encouraged him not to give up hope in his arduous and much-contested efforts. None of the emancipated Jews of Vienna was prepared to side with him: Schnitzler withdrew after some initial interest and Beer-Hofmann was no more than a passive partisan, while Chief Rabbi Güdemann withdrew his earlier consent and in the end explicitly condemned Herzl's undertaking.

It is impossible to exaggerate the self-sacrificial nature of Herzl's endeavours in the Zionist cause once he had embraced it and set it out in his brochure *Der Judenstaat* (The Jewish State, 1896). Tirelessly lobbying countless rulers, statesmen and millionaires; constantly travelling within Europe and in the Middle East; organizing and chairing six Zionist congresses in the same number of years, and thereby encountering his worst opposition from within the ranks; suffering Karl Kraus's corrosive attacks as well as shocked resistance from the *Neue Freie Presse*, for which, however, he continued to work; even churning out an occasional light comedy to make some money and keep his name afloat – all this systematically ruined the constitution of a man who before he began his campaign had enjoyed good health.

Bertha von Suttner, the great humanitarian, worker for peace and protector of the Jews, compared Herzl in his physical heyday to an 'Assyrian king of majestic height'. Yet within less than a decade he had spent all the strength he ever had. When, his resistance broken down, he died of pneumonia at the age of forty-four, he had not yet managed officially to secure for his brethren so much as one square metre of the promised land. But as his biographer Amos Elon has so movingly written, even as Herzl was being buried in the cemetery of Döbling near the green slopes of the Vienna woods, young Jews in small towns and villages in Russia and Poland were doing up their bundles and packing their cardboard suitcases to make their way, singly and clandestinely, to Ottoman Palestine. Among them was Ben Gurion, the future first prime minister of Israel. Although the Balfour Declaration of 1917 promised the Jews a 'homestead' in Palestine, the holocaust had to happen before their state came into being. Weininger's dictum that the Jew, 'asocial like woman', would 'never be capable of founding a permanent state or a permanent society' but would rather 'join movements undermining the constitutional state like anarchism and communism', was proved to be the same pernicious rubbish that so many of his other assertions had been.

History has shown, on the other hand, that of the three behavioural patterns open to Jews of the diaspora, at least in central and eastern Europe – to remain on an island of orthodoxy within their country of residence; to aim at being its loyal citizens while retaining their own religious or ethnic allegiance; or gradually, and in the end completely, to merge with its population through mixed marriages and the shedding of their ancient belief – only the last one had and still has a chance of working. When Hitler came to Austria a smallish number of families founded by a

Jewish ancestor and still bearing his name were exempted from persecution owing to their small percentage of 'contaminated' blood. (Even now, only those not visibly recognizable as Jews can hope never to encounter the aggressive spite of anti-Semitism, ever lying dormant in some sections of the community. 'The womb is fertile yet from whence that crept,' wrote Bertolt Brecht. Not much has changed in this respect since his death in 1956.)

One clan which survived relatively unharmed throughout the Third Reich was that of the Wittgensteins. Having taken their name early on from the German princely family Sayn-Wittgenstein (much as southern Negroes in the States were called after the master they served), they had settled in Austria and come to wealth in the course of the nineteenth century although, surprisingly, they were not ennobled like so many others of their kind. Karl Wittgenstein, the philosopher's father, grew up in comfortable circumstances, ran off to America as a young man, and after his return to Vienna in 1867 built up a fortune of his own in the iron and steel industry. A man of artistic leanings, he financed the Secession building when it was put up in 1897. Of his eight children, apart from Ludwig, Paul the one-armed pianist became famous, Margarete was immortalized through her portrait by Klimt, and two or possibly three of the sons committed suicide. Nowadays their descendants, who have married into Christian families and embraced the Lutheran faith (some of them having served in the Austrian army even after it had been incorporated into Hitler's Wehrmacht), are no longer willing to be reminded of their antecedents. Ludwig, who was a Catholic, at one time seriously considered becoming a priest. It is as well to remember that Hofmannsthal's brother-in-law, the painter Hans Schlesinger, entered a religious order, and that he himself was buried, according to his wishes, in the frock of the *Tertius Ordo* of the Franciscan brotherhood.

In view of what has been said earlier about Weininger, it is embarrassing to have to report that he was named by Wittgenstein as one of those whose trains of thought he had 'passionately adopted' in his 'work of clarification' – others including Schopenhauer, Bertrand Russell, Karl Kraus, Adolf Loos and Oswald Spengler. A mixed parentage indeed, for it contained men of strictly scientific and logical bent together with others who relied upon speculation and a priori statements. Both left their traces in his philosophical work. While in his earlier writings Wittgenstein exemplified the former mode of reasoning, later, despite his continued insistence on linguistic purity as the premise of all reflection, he permitted himself the search for the *Wesen* (substance) of language – a metaphysical quest. He even used the word he had formerly outlawed from all his deliberations: 'Like everything metaphysical the harmony of thought and reality is to be found in the grammar of language.'

More than any other of his contemporaries, Wittgenstein was a true eccentric. After studying mechanical engineering he went to England in 1908, sitting at the feet of the philosophers Bertrand Russell and G.E. Moore for some time. Soon he detected within himself as many differences from their thinking as points of agreement with it. When five years later his father died in Vienna, Ludwig Wittgenstein immediately gave away his sizeable inheritance, and after the outbreak of war he hastened to join the army. In the intervals between active service, he immersed himself in Tolstoy's Gospel commentaries, toyed with taking holy orders, battled with depressions and suicidal attacks, and tried to formulate the tenets of his philosophy. Finally he ended up in an Italian prison camp, where he completed his *Tractatus Logico-Philosophicus*, the only one of his written works – apart from a dictionary for elementary schools – that he would ever see in print. In the twenties he lived an utterly frugal life as a teacher in the Lower Austrian hills, where he loved but overtaxed his small pupils and boxed their ears, which in the end led to his resignation.

After retiring for a while to a Viennese convent as a lay gardener, then building the house for his sister, which owing to its rigorous functionalism and austerity has been called 'logic turned into stone', he settled in England and taught philosophy at Cambridge. During the Second World War he worked as a hospital porter and on the *Philosophical Investigations*, the second major documentation of his thoughts and beliefs. A year or two later, having found temporary peace and the 'simple life' in remote spots in Ireland, he realized that he had cancer. He faced death stoically and assured the physician who cared for him in the terminal stages of his illness that he had had 'a wonderful life'. Nothing has ever been known of a deeper friendship or even a love relationship between Wittgenstein and anyone, man or woman. Whatever inclinations he may have had were doubtless sublimated. Because he labelled himself a 'non-Christian evangelist', when questioned about his religion by a villager of Trattenbach, he is believed by his biographer W.W. Bartley to have attempted something like an imitation of Christ. This may be somewhat wide of the mark. But Wittgenstein does seem to have attempted at least an imitation of Tolstoy, and (despite his mental arrogance and sudden rages in which he was driven to beat little children) to have aimed at a life of self-denial, holy poverty, charity and morality – whether Christian or Kantian.

Ethics were the overriding factor in his thought and work. He even insisted in a letter about the *Tractatus* that 'the book's point is an ethical one', although the visible part of it is devoted to the purging of metaphysics from philosophy. To his famous comment on the work that 'it consists of two parts: the one presented here plus all that I have not written. *And it is precisely the second part that is the important one,*' he added that the ethical was 'determined in it, as it were, by inner limits'. In the *Tractatus* itself he maintains that ethics are inexpressible, which is consistent with Wittgenstein's differentiation between meaningful and meaningless statements. But when he adds that 'Ethics are transcendental', this shows his tendency even in this early work to peep beyond the borders of language into something indescribable and unfathomable which cannot, however, be excluded from the philosopher's domain. In this tendency Wittgenstein was at variance, as we shall see, with the Vienna Circle of logical positivists, many of whose concepts he shared and even formulated before they did. These included the view of philosophy as an activity not a theory, the activity being a critical analysis of language during which the sayable is separated from the unsayable, the meaningful from the meaningless. He also, like the Vienna Circle, understood philosophy as something outside science, always either above or below it, never inherent in it. Once the logic of language is uncovered and understood, he emphasized, certain questions can simply no longer be put. Everything meaningful that can be said can be said only within the limits of language. However, meaningful statements can only point at what they have in common with reality; they cannot express reality itself. One of his most famous sayings is usually quoted in a simplified form: 'The limits of my language mean the limits of my world.' In fact he wrote in the *Tractatus*: 'That the world is my world is evident in the fact that the limits of language (the language I alone understand) mean the limits of my world.' Somewhat more complicated, but also more faithful to the precision of his every utterance.

It is true that despite this the *Tractatus* contains some obscure or opaque clauses (even Moore and Russell were assumed by the author not to have understood it fully), but on the whole it made crystal clear the main issue with which Wittgenstein, and at that time the logical positivists, were concerned: the task of philosophy was analysis, not speculation. It was there to remove the metaphysical cobwebs which through the ages had shrouded all great issues in mankind's attempts to crack the riddles of the universe. It did so by setting aside those problems that could not reasonably be solved. Whatever up to now had been thought by the layman to be the business of the philosophers – the existence or non-existence of God, ethical values, the question of free will or determinism, the nature of consciousness and the meaning of life – was now considered incapable of being tested empirically, and as such was therefore impenetrable even to the greatest minds and better excluded from serious contemplation. This was so complete a break with philosophical tradition that even the young Wittgenstein, let alone the author of *Philosophical Investigations*, left loopholes for the transcendental to creep back in. The famous last sentence of the *Tractatus*, *Wovon man nicht sprechen kann, darüber muss man schweigen* (rendered by the English translators not as 'about what' and 'about that' but as '*whereof* one cannot speak, *thereof* one must be silent') was contested by the most rigorous member of the Vienna Circle, Otto Neurath. When it comes to metaphysics, he said, 'one must indeed be silent, but not about anything.'

In conclusion, a chapter devoted to the most remarkable and prolific ideas that emanated from Vienna before it was swallowed up, temporarily but no less fatally, by Hitler's Third Reich, must subject the group of philosophers known as the Vienna Circle to a brief scrutiny. This had formed around the impressive figure of Moritz Schlick, a native of Berlin and, it was said, an aristocrat, though he never used his title. He was a friend of Bertrand Russell and a follower of the mathematician Gottlob Frege. Like these scientist-philosophers he saw himself in the tradition of English empiricism and aimed at a meticulous clarity of thought. If at heart he was poetically, even metaphysically inclined, as his foremost collaborator and spiritual heir Friedrich Waismann has asserted, he did not allow this tendency to dominate his philosophical argument. Much of what was later thought to be characteristic of logical positivism was set out by him in 1918 in his *Allgemeine Erkenntnislehre* (General Theory of Knowledge), thus forestalling some of the tenets of Wittgenstein's *Tractatus*. When four years later, simultaneously with Karl Bühler, Schlick received a call from Vienna University, he gathered around himself a number of like-minded thinkers, among them – besides Waismann – the philosophers Rudolf Carnap, Otto Neurath, Herbert Feigl and Viktor Kraft as well as the mathematicians Hans Hahn, Karl Menger and Kurt Gödel.

There is no doubt that, appearing almost at the same time as Schlick took up his chair in Vienna, the *Tractatus* greatly influenced him and his group, though Wittgenstein, the lone wolf, could never be considered a member of the Vienna Circle. In fact, he and Schlick did not meet until the late twenties, shortly before he removed himself to England. Even so, for some years they maintained contact with each other, and Wittgenstein's theses were regularly discussed in Schlick's seminar – the most stimulating meeting place for selected students and postgraduates of philosophy. The members of the circle were by no means in complete agreement on matters of politics, ethics or even problems of language. But they all ruled out even more strictly and unconditionally than Wittgenstein speculation on issues that could not be meaningfully expressed and statements on facts that could not be verified.

Indeed, the possibility or impossibility of 'verification' became the sole criterion for the Vienna neo-positivists in deciding whether a question could be answered or was even worth asking. However, in a series of lectures delivered at London University in 1932, Schlick made it quite clear that he and his group would 'call a proposition verifiable if we are able to *describe* a way of verifying it, no matter whether the verification can actually be carried out or not'. It is with some emotion that one now reads the reason he gave for this wider application of the term: 'Take the statement: "On the far side of the moon there are mountains 10,000 feet high." It is not improbable that no human being will ever be able to verify or falsify it, but what philosopher would be bold enough to declare the sentence to be devoid of meaning!' One can only admire the caution of the scientist who held theoretically possible what at the time seemed quite improbable.

Moreover, one finds in this passage the word 'falsify', which (Sir) Karl Popper, a former pupil of Schlick and also Bühler, was to employ in his own method of distinguishing between what he preferred to call 'scientific and pseudo-scientific' propositions. In his adherence to a 'critical rationalism' Popper remained in the main stream of the empiricists. But in many ways he differed fundamentally from the Vienna Circle – not merely in his insistence on falsification instead of verification as the only valid method for testing a statement, but also in his belief that a distinction between meaningful and meaningless sentences made no sense, since any debate about 'meaning' must itself contain meaningless sentences.

Popper's only publication during our period, *Logik der Forschung* (The Logic of Research), 1934, though containing some such strictures of Schlick's (and Wittgenstein's) tenets, appeared in a series devoted mainly to papers of the Vienna Circle. He was thus for a long time taken to be a somewhat dissenting member of that group instead of an opponent. Despite the fact that in his autobiography Popper admitted responsibility for the fact that nowadays 'logical positivism is dead', he also scattered flowers on its grave: 'The Vienna Circle was an admirable institution ... Its dissolution was a most serious loss.' He also stressed that he owed a debt of gratitude to Schlick and his co-editor, Philipp Frank, 'who had accepted my book in spite of its severe criticism of their views'. In its 'general attitude, the attitude of the enlightenment', Popper to this day feels 'very much at one with the Vienna Circle'. And though the fact that for some reason he was never invited to Schlick's private seminar still seems to rankle, it is unthinkable that he could have been unaffected by the sheer goodness and integrity of the man.

As one who, some years later than Popper, was Schlick's pupil at Vienna University, I can testify personally to his great qualities as a teacher, to his lucid simplicity in explaining complicated trains of thought, to his cheerful and patient unravelling of scholastic conundrums which had haunted philosophy for centuries. However, it was for more reasons than that of his utter scientific honesty that Schlick became a paradigm and guiding light to most of his students for the rest of their lives. He was a truly modest, almost diffident, trustingly childlike man who loved his fellow human beings just as much as he strove towards a reasonable, logical view of the world. While he believed that rules of ethics could not be laid down – ethical statements being emotive not descriptive – and that moral behaviour could be based on merely utilitarian principles, Schlick's own humaneness was the best example of how to deport oneself honourably and charitably in all things. To him the sum of wisdom was St Augustine's saying 'Ama et fac quod vis' – if moved by love whatever you do will be well done. All the evil and the tragedy to come in Vienna was foreshadowed when in June 1936 Moritz Schlick was murdered on the steps of the philosophy faculty by a half-demented student. After this anything could happen. And almost everything did.

Left *Sigmund Freud with his daughter Anna.*

Below left *Richard Weininger.*

Below *Otto Weininger.*

Opposite *Theodor Herzl with his children.*

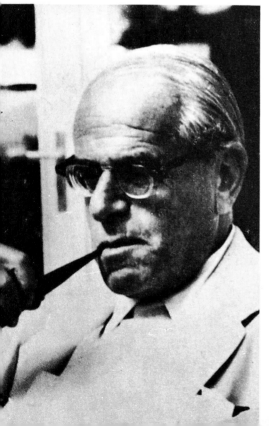

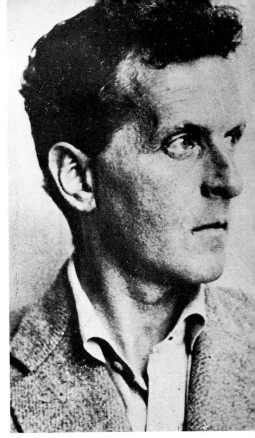

Above
Ludwig Wittgenstein.

Above left *Moritz Schlick.*

Left *Egon Wellesz and his family..*

Opposite above left
Gustav Mahler.

Opposite above right
Arnold Schönberg.

Opposite below left
Alban Berg.

Opposite below right
Anton von Webern by Max Oppenheimer, 1910.

10

THE HOLIEST
OF ARTS

Vienna is and always has been a city saturated with music – though by no means at all times has it been the musical capital of the world. Of its host of serious composers from the seventeenth to the nineteenth centuries very few, however, were natives (such as the three baroque emperors Leopold I, Joseph I and Charles VI); there were none among the 'Vienna classics' Haydn, Mozart and Beethoven, and only one of their peers, Franz Schubert, was in every way a true Viennese. Light music, on the other hand, is indigenous to a far greater degree. It seems to spring naturally from the city's soil and to flow over into the most sublime works written there. In fact as a contemporary Austrian writer, Hans Weigel, has pointed out, in Vienna there is less than one step from the sublime to the ridiculous (or risible), and indeed utter harmony between the two.

The dualism of the lofty and the lowly, of court art and popular art, which was so characteristic of the development of theatre in Vienna, never caused such a conflict in music as there had been between the *Kasperl* plays and the idealistic drama imported from Germany. In Schikaneder's *Magic Flute* Austrian folk humour walks hand in hand with exalted humanism, as Papageno does with Tamino. And it is not to the prince but to the plumed birdcatcher, surely a cousin of Hanswurst and Arlecchino, that the most beautiful verse about man and woman united approaching divinity is entrusted. Hofmannsthal's *Ariadne auf Naxos* again represents a successful attempt to wed a solemn Greek myth to an Austrian version of *commedia dell'arte*. The young composer – from whose belief in the holiness of music this chapter's title is borrowed – admires the prima donna who is to sing Ariadne, but he falls in love with the coquettish Zerbinetta. For, as he stresses in his panegyric to it, his art 'assembles all kinds of courage like cherubim around a radiating throne'.

All great music written in Vienna, whether by immigrants from Bonn and Hamburg or by those from nearer places such as Bohemian Kalischt, Salzburg and Linz, contains elements of local dances, songs and tunes. Not only Beethoven's *Pastoral Symphony* but also his seventh – in the hurdy-gurdy motif of its second movement – owe part of their inspiration to the composer's residence among the ordinary people, and to his frequent walks on the hilly slopes of what are now the outlying districts of Vienna. Bruckner's *Ländler* temper the heroism of his monumental symphonies, while Mahler's ditties or marches (though transposed into a minor key) mitigate the basically tragic nature of his works. As for Brahms, who unlike that other north German, Friedrich Hebbel, shed much of his Teutonic earnestness if not his innate melancholy after settling in the Austrian capital, his speedy adoption of its playful rhythms is startling. Three years after his arrival in 1862 he wrote sixteen waltzes (op. 39), and in 1869, shortly after completing his heart-rending *German Requiem*, he composed the *Liebesliederwalzer* for the relief of his own feelings.

Even the Second Vienna School (successor to the first classical one), though it shed the tradition of tonality and exposed itself to the (false) accusations of being 'cerebral', 'mathematical' and even 'sterile', had roots in the city's musical traditions which cannot be ignored. Not only did all these composers, especially Schönberg and Webern, conduct or indeed orchestrate Johann Strauss's scores and other dance and operetta music, but they also – particularly Alban Berg – retained enough of the sensuousness and the melodic colour of Schubert and Brahms to assure a continued adherence to the *genius loci*. Moreover, as the ingenious friend and interpreter of Schönberg, Theodor W. Adorno, has pointed out, the degree of liberty allowed to the composer by the twelve-tone system tallies with the casual *laissez-faire* attitude inherent in the Viennese character and in its every artistic manifestation. It is as well to remember that among those who, though professing not to understand it, supported the 'new music' of the Second Vienna School when it encountered heavy attacks and derision, was Franz Lehár, operetta's 'silver king'.

During the 1880s, the musical world of the capital was riven by the conflict between Wagnerians and Brahmsians – inadequately described as believers in progressive forms of this art on the one hand and established ones on the other. If it is true that all modern music sprang from the abandonment of tonal meaning in *Tristan and Isolde* (which had in fact been foreshadowed in the overture to *The Flying Dutchman*), then Bruckner, Mahler, Hugo Wolf and the explorers of free tonality must be seen as followers of the Wagner line. On the other hand, though Brahms was certainly an impressive end product and even the ultimate exponent of high romanticism, rather than a friend of the *Neutöner* ('new sound' composers), he is known to have influenced the young Richard Strauss no less than did Wagner. In fact, despite the deep gulf and acrimonious controversies which at that time divided Vienna's music-lovers (the most loyal advocate of Brahms and vehement opponent of Wagner being the critic Eduard Hanslick, who is remembered less for his excellent musical essays than for being pilloried as Beckmesser in *Die Meistersinger*), no strict boundaries can be discerned between one school and the other. Gustav Mahler felt the impact, as much as Strauss, of the German romantics, of whom Brahms was the last great master. And Mahler, 'contemporary of the future', as he has been called, is the composer in whose work was most palpably expressed the *Zeitgeist* of the *fin de siècle*, with its nervousness, its intoxication with colour, its eclecticism, its *Weltschmerz* and its ecstasy.

Like Freud and Karl Kraus, Mahler was born in what is now Czechoslovakia, more precisely in the Bohemian village of Kalischt from which his father moved across into Moravia when Gustav was a few months old. Most probably, as was the case with many other Jewish families in this part of the empire, their forebears had at some point been evicted from Vienna and moved up north, or settled there directly on their trek eastwards from some ghetto or settlement on the Neckar or the Rhine. There is no evidence of any ancestors having come from Poland. Gustav's mother, according to his wife Alma, was 'a girl from a better-class Jewish house called Frank', who in spite of a very unhappy marriage bore her husband twelve children, six of whom died at an early age. Gustav was the eldest surviving son. The composer's father, Bernhard, whose mother had been so poor that she peddled household linen around the villages, came into modest wealth, shed his orthodox belief and strove to acquire a cultural education. At Iglau, a German-speaking enclave in Moravia, this would have been achieved mainly through reading the works of Goethe, Schiller and Heine which, in dark green or scarlet uniform editions, graced the bookshelves of every middle-class home.

There have been many attempts, by National Socialist ideologues as much as by fervent Jews, to pinpoint and describe the Jewishness of Mahler's music – the latest, undertaken by one of its greatest interpreters, having a force of conviction unmatched by former friends or foes. In a series of televised talks Leonard Bernstein has gone so far as to describe Mahler's life as 'one long Day of Atonement', in which he tried to make amends for being ashamed of his Jewishness. In Bernstein's introduction Mahler is made to recall his early days as 'a small German-Czech-Moravian-Jewish-Polish-Austrian boy', and describes his parents as orthodox. Neither the Polish connection nor the orthodoxy is borne out by any biography of the composer. As Bernstein goes on to analyse certain of Mahler's harmonies in terms of their 'undeniable gipsy, Hungarian, Arabian flair', their 'oriental lachrymose Phrygian key' or their 'Jewish sobbings and sighings', his arguments become progressively more laboured. It is true that in Bernstein's own highly emotional renderings of the scores Mahler's music may evoke associations which had not been present when the same works were interpreted by other – equally Jewish – conductors such as Otto Klemperer or Bruno Walter.

It must be assumed that Bernstein, whose father emigrated from Russian Poland to the United States early this century, without setting foot in the Austrian empire, is not really familiar with the world of central European Jewry in Mahler's time. Ignoring the degree to which these people had achieved a symbiosis with their Christian countrymen and absorbed the German and Austrian cultural past, sometimes within the span of one generation, he jumps to conclusions based on his own personal history. The deep romantic melancholy of Weber and Schumann, the age-old anguish and torment emanating from *Grimms' Fairy Tales* and more especially from *Des Knaben Wunderhorn* (The Youth's Magic Horn), the collection of German folk songs edited by A. von Arnim and C. Brentano, many of which Mahler set to music, are alien to Bernstein's background and experience – how otherwise could he attribute those 'chromatic laments' to the composer's atavistic 'ghetto loneliness'?

It is true that a traditionalist, say a Brahmsian, would perhaps have felt ill at ease when a mood of gaiety or even of humour in Mahler's music was abruptly broken by some dissonance. Indeed anti-Semites, who abounded in *fin de siècle* Vienna, might have put it down to that *goût juif* which became a byword in their vocabulary at that time. However, as Adorno has stressed, it was the arch-anti-Semite Wagner who had first waived the rule which had obtained up to the era of high romanticism, that in harmonic expression 'dissonance stands for the negative, for pain, consonance for the positive, for fulfilment'. In Wagner, who enjoyed nothing as much as suffering, sweetness is distilled from discordant notes, while happy chords are often modulated into minor keys. There is no doubt that this innovation, like so many others, was adopted devotedly by others of Wagner's disciples such as Bruckner and Hugo Wolf. An incident in Gustav Mahler's childhood, nothing to do with 'ghetto loneliness', led to his particular – and perhaps exaggerated – use of a similarly inverted technique. As he recounted to Sigmund Freud, who once consented to a kind of lightning analysis of Mahler, young Gustav had often witnessed terrible rows between his parents. After one of these he had rushed out into the street and encountered a hurdy-gurdy man grinding out some shallow ditty. This bond between the tragic and the trivial, he later felt, had dominated his life even at its most inspired moments, and possibly prevented him 'from reaching the highest rank of creativity'.

No one could deny, of course, that Mahler's music contains Jewish elements, just as it contains Slav, Viennese, German and purely Christian elements. The complexity of them all is what makes him an Austrian composer, in many intrinsic as well as superficial respects. Like Mozart, Gustav Mahler was a child prodigy. And like many others among his countrymen after Beethoven, he found his powers failing when it came to writing a tenth symphony, though a short score was found in his papers. At the age of four he had begun to improvise on a piano he discovered in the Frank family's attic. Later his father bought one too, both as a status symbol and for his talented boy to play on. At eleven Gustav began to study music in Prague. Four years later he was allowed to enter the Vienna Konservatorium. For a short while he learned counterpoint from Bruckner, but it was less as a teacher than as a composer that he revered him. When his master's third symphony was greeted – presumably by Brahmsians – with hoots of laughter, he was present to applaud. With his friend Rudolf Krzyzanowski young Gustav was commissioned to prepare a piano score for publication. Later, in appreciation of the understanding he found in Mahler, Bruckner presented him with the manuscript of this symphony.

It was under the influence of Bruckner, the deeply religious church organist and Wagnerian from Linz (rather than the 'talmudic quality of his dualistic spirit, his rabbinical either-or', as suggested by Bernstein), that Mahler wrote his own highly dramatic *Lieder* and grandiose symphonic works. The first opus, *Das klagende Lied* (The Song of Complaint), a score for soprano, contralto, tenor and mixed choir supported by a large orchestra, was inspired by Ludwig Bechstein's gruesome tale of a dead man's bone which is carved into a flute, and of its own accord starts to sing, accusing the king of having murdered his own brother. It was not supposed to be an opera but a 'fairy tale for the concert hall'. When the work was performed twenty years after it was written, in 1900, a Viennese critic wrote that 'compared with the collapse of the castle at the end, *Twilight of the Gods* was a local incident'. Mahler, *Spätromantiker* (late romantic) – a label to which he has often been reduced – early on demonstrated a lust for luxurious, superabundant sound and a gigantic power of expression which was stimulated by the Bayreuth of Richard Wagner, not by that of Jean Paul.

The affinity he felt on the other hand with *Lied* composers, from Schubert and Schumann to Brahms and even Hugo Wolf, reveals the romantic in Mahler as much as his fascination with German folklore, its sinister profundities and irrational cruelties. Mahler the composer, as distinct from the conductor and opera director, was prone to all kinds of mysticism, whether of Germanic, Christian or Gnostic origin. With one of his first loves, the great singer Anna von Mildenburg, he frequented for a while the circle of Siegfried Lipiner, a philosopher much esteemed by Nietzsche and Wagner. This extraordinary man, librarian of the Austrian Parliament and a secretive author who finally burned all his manuscripts, preached to audiences of admiring friends on the great classical works of art and their inner meaning, on Persian and Chinese mythology, on eschatological problems, and very decidedly against that positivism which in the eighties had begun to take hold of scientific thought. Lipiner's influence on Mahler can be detected in much of his music – in its purely abstract transcendental elements as much as in its Christian components. A converted Jew, Lipiner was himself engaged for a long while in writing a drama cycle called *Christ*. And though it was not due to him alone that Mahler introduced motifs from the New as well as the Old Testament in his symphonies, Lipiner certainly strengthened the composer's spiritual and indeed religious leanings, which found their supreme expression in his second symphony, the *Resurrection*.

Born in 1860, Mahler died in 1911 – not as short a life as Schubert's or Mozart's, but brief for a man who wrote twelve titanic orchestral works and dozens of songs. Many of these had been stimulated by *Des Knaben Wunderhorn*, and the most heart-rending cycle of them all, *Kindertotenlieder* (Songs on the Deaths of Children), composed between 1901 and 1904, had been taken from posthumously published poems by Friedrich Rückert. No doubt these beautiful dirges contain some of the deep sorrow he had felt in his youth at the death of his favourite small brother Ernst. But he could not have foreseen that his first-born and most beloved daughter, Maria Anna, would be taken from him at the age of four in 1907. A short life, finally, for a man who was able to devote no more than two months of each year to composing, while the rest was taken up by his main career as a conductor and musical director all over Europe. From Slovenian Laibach he went to Moravian Olmütz (to use those cities' German names at the time of the empire), then to Hessian Kassel, to Bohemian Prague, to Saxonian Leipzig, to Hungarian Budapest, to north German Hamburg and finally to Vienna where, for the ten years between 1897 and 1907, he held the most coveted artistic post of *Hofoperndirektor*.

One of the triumphs of his vocation as an interpreter of other people's music was his London season with the Hamburg Opera Company in 1892. At Drury Lane he conducted Wagner and Beethoven. And in spite of George Bernard Shaw's critical reviews – though Shaw conceded that Mahler knew the scores 'extremely well' and 'set the pace with excellent understanding' – the audiences worshipped him. Pierre Boulez summed him up as an 'extraordinary and difficult, pitiless and eccentric conductor' – and this despite his aim at a 'faithful' rendering of every work. His *Don Giovanni* in Budapest, two years before London, had so impressed Johannes Brahms that he is said to have called Mahler a *Teufelskerl* (devil of a fellow), which in German is a compliment. In later years, when he spent his summer at Austria's Attersee, he repeatedly visited Brahms at the latter's holiday resort at Ischl.

While appalled by Mahler's music, especially his second symphony, Brahms never lost respect for him as a conductor, and in 1897 could be quoted as an admirer by Count Apponyi in a letter to the management of the Hofoper supporting Mahler's candidacy for the musical directorship. Many strings had to be pulled until he was accepted, as there had been the usual intrigues, such as exist to this day, against anyone audacious enough to set their sights on this appointment. From Bayreuth Cosima Wagner protested against the Jewish Wagnerian getting the post. For his Jewishness was the chief obstacle to be overcome. (In this the Austrian *Herrenhaus*, the upper chamber of Parliament, proved less squeamish, having accepted the unconverted Julius von Gomperz into its ranks). As in Maria Theresia's day, Mahler's impediment could still be conquered by baptism. It is to his credit that, while imbued with Christian hagiography and articles of faith, he had to be 'dragged to church' by his friends to effect, purely for convenience's sake, the necessary rite.

As chief conductor of the Court Opera, and before long as its overall 'artistic director', Mahler the mystic proved himself the precise perfectionist he had always been as a performer. His famous utterance when trying to put a stop to that *laissez-faire* attitude of his musicians and singers, so favourably viewed by Adorno, has to be quoted in full, as it is usually reduced to the aphorism 'Tradition is slovenliness' (*Schlamperei*). In its original, qualified form, his reprimand was: 'What you theatre people call your tradition is nothing but your indolence [*Bequemlichkeit*] and slovenliness.' In fact Mahler was far from shunning tradition. While insisting that each work should be 'reborn' in every performance, he also forced his orchestra 'to play exactly what is in the notes'. It is true that he sometimes stretched his point by employing, in the case of Beethoven for instance, a surplus of instruments. But he maintained that had the composer been neither deaf nor unaware of modern means of expression, he would have wished to alter his orchestration in a similar way.

Mahler's era at the Hofoper is considered in retrospect to have been one of its most glorious periods, despite the difficult climate produced by his reforms (he revitalized the stage through new designs by the Secessionist artist Alfred Roller and directions aimed at coordinating action and music in a way that had not been attempted before, removed the claque which had tyrannized the house, and imposed a rule forbidding latecomers to enter during the performance, from which not even archdukes were exempted). He purged Wagner's scores of the cuts that had been made for the listeners' and musicians' comfort, he introduced new works by Richard Strauss, Saint-Saëns, Smetana, Tchaikovsky, Pfitzner and Zemlinsky as well as the operetta composer Offenbach's *Tales of Hoffmann* – a daring feat. And although he was forbidden by the censor to stage Strauss's *Salome* and himself hurt his old friend Hugo Wolf by delaying the premiere of his only opera, *Corregidor*, until it was too late, Mahler's repertoire, apart from the classics and Wagner, was as advanced as his period allowed. (Not fear of its new sound, but lack of faith in the quality of Wolf's *Corregidor* had made him hesitate, and when he did put it on, six months after poor Wolf had died of paralysis, its modest success did not prove lasting.) All in all, it was the hard-won perfection of every opera performance which made his decade memorable. And it was this battle for perfection that finally he lost.

Having been forced out by intrigue in 1907, he fled to the United States before the end of the year. It had been a terrible year for Mahler. In March he had first handed in his resignation as opera director. In July his daughter Maria Anna had died. Then his own heart disease was diagnosed. Even so, he went on working at his ninth symphony, later known as *Das Lied von der Erde* (Song of the Earth) and posthumously performed. An attempt by Prince Montenuovo, head of the imperial theatres, to make Mahler reconsider his relinquishment of the directorship, was rejected by him. Even a 'historic petition' to make him stay, signed by Freud, Schnitzler, Klimt, Schönberg, Stefan Zweig and others, was unsuccessful. At the Westbahnhof, the station from which he left Vienna in December, between one and two hundred people saw him off, among them Schönberg and all of his circle, many of Mahler's singers and orchestra musicians, Roller and Klimt. Mahler was in tears. From America, he wrote the following year to his friend Countess Wydenbruck: 'Homesickness has plagued me the whole time. Unfortunately, contrary to my wife who would like to stay here forever, I am a confirmed Viennese.' This feeling was to be echoed later by many refugees from Hitler, those of Jewish descent proving to suffer more deeply than their gentile compatriots from nostalgia for their native cities or lands.

For the rest of his life Mahler subjected himself to the strain of alternating between the two continents, since he refused to spend his summers anywhere but in the Austrian countryside. Ceaselessly travelling, conducting and composing, the sick man burnt himself out. His immensely prolific but fundamentally tragic and tortured life ended in May 1911. Not quite a decade earlier, on a concert tour in Paris, his name had been billed as 'Gustav Malheur'. Despite Mahler's marriage to a beautiful and adored wife, his worldwide fame and the satisfaction he drew from his own creative achievements, that unintended twist to his name was not too wide of the mark. Pierre Boulez has spoken of the 'inherited gloom of all Jewry' and of the 'mood of impending doom' in the last years of the Austrian monarchy, which overshadowed Mahler's existence. As we have seen, similar deep leanings towards melancholy are inherent in the German romantic mind. Yet it is not merely as another *Spätromantiker*, but as an innovator and precursor of modern music that posterity is now ready to view him.

Not so much from a sentimental, geographically determined attachment – as, again, Boulez has suggested – but more from a feeling of profound admiration and inner affinity, Schönberg and his disciples gathered around Mahler in his last years and paid him their respects after his death. On their funeral wreath they wrote, 'Bereft of the saintly human being Gustav Mahler, we are left for life with a never-to-be-lost example of his work and impact.' Schönberg's *Harmony Manual*, finished late in 1911, was dedicated 'to the memory of Gustav Mahler ... This martyr, this saint'. The word was used again and again by his young admirers, as by Anton Webern in a letter to Alban Berg in September of that year. For Berg, Mahler was one of the 'sacrosanct masters' of an 'unimpeachable tradition'. He too spoke of 'holy Mahler' and held his example as a lifelong ideal. During Mahler's years at the opera 'we young people learned to love perfection in him ... no one, nobody else in his time had a similar power over us'.

Egon Wellesz, the third of Schönberg's earliest pupils after Webern and Berg, has given a moving description of the 'spell' exercised on him by Mahler. While Schönberg, Zemlinsky and Webern, according to his memoirs, were not totally won over to Mahler's music until 1904, at a performance of *Des Knaben Wunderhorn* and *Kindertotenlieder*, Wellesz had been his 'passionate follower' from the earliest symphonies. When in May 1920 he and his wife travelled to Holland, together with Webern and the Schönbergs, to attend the first post-war Mahler festival, it was – like the pilgrimage of Webern and others to the posthumous first performance of *Lied von der Erde* in Munich late in 1911 – an expression of undiminished loyalty to their patron saint.

At this point, before looking more closely at Schönberg and his school, some basic remarks must be made regarding the musical taste of Vienna. In a city where every inhabitant, since time immemorial, has grown up hearing, singing or playing music, and before long judging it, appreciation of this art is ruled by a common denominator rather than by a selective and progressive élite. It was therefore always with reluctance, and frequently not even with the initial support of the critical pundits, that innovative composers were accepted in Vienna. The two bastions of music in performance, the opera house and the concert halls of the Musikverein (to which in 1913 was added the second great concert building, the Konzerthaus), relied on their regular audiences who were prepared to love what they knew but recoiled from the unfamiliar.

In both places members of the Vienna Philharmonic reigned supreme. Always one of the world's three greatest orchestras, and more often than not the foremost, it liked to indulge in its own consummate harmonies and exquisite sound, especially of its unsurpassed strings, in rendering time-honoured masterpieces, rather than run the risk both of losing their perfection through playing new and controversial works, and of being identified with them. If Brahms was supposed to have written his symphonies for the Vienna Philharmonic, Gustav Mahler and his successors quite obviously did not. The orchestra's *Abonnement-Konzerte* at the 'Golden Hall' of the Musikverein – subscriptions for which, passed from generation to generation, were said to be the only patent of nobility left after 1918 – were rituals of tradition and remain so to this day. If, riding high on that vogue of 'Vienna around 1900' which is sweeping the capitals of the western world at present, Austrian politicians cheerfully endorse the claim that all modernity was born and cradled in this city, it is as well to remember that as far as music went Vienna had to be dragged into the twentieth century.

The 'battle' between Brahmsians and Wagnerians must be seen in the light of this state of affairs – though it concerned the music-loving public more than the musicians. Arnold Schönberg began as an enthusiastic follower of Brahms whose influence can be traced in early works, such as his sextet for strings *Verklärte Nacht* (Transfigured Night, 1899). On the other hand, the same work owes much to the 'technique of Wagner', as the composer himself has asserted. Before he left the realm of strict tonality in about 1907, Schönberg did not encounter more than the usual lack of understanding. Even so, in order to combat this general attitude, in 1904 he felt bound, together with his friend and brother-in-law Zemlinsky, to set up an 'Association of Creative Composers' (*Verein der schaffenden Tonkünstler*). Its manifesto stated that 'works of contemporary composers, especially those of Viennese ones,' were 'hardly taken note of within the musical life of Vienna'. The city, so it was said, 'was no platform for novelties', except for operettas 'where Vienna without doubt was dominant.'

When he founded the association, Schönberg had already spent three years in Berlin in order to escape the conservative climate of his native city. It seems that Mahler was the last great composer to feel homesick for a place where he had met with prejudice and disparagement. Members of the Second Vienna School often felt happier when away from Vienna, although they used to drift back from sheer force of habit after spells abroad. During his second span of a few years in Berlin, in 1912, when he was working on *Pierrot Lunaire*, Schönberg received a call to join the Vienna Musikakademie as a full professor. He declined. 'I cannot live in Vienna at the moment. I have not yet got over the harm done to me, I am not yet reconciled. And I know I would not last two years. I know that shortly I would have to face the same battles which I wanted to avoid.' At about the same time Anton von Webern, who had returned to Vienna after some months at Danzig, wrote to Alban Berg: 'Here it is terrible. It is a crime to breathe such air. It is totally unworthy of a human being to exist like this.'

The reason for these utterances was the truly vituperative opposition of the Vienna public to Schönberg and his disciples – an opposition which, for the first time in this city, repeatedly led to open scandal in the concert halls. With the introduction of musical forms that ousted those of the past as decisively as Wittgenstein and Schlick were to purge metaphysics from philosophical thought, a new element of rancour and spite had entered the relationship between composer and audience. It is fair to say that anti-Jewish feeling had little to do with it. Neither Berg nor Webern gave grounds for these sentiments, and when it came to the twelve-tone technique it was generally accepted, and never denied by Schönberg, that Josef Matthias Hauer had been the first to think of employing it. Moreover, the rift did not appear until after the break from tonality. When young Schönberg, born in Vienna in 1874 to a Jewish merchant who had come to Vienna from Pressburg more than two decades before, began to study composition with Alexander von Zemlinsky, he had no intention of deviating from the line that ran from Brahms, Wagner, Liszt and Bruckner down to his contemporary Hugo Wolf.

Zemlinsky himself, only two years his senior, did not strictly belong to the Second Vienna School, since he never followed them on their arduous path into atonality. Indeed, his musical kinsman was Richard Strauss, whose colourful impetuosity can still be detected in Zemlinsky's late operatic music, as in his *Florentinische Tragödie* (Florentine Tragedy, 1917) and *Der Zwerg* (The Dwarf, 1924), after Oscar Wilde. In this context we can give only perfunctory attention to Strauss, although he wrote the most Viennese of operas, *Der Rosenkavalier*, and the most sugary of Vienna ballets, *Schlagobers* (Whipped Cream). His presence in Austria's musical world, especially that of opera, was overwhelming. From 1919 to 1924 he was director of the Staatsoper (as it was now called) and even acquired Austrian nationality before the country was swamped by his compatriots. If for no other reason than his long alliance with Hugo von Hofmannsthal, he cannot be excluded from this survey. However, his Bavarian robustness, dynamic gusto and, within the rich and brilliant fabric of his musical inventions, occasional lapses into crude taste are more than three hundred miles away from the Vienna of our period. He came nearest to this spirit when yielding to his librettist's elegiac moods or elegantly sublimated emotion – as in the Marschallin's soliloquy on time and evanescence, or the truly celestial trio in *Der Rosenkavalier's* third act.

The fact that Richard Strauss continued to influence Zemlinsky and another Austrian contemporary, Franz Schreker, until well into the thirties is ample proof that these two highly gifted musicians stayed outside the Schönberg school during the period of its 'atonal' and dodecaphonic development. In all his early masterpieces, *Verklärte Nacht, Pelleas und Melisande* and even *Gurre-Lieder*, which were begun in 1900 though orchestrated much later, Schönberg himself owed a great deal not only to Brahms and Wagner but also to Strauss – who had actually drawn his attention to Maeterlinck's drama. Unaware of Debussy's opera after that work, Schönberg instinctively translated it into the form of a symphonic poem which – in contrast to the subtle impressionism of the French composer – brought out the dramatic passion of the lovers in the original play. The great divide must be dated to about 1907 when his *String Quartet in F sharp minor* (op. 7) was first performed at the Bösendorfer Saal in Vienna by the famous Rosé Quartet led by Mahler's brother-in-law, soon to be followed by his *Kammersymphonie* (Chamber Symphony) (op. 9) by the same ensemble and the wind instrumentalist of the Hofoper orchestra.

Both works, though written somewhat earlier, hit Vienna with the full force of their novelty. Gustav Mahler's wife has left a vivid account of both occasions. At the first, a critic she calls K. (most probably Julius Korngold) shouted 'Stop it!', whereupon the audience broke into 'a whistling and yelling such as I had never heard before or after'. Mahler himself got into a tussle with a hisser who, after being driven to the door by Alma Mahler's step-father, the painter Moll, uttered a parting shot: 'Calm down, I hiss at Mahler too'. When the same symphony was played in the 'Golden Hall', people began noisily to move their chairs and leave in great numbers. Mahler got up and commanded silence. At the end he stood in his box and applauded until the last opponent had left. Then he drove home with Alma, discussing Schönberg with her for the rest of the evening. Having recognized his genius on hearing *Verklärte Nacht* and *Pelleas*, he now confessed: 'I don't understand his music. But he is young, perhaps he is right. I am old and may no longer have the ear for his music.'

When the next big scandal broke in 1913 (the year, incidentally, in which Stravinsky's *Sacre du Printemps* was howled down by the first night audience at the Théâtre des Champs-Elysées in Paris), Mahler was no longer there to champion the new composers. On the last day of March that year Schönberg conducted, again in the golden temple to classical music, his own *Chamber Symphony*, orchestral songs by Zemlinsky, Webern's orchestral pieces op. 6 and two of Berg's 'Songs with Orchestra after Picture Postcard Texts by Peter Altenberg'. The first two pieces had been played to whistling and jeering, and fighting had already broken out in the gallery. Webern shouted from his box for the 'rabble' to be evicted from the hall, and the audience demanded that all three composers should be committed to the lunatic asylum. After the Berg cycle had been interrupted and the concert broken up, blows were exchanged by the composer of *Walzertraum*, Oscar Straus, with the founder of an avant-garde Society for Literature and Music. In the course of the ensuing court case a 'practising doctor', so Egon Wellesz has recalled, declared that the effect of the music was 'for a certain section of the public so nerve-racking, and therefore so harmful to the nervous system, that many who were present already showed obvious signs of severe attacks of neurosis'.

By that time, it seems, psychological terms had begun to infiltrate everyday language in a vulgarized way. Four years before, Schönberg had expressed the unconscious in his monodrama *Erwartung* (Expectation), to a libretto by Marie Pappenheim, a relative of Bertha Pappenheim whose analysis by Freud – made public under the pseudonym Anna O. – left traces in the script. This work was not to be performed until the twenties. In considering the rumbustious March concert, it is as well to remember that only a month earlier Schönberg's *Gurre-Lieder* had brought him his first big success in the very same Golden Hall of the Musikverein. (His snubbing of Oscar Straus on that occasion with the words 'I don't talk to operetta composers' may have prompted the latter's revenge in March.) In the *Gurre-Lieder*, of course, Schönberg's musical idiom had not deviated too far from tradition. Even his *Chamber Symphony*, provocative though it appeared, was among the last of his compositions in which he made use of strict tonality. Meanwhile, with his musical dramas *Erwartung* and *Die Glückliche Hand* (The Hand of Fate), with his orchestral work for soprano *Herzgewächse* (Offshoots of the Heart) and finally with his

Pierrot Lunaire, he had entered a new region which is no longer called 'atonal' but is now better described as having 'free tonality'. After one more composition, *Vier Lieder für Gesang und Orchester* (1913–16) there followed what may be called a 'creative interval' of some years.

In this chapter, unlike the preceding one, a natural hiatus seems to offer itself at the time of the First World War and the period that followed it. Up to then, Anton von Webern, Alban Berg and (for a much shorter while and far less closely) Egon Wellesz remained Schönberg's main disciples. Although they were free to develop their own compositional technique, their master's overwhelming example asserted itself in their work. Webern has stressed that Schönberg taught 'no style at all', that he preached 'the use neither of old nor of new artistic means'. Even so, while Webern's early works, prominent among which were the *Quintet with Piano in C major* of 1906, several sets of *Lieder* after poems by Stefan George and Rilke, and orchestral pieces which included those mocked at the March concert of 1913, are characteristic of that sparse, tender, colourful but almost unearthly delicacy and sensitivity which would become his hallmark, they also bear the unmistakable imprint of the Schönberg school. Alban Berg, his friend and junior by two years whose most important compositions were written during and after the war, displayed in his work especially the melodiousness which even in its dodecaphonic phase, despite the baseless calumnies directed against its 'abstract', 'intellectual' nature, was a prerequisite of the Second Vienna School.

Early on, and before he came under Schönberg's spell in 1904, Berg had been greatly impressed by the theatricality and instrumental artistry of Richard Strauss. This would not be forgotten when he began to write his opera *Wozzeck*. In the *Lieder* he wrote after poems by Alfred Mombert and Peter Altenberg, Berg's own capacity for profound and intense feeling found adequate expression. The third Mombert *Lied* was his first free-tonal composition. In the five *Lieder* after picture postcards by Altenberg – two of which were played at the March concert – he had made use of an aphoristic brevity reminiscent of Webern, but so filled with ecstatic passion that the songs were too much for his audience to bear. When in 1914, after attending a stage performance of Büchner's *Woyzeck*, he felt driven to render that gripping drama in music, Schönberg's *Pierrot Lunaire* was the model he had in mind.

Egon Wellesz's personal, musical and professional life differed from those of his contemporaries Berg and Webern in many ways. While they, like their master Schönberg, saw their vocation solely in the practice of music, whether as composers or – for bread-winning purposes – as conductors, orchestrators or private teachers, Wellesz grew to be a famous scholar as well as a creative musician of renown. Unlike Webern, who had also studied music with the great musicologist Guido Adler but had no wish to take up an academic career, he had acquired the status of *Dozent* (lecturer) at Vienna University. His interests led him first to the exploration of the baroque era, and later to that of ancient music. While teaching he went on studying Gregorian chant as well as art history, theology and especially Greek palaeography. By 1917, having been spared military service for medical reasons, he had found the key to the decoding of Byzantine musical notation.

Although the least-known of Schönberg's earliest pupils, Wellesz can be seen almost as the perfect prototype of those cultured Viennese with Jewish antecedents who made vital contributions to the city's most fruitful era in modern times. His parents had come to the capital from Hungary long before his birth in 1885. He belonged to the Catholic church, but owed his allegiance and inspiration to the religious and cultural manifestations of all ages. A man of encyclopaedic knowledge and cosmopolitan outlook, moreover, he aspired to the 'universality' ordained by Goethe. Like Alban Berg – who admired Karl Kraus and befriended Adolf Loos, Oskar Kokoschka, Peter Altenberg and Egon Friedell – Wellesz kept in close touch with the eminent writers, painters and architects of his time. He met them mostly at the house of Eugenie Schwarzwald, an outstanding teacher and philanthropist. At the girls' high school she had founded in 1901 Schönberg, Loos and Kokoschka all taught their craft at one point or another. Wellesz's fiancée, Emmy Stross, later to become an art historian, had been among her first and favourite pupils. Another class at the Schwarzwald School could boast the future wives of three eminent men (Brecht, Zuckmayer and Berthold Viertel) – all three of them writers or actresses to be.

Bliss was it in that dusk to be alive. During the last decade before the war the Viennese – proud inhabitants of a country at least equal in rank to the other European powers – still felt cushioned from the rest of the world by a sizeable expanse of home soil, but at the same time open to every kind of cultural influx from north and south, east and west. The slogan 'joyful apocalypse', coined by the writer Hermann Broch in an essay on Hofmannsthal posthumously published in 1955, may be applicable in retrospect. Some of those who were young at the time were still alive, until recently, to tell a different story – the story of a heightened awareness of the 'synaesthetical' possibilities and demands of the *Zeitgeist*, of the knowledge that all the arts are interrelated and able to reflect each others' discoveries. Anton von Webern, the son of an ennobled but rather impecunious Tyrolean civil servant, had to earn his living conducting at smaller opera houses away from the capital. But Berg, who had come into a modest inheritance, and Wellesz, son of a prosperous industrialist (who for a while made him work in his office), were able to enjoy the stimulating company in Vienna of their great contemporaries.

These were not always affluent or even recognized. When the Austrian Ministry of Education, in 1912, terminated Oskar Kokoschka's short spell as teacher at the Schwarzwald School because he lacked the necessary qualifications, the headmistress went to plead for him: 'Your Excellency, Oskar Kokoschka is a man of genius: it is simply not yet known.' Whereupon the Minister replied: 'Men of genius are not provided for in the syllabus.' So Dr Schwarzwald commissioned him to paint a portrait of Egon Wellesz, which now hangs at the Smithsonian Institution in Washington DC. The artists themselves knew their own worth. In a mixture of self-confidence and resignation, Schönberg predicted that 'the second half of this century will spoil by overestimation what good the first half left of me by underrating me.' Poorer than any of his pupils at the time and forced to score the most banal of operetta music, he trusted that his time would come. Meanwhile, even if nobody commissioned anyone to paint him, his young friend Gerstl had done so anyway, while Schönberg himself, during the short time in which he practised this craft, painted the famous full-length picture of Alban Berg.

His three earliest pupils began their studies with Schönberg in about 1904–5, ending them at different times but, in the case of the first two, never losing touch with their teacher for long, despite his or their absences. Schönberg's great works in traditional or free tonality are still as popular as his later dodecaphonic ones. Berg's *Altenberg-Lieder*, his *String Quartet*, op. 3, and his clarinet and piano pieces can be heard on concert platforms. Webern's subtle and transparent chamber music, up to op. 11, is less often performed, as is also the case with Wellesz's pieces for piano, such as *Der Abend* (Evening), which had been so greatly admired by Béla Bartok when performed at Budapest in 1910. Sixteen works of his, including a string quartet and an orchestra suite, were composed before war broke out. But the true masterpieces of the Second Vienna School remained to be written. *Moses und Aron, Wozzeck*, Webern's symphony op. 21 (to name the best-known of his works) and Wellesz's opera *Alkestis*, after a verse drama by Hofmannsthal, all came into being in the course of the twenties or early thirties – at a time when tremendous hopes were entertained, or had already been dashed, for a lasting republican peace.

Not three but nine self-confessed pupils of Schönberg, augmented by the painters Kandinsky and Gütersloh, had combined in 1911 to pay homage to their teacher in a slim volume which was published in the following year. One of them, Erwin Stein, was to act as a promoter and champion of Schönberg and his school in both Vienna and London. Another, Robert Neumann, had invented a tempered scale of fifty-three tones which was not heard of again. The other musicians, apart from the illustrious three, are also now forgotten. After the Great War a new generation, born at about the turn of the century, was preparing to join them. When they came out into the open they were found to have been nurtured in the twelve-tone technique – contemplated by Schönberg in secret for a great number of years but sprung on his nearest entourage in February 1923. Since the meeting with Josef Matthias Hauer that sparked off his complete conversion to serial music occurred in 1916, it should be mentioned at this point.

In a talk given in Washington on 'The Origins of Schoenberg's Twelve-Tone System', Egon Wellesz has described Hauer's first visit to him with some of his compositions. 'Never', said Wellesz, 'had I seen such a mixture of amateurish writing without any experience in harmony and counterpoint, yet with passages of indisputable originality.' These works were taken to Schönberg, who had already occasionally used the serial technique but, according to his faithful follower Wellesz, was now moved by 'the impulse given to him by Hauer to adopt a twelve-tone series as the basic new principle of composition'. What is known as the 'priority dispute' in musical history was not, at first, seen as such by the two protagonists. Hauer, nine years younger than Schönberg, wrote to him after the two men had met and discussed their respective ideas, that there was 'no musician except you in the whole world with whom I would like to collaborate so willingly, absolutely without reserve and sincerely'. He also suggested the founding of an 'atonal school' which Schönberg would lead and Hauer would teach at on a lower level. If Schönberg declined, it was from the conviction that Hauer's theories and mystically worded laws were false. He finally summed up their differences by asserting: 'He had found a possibility, I had found the key to many possibilities ... He looked for a solution in the cosmos. I confined myself to the available human brain.'

In later years Hauer's lack of success turned his attitude towards Schönberg into bitterness. The birth of dodecaphonic music, however, now considered to be the hallmark of the Second Vienna School, must be placed firmly in the post-war period. When soon after the war Egon Wellesz decided to write a biography of his teacher, the last work he commented on was *Vier Orchester-Lieder* (Four Songs with Orchestra) op. 22, dated between 1913 and 1916. Of *Die Jakobsleiter* (Jacob's Ladder), an oratorio that was to remain unfinished, Wellesz at that time knew no more than the poem Schönberg had published and some 'extensive sketches for the music'. In a final analysis of his teacher's artistic progress, Wellesz distinguished between three creative phases.

In the first, he carries the melodic-harmonic development of the romantic style to its utmost point. In the second, from op. 7 (the *String Quartet in F sharp minor*) to op. 22, he turns towards the classical forms and in the third period, from op. 23 (*Five Piano Pieces*, 1920–1923), we find him bringing order to the newly-won tone-material and establishing rules for it. These rules naturally are not acquired in an abstract manner, but are the results of a technique found in various works of the second period.

No mention yet, in 1921, of the particular serial system which at that time, as we now know, was brewing in Schönberg's mind. When Egon Wellesz reissued his Schönberg biography, the first ever written, fifty years after the German edition appeared, he gave it the subtitle 'The Formative Years'. Unlike developments in literature and the visual arts, in music the great leap forward did not take place in Vienna's golden autumn, but in the wintry days of the First Republic, one of the most troubled and frustrating periods in Austria's long history.

II

IN VINO VERITAS

Seven months after the fateful battle of Königgrätz, when the net proceeds of many cultural undertakings were still shared between the families of Austrian soldiers killed in the war with Prussia, the waltz *The Blue Danube* by Johann Strauss the younger was first performed at the annual ball of the male choir of Vienna's Männergesangsverein. It was carnival time. But military defeat and its economic consequences dampened the spirits of the Viennese, and they refused to be coaxed into a light mood even by the music of Strauss – especially if the words urged them to stop moping and brooding:

> Cheer up, Viennese!
>> Oh yes? Why so?
> Just look around!
>> I beg you, why?
> A ray of light!
>> Can't see a thing.
> Carnival's come!
>> Ah well, so what?
> Defy the times!
>> Oh Lord, the times!
> Defy the gloom.
>> How very wise!

The lovely, lilting, endless melody of the waltz, the 'heavenly length' it shared with some works by Schubert, was marred for the listeners by the silliness of its underlying words – written by a certain Josef Weyl – which half mocked their despondency and half exhorted them, without any good reason, to 'dance, yes, dance, yes, dance!' What in later years was to be known as Austria's unofficial anthem failed miserably in February 1867. Not quite twenty years before it had been easier for Johann Strauss the elder to win instant acclaim with his Radetzky March in honour of the eighty-two-year-old Field Marshal's victory over the Lombardian

rebels at Custozza. When Haydn's beautiful *Kaiserhymne* had been abandoned after the fall of the Habsburgs (and immediately snapped up by the
Germans, who used it for their *Deutschland, Deutschland über alles*), those
two striking tunes by Strauss father and son, the one soft and soothing,
the other rousing, went on stirring patriotic feelings in the Viennese far
more readily than the anthem of either the First or the Second Republic
was able to do.

That rare phenomenon, the Strauss dynasty, has its counterpart only in
the field of serious and sacred music. The family of Johann Sebastian Bach
brought forth as many eminent composers as four generations of Strausses
produced eminent musicians in the lighter vein. They were true Viennese
in the sense that both their Hungarian and their Jewish forebears had
mixed with simple folk from the capital or the country who did not yet
all bear indigenous names. In 1762 the Catholic marriage licence of Johann
Strauss the elder's parents – suppressed by the Nazis, but rediscovered
after the war – gave the following details:

The worthy Johann Michael Strauss, footman to His Excellency Field-Marshal
Count von Roggendorff, a baptized Jew, single, born at Ofen [part of Budapest]
in wedlock of Wolf Strauss and Theresiae uxoris, both deceased in the Jewish
faith; with the worthy and virtuous Rosalia Buschinin, born at Gföll in Lower
Austria, legitimate daughter of Johann Georg Buschini, a former gamekeeper,
and Eva Rosinae uxoris.

Their son, Franz Borgia, married the daughter of a Viennese coachman,
who gave birth to the founder of the musical dynasty. Its latest, but
perhaps not the last offshoot is Eduard Strauss, great-nephew of the 'Waltz
King', born in 1910, who until recently conducted light music with his own
orchestra. In the eyes of the world, however, there is only one Johann
Strauss, the younger, to personify all that is joyful, carefree, vivacious and
indeed exhilarating in Viennese music. No one would expect his private
life to have been as untroubled. Yet on the whole, his seventy-four years
on earth were happy and filled to the brim with work, love, play, far-flung
travel and global idolatry. After a difficult childhood spent in a tenement
house in the Leopoldstadt teeming with seventy-six families besides his
own, Johann was deprived at the age of thirteen of his famous father, who
had left his wife and six children for a pretty young milliner. He was
distinctly discouraged by the elder from following in his footsteps.
Although he had formed his own waltz band and given his first concert
at nineteen (at the renowned garden-restaurant Dommayer), thereby
deepening the rift with his father, it was only after the latter's death five
years later that he was able to come into his own. At the memorial service

he led his father's orchestra in playing Mozart's *Requiem*, and two weeks later became its conductor and his successor, never to look back again.

Even phenomena like the Bach and Strauss dynasties do not spring inexplicably from a void. Recorded music-making had been going on from Vienna's earliest days when, after the fashion of the minnesingers, local minstrels and street troubadours improvised their rhymed and sung narratives. The oldest musicians' guild, the St Nicholas Brotherhood, which also contained lay members, was founded in the city in 1288. But whether created and performed within clerical or lay circles, from their beginnings Austrian folk songs were linked with the drinking of wine. The vineyards around Vienna had been planted by Roman legionaries, probably as tradition has it during the reign of the Emperor Probus in the third century AD. The art of tending them was not lost even in the dark ages. A millennium after Probus the word *Heuriger* – meaning both the season's freshly pressed wine and the vintner's inn where it was consumed – appeared in the city's archives. It was in the small, open-air taverns in the foothills around Vienna that its *Heurigen* songs were born, handed on to posterity and constantly enriched by new creations, the originators of which successively sank into the oblivion of ancient history.

In the second chapter mention was made of the German schoolmaster Wolfgang Schmeltzl, who in 1548 described the Vienna of his day. Of its musical pursuits he wrote: 'There are many singers, lyres too / Diverse company, pleasures bountiful / More Musicos and instruments / Surely cannot be found in any place.' (His ancient word for lyre or string-music, *saytenspil*, in its modern form was Gustav Mahler's favourite term of endearment for his wife Alma.) In the sixteenth century, after the first Turkish siege, and in the seventeenth, after the second, popular ditties concerned with war and victory for a while replaced those on the usual themes, which were Vienna, wine, death and the golden, irretrievable past. During the great plague of 1679 the first true *Wienerlied* is said to have been made up by a bagpiper called Marx Augustin. Somewhat inebriated, he fell into a pit dug in the middle of town for victims of the disease. After waking up among corpses and crawling out unharmed, he is supposed to have written and composed a jubilant dirge about the plague and his own survival, whose refrain has become immortal: 'Ei, du lieber Augustin / Alles ist hin!' (Oh my dear Augustin, everything's gone).

Most of the famous wine-songs which are sung to this day came into being in the Biedermeier, when the people of Vienna began to swarm out into the countryside and to frequent the *Heurigen* inns in great numbers. With the growing prosperity of the lower-middle classes during the next decades, many amusement places and dance establishments catering for their tastes were opened in Vienna. Players of the harp, zither and guitar appeared there, and pretty *chansonnières* like Antonie Mannsfeld, Fanny Hornischer and Louise Montag, now legendary, performed the new popular songs and *couplets*, written to satisfy an ever-growing demand. One of them, the racy 'Fiakermilli', friend of those cab drivers who played so large a part in Viennese life before the advent of the motor car, found her way into Hofmannsthal's opera *Arabella*, where she hands the bouquet offered to her as Queen of the Ball to the young countess, and then starts yodelling to the strains of a waltz written not by Johann Strauss but by Richard Strauss.

More and more *Wienerlieder* and *Heurigenlieder* – the distinction is hard to define – were created throughout the nineteenth century, thinning out slowly, though by no means disappearing entirely in ours, as first the cinema and then television usurped people's leisure time. Among the themes they dealt with nostalgia for bygone and better days took preference over those of a fragile *joie de vivre* tinged with thoughts of death, of local pride and the hope of drowning one's sorrow in plenty of *Heurigen* wine. In 1868 this lament was heard for the 'good old times' in Emperor Francis's golden age:

> Our Ring has lovely houses
> Splendid palais where'er you look,
> Large shop-windows, grand illuminations
> Even an alley to ride along.
> Omnibuses and horse-drawn coaches
> For our traffic have we now
> But the good old times will never,
> Never ever come again.

In the following verse the refrain is altered to 'But our good old twenties we will never, / Never ever see again', and in the last – more cautiously worded – it becomes: 'But a general like Radetzky / They won't easily find again.'

Every decade took a fresh look, not forward but some way backward, to when things were brighter, amusements jollier, people friendlier and true love more easily to be found. In a song written in the eighties a young girl is described returning by carriage from a garden-restaurant:

> Still hearing the boisterous waltzes,
> The waltzes by Lanner and Strauss,
> Her heart full of tender feelings
> From Dommayer now she comes home,
> Her blue eyes like violets sparkle

> With pleasure and happiness.
> So that's how it was in 'thirty A D,
> In the golden and leisurely days.

The Viennese were even able to yearn for a time when freedom of thought was denied them but taxes were lower:

> Twenty-five or thirty years ago, what a life we had then,
> With no lack of work and no price increase,
> How we all used to long for freedom before '48.
> Now we have a lot of freedom
> And God knows what else
> But are laden with taxes.
> That's the end of it.

Like Alice in Wonderland, who complains about jam yesterday and jam tomorrow, but never jam today, the Viennese, at least in their *Heurigenlieder*, denied the possibility of any enjoyment of the present. In view of this even the prospect of death could be glorified:

> One day when I die, die, die
> *Fiacres* must carry me,
> Must play the zither for me,
> That's what I love, love, love.
> Play a dance loud and clear,
> Merry we'll be.

It was in a *fiacre* that the unhappy Crown Prince Rudolf drove to the small country castle at Mayerling, there to commit suicide with his mistress, Baroness Vetsera. It was a *fiacre* cab-driver who finally married the demi-mondaine singer 'Fiakermilli' in real life. And it is another who in Schnitzler's comedy *Komtesse Mizzi* carries off the mistress of Graf Arpad Pazmandy, when she is pensioned off by the *corps de ballet* and unwilling to go on living as a kept woman. No wonder that many *Fiakerlieder* exist, the best-known and most rousing of them being written and composed by a gentleman called Gustav Pick in the mid-eighties. It was the famous comedian Girardi's favourite recital piece and has lost none of its popularity since. 'My blood', it ends, 'is as airy / And light as the wind. / A true child of Vienna, / That's me.'

No other songs by Gustav Pick have survived though he is said to have written many others, but the one sufficed for a street in Vienna now to bear his name. He was a *bon vivant* and a man of leisure who had never studied music but practised it as a hobby, being equipped with independent means. In fact he was a member of that *haute juiverie* which in his time already played an important part in Austrian cultural life. His mother had been a Baroness Schey, and he was related to the Thorsch family whose private banking house was second only to that of the Rothschilds. Two Thorsch girls had married two sons of Heinrich von Ferstel, architect of the Votivkirche and of the new Vienna University. In Gustav Pick, then, we can see another example of that integration which led Jews who were ready to adopt the way of life, sentiments and manners of those in whose midst they dwelt, to identify with a 'true child of Vienna', and indeed to turn into genuine Viennese themselves.

Soon after their new rhythm had caught on and been taken up by serious composers such as Schubert and Weber, the most beautiful waltzes were written by Josef Lanner and the elder Strauss, who conducted them while playing the first violin. These two men of genius loved each other and worked together until they separated around the middle twenties and became competitors. The sweetness of Lanner's melodies and the dynamic temperament of Strauss were to be combined in the music of Johann the younger. But when half a century later, in 1907 to be exact, another Straus, this time spelt with a single s, produced an operetta entitled *Ein Walzertraum* (A Waltz Dream), it turned out that a Jewish composer had the same delicate and mellifluous harmonies at his command, and even the same charming *naïveté* that had seemed a prerogative of Vienna's innate musicality.

The most complete collection of old songs and dances was published in several volumes from 1912. In his foreword its editor, Eduard Kremser, warns his readers against neglecting their 'home-grown treasures', and composers against introducing new *Wienerlieder* with 'modern harmonies' and 'Frenchified melismata'. It could be, he adds (perhaps in his choice of words displaying the influence of Burgomaster Lueger, not two years dead at that time) that 'the recent arrival [*Zuzug*] of foreign elements which have infiltrated the Viennese people of late, has created a population to which the *Wienerlied* is alien'. Even so, 'there is no danger from that side. Experience has taught us that the offspring of these foreigners usually turn into dyed-in-the-wool Viennese; indeed, that they try to be even more Viennese than the natives, if that is at all possible. For this is the charm', Kremser concludes, 'of our city, to captivate everyone living within its walls.' These lovely tomes contain many reproductions of water-colours and drawings by Hans Larwin and the Secessionist Josef Engelhart, depicting cosy groups of wine drinkers at the *Heurigen*, pretty washer-women, street musicians in overgrown courtyards and revellers lighting their way back from the suburbs with Chinese lanterns, which show the authentic face of a Vienna worthy to be remembered and preserved.

In the Kremser collection the *Heurigen* musicians are invariably shown as a trio of violin, accordion and either guitar or clarinet – the 'sticky-sweet little bit of wood'. In fact the 'classic' *Heurigen* band was a quartet of two violins, bass guitar and accordion or G clarinet, and its tradition was founded, fairly late in the nineteenth century, by the brothers Schrammel. In 1878, Johann and Josef began to play at the inns in the village of Nussdorf, but soon moved on to one of the garden-restaurants most favoured in the *fin de siècle* by the upper middle classes and aristocracy, the Güldene Waldschnepfe (Golden Snipe) in Dornbach. With the guitar player Strohmayer and the clarinettist Dänzer they also went on concert tours or performed at the houses of the rich, including the Crown Prince's hunting lodge. Theirs was considered a great art to be handed on to later generations of Schrammels. And when the family was no more, other musicians took up the tradition under the name of *Schrammelmusik*. The permanence of such institutions in Vienna is vouched for by the fact that four of the best instrumentalists of the Vienna Philharmonic Orchestra have formed a new *Schrammel* quartet, which on fine summer Sunday mornings plays to enraptured audiences at one of the most charming old *Heurigen* inns in suburban Heiligenstadt.

The waltz, derived from the *Ländler* which occurs in Mozart, Beethoven and Schubert, most probably first flourished in Vienna. As was shown in an earlier chapter, the Irish tenor Michael O'Kelly (or Kelly, for professional purposes) recorded its vogue around 1786, only six years after the death of Maria Theresia. This would seem to exonerate Richard Strauss from his supposedly anachronistic use of the waltz in *Rosenkavalier*, which is set in her reign. Although the triple-time dance swept Europe and America after the battle of Waterloo, the Viennese waltz, with its special 'grace, lightness, melodic charm and piquancy', seems linked for ever with the Austrian capital. Its ritual celebration – introduced curiously enough during Hitler's short reign – takes place annually at the New Year's Day Concert of the Vienna Philharmonic Orchestra, which always ends with the two 'unofficial anthems' by the elder and younger Strauss. Like the *Wienerlied* and *Heurigen* music, the waltz was rooted and is best preserved in Vienna, its rightful domain. This cannot be said of the operetta, although Austrian composers have added more than their share to the world's repertoire. Despite its precursors in the Viennese *Singspiel*, operetta was derived more directly from the French *opéra comique*, from Auber and Florimond Hervé, and its true begetter was a Parisian born in Cologne – the great Jacques Offenbach.

Johann Strauss the younger, whose *Fledermaus* was to become the epitome of Vienna's 'golden operetta', had to be forced by his wife, his publisher and his manager to take an interest in the genre. In the sixties Offenbach himself, while visiting a fête at the Viennese Writers' and Journalists' Union 'Concordia', had told him casually: 'You should write operettas'. Strauss did not take this any more seriously than it was meant. But from that moment Jetty Treffz-Strauss made him read all the libretti submitted to him by the director of the Theater an der Wien, until at last he gave in. Without Jetty, *Die Fledermaus* would never have been written. Henriette Chalupetzky, as she was called at birth, was a former singer and, before Strauss married her, the official mistress of Baron Moritz Todesco, a brother-in-law of the Baroness Sophie whose salon has been mentioned before. Jetty had borne the baron several children, lived in his house and received his guests; but she could not be his legal wife, for no civil marriage was possible at the time and Todesco had promised his dying father that he would never leave the Jewish faith. When the famous and dashing Johann Strauss, nine years her junior, fell in love with Jetty, she flew into his arms, and was generously released by the baron.

In a marriage lasting seventeen years she devoted to him all her time and talents. 'Jetty is indispensable,' wrote Johann's brother Josef to a friend, 'she writes all the bills, copies all the orchestra parts, looks after the kitchen and watches over everything with admirable diligence and amiability.' Despite the energy with which she furthered her husband's career, however, Jetty could not at first find the right libretto to match his musical imagination. An initial attempt, *The Merry Wives of Vienna* (based on the text of one Josef Braun who also supplied the Belgian-Austrian Franz von Suppé with successful plots), was withdrawn by Strauss because the singer Josefine Gallmeyer was not available for the leading role. The next, *Indigo and the Forty Thieves*, a 'waltz operetta with reminiscences of Offenbach', as it has been called, was well received despite its patchy text, which caused the Viennese to quip that the forty thieves had in truth been forty librettists. The third work by Strauss in that genre, entitled *Carnival in Rome* and again based on a story by Braun, was more of a lyrical opera in the vein of Gounod, full of lovely *Lied* motifs. After Gallmeyer, the second great singer of light music in the seventies was Marie Geistinger. By taking over the soprano part she helped Johann Strauss to his first triumph on the musical stage. And then, in April 1874, came *Die Fledermaus*.

The three opening chords of the overture, fired off in quick succession in E, E sharp and F sharp, have been likened to three champagne corks popping, followed by a flow of effervescent music. Indeed, with the famous *Champagnerlied* of its finale, second only to Don Giovanni's aria in the first act of Mozart's opera, *Die Fledermaus* has been called the 'Champagne operetta' and is sometimes seen as the truest expression of

Above *A washerwomen's ball,
painted by Gause in 1898.*

Left *Johann Strauss and
Johannes Brahms at Ischl
in the 1890s.*

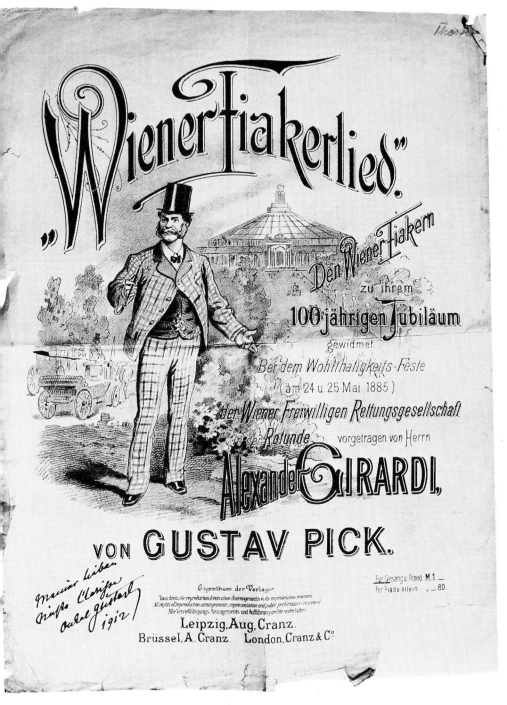

Fiakerlied, 1885.

joie de vivre in all musical history. It is as well to remember, therefore, that like the Blue Danube waltz it was written after a crushing defeat, this time an economic one – the fatal crash of the Vienna Stock Exchange on 'Black Friday' in May 1873. As had been the case six years earlier, it was not so much an enemy or fate that had to be conquered, but rather a black mood in the country. And so the leading tune in *Fledermaus* – which had been scripted by two Viennese after the French vaudeville *Réveillon* – was sung to the words: 'Happy is he / Who forgets / What no longer / Can be changed'. No *veritas* in champagne, but at least a merry delusion. Even so, Vienna at first refused to accept such solace, and after sixteen performances the operetta was taken off. Typically enough, after Berlin took it to its heart a few months later, playing it over a hundred times running, it came back to the stage of the Theater an der Wien in the autumn to a rapturous reception.

Jetty Strauss died – it is said from grief over a profligate son – before her husband's subsequent masterpieces, *Der Zigeunerbaron* (The Gipsy Baron), *Der lustige Krieg* (The Merry War) and *Eine Nacht in Venedig* (A Night in Venice), justified her faith in his great gifts for the dramatic genre. Johann himself was five months in his grave when *Wiener Blut* (Viennese Blood), adapted by Josef Müller after music from his estate (which was administered as diligently by his third wife Adele as it would have been by Jetty), was put on in October 1899. It was not until 1949 that the ultimate Strauss operetta, *Walzerzauber* (Waltz Magic), had its first performances at Mannheim. The 'golden' period of Viennese operetta thus did not end until the middle of our century. Its first representative was not Strauss, but Franz von Suppé, who had been born in the Dalmatian town of Split but brought up in Vienna by his Austrian mother. His operetta *Das Pensionat* (The Boarding School), written in 1865, was an initial attempt to follow in Offenbach's footsteps, and *Die schöne Galathee* (The Fair Galatea) a more successful one. Two other prolific composers of the time were Carl Millöcker, whose greatest achievement was *Der Bettelstudent* (The Beggar Student), written in 1882, and Karl Zeller, whose *Der Vogelhändler* (The Bird-seller) rounded off the era eight years before the posthumous *Wiener Blut*.

Although there was no break in the tradition, for some reason it is customary to date the 'Silver Operetta' to the time after 1900. Its most perfect example is of course Franz Lehár's *Merry Widow*, which first saw the stage in 1905, the year of Schönberg's *String Quartet in D minor* and Mahler's *Seventh Symphony* (which was not performed until 1908). Lehár can be seen as a true child of the empire. His father came from Moravia, his mother was a German living in Hungary. Although he studied in Prague and did not settle in the Austrian capital until he was a grown man, he is considered the second master of Viennese operetta after Johann Strauss. Before and after *The Merry Widow* he wrote such immortal works as *Der Rastelbinder* (The Tinker), *Der Graf von Luxemburg* (The Count of Luxemburg) and – perhaps inspired by *The Mikado* – *Das Land des Lächelns* (The Land of Smiles). His last decades were spent at a pretty villa at Ischl, the small spa which, as well as housing the emperor's summer residence and attracting celebrities such as Johannes Brahms during the fine season, was also the annual meeting place for composers of light music and their librettists from the *fin de siècle* to 1938.

Two years after *The Merry Widow* came *Ein Walzertraum* by Oscar Straus – the text of which had been furnished by the *Jung-Wien* author Felix Dörmann and was said to have been improved by other members of his circle, including Hofmannsthal. The ridiculous notion that 'Jewish music' is written by composers of that descent, long ago refuted by Felix Mendelssohn–Bartholdy, was disproved again and again in the Vienna of our period in the fields both of serious and of light music. Of the four 'Silver Kings' of operetta, three – Oscar Straus, Leo Fall and Emmerich Kalman – were of Jewish stock. Countless minor ones, especially in the years of the First Republic, confound that theory equally well. Like any other talented citizens born or at least bred in Vienna, they produced the charming inanities which are the hallmark, indeed the prerequisite, of the libretti, as well as the lilting melodies and stirring rhythms that have proved to have such lasting appeal. Some of them, such as the Hungarian-born Kalman, began to dominate the genre before the end of the Great War. His *Csardasfürstin* (Princess of the Csardas), which some feel is on a par with Strauss's *Gipsy Baron* as far as Magyár temperament and musical inventiveness are concerned, was first performed in Vienna in November 1915 – after the first heavy defeats of the Imperial and Royal Army on the eastern front and the introduction of food rationing in the Austrian cities.

In his early days Leo Fall, born in Moravian Olmütz, had belonged like his friend Franz Lehár to the species of military bandleaders who were immensely popular throughout the empire. He had no wish, nor was there any need for him to abandon the faith of his forefathers. Two of his best-known works, *Der fidele Bauer* (The Happy Countryman) and *Die Rose von Stambul* (The Rose of Istanbul), were written before 1918. Like the hits from *Csardasfürstin*, the theme song of the 'Rose', bellowed out in all the officers' casinos at the base and at the front, became as popular as *Lili Marlen* was to be in the Second World War. Hermann Broch's term 'joyful apocalypse', though a far from accurate description of the state of Viennese emotions up to the outbreak of war, is certainly applicable once they were engulfed by it. Tenaciously, in the midst of an ever-growing cataclysm, they clung to the shallow and naïve amusements so many had always preferred to more profound and sophisticated ones. Let the martial spirit of their German comrades-in-arms be roused by *The Watch on the Rhine*: Austrians indulged in Kalman's sentimental ditty *Machen wir's den Schwalben nach / Bau'n wir uns ein Nest* (Let's do it like the swallows / Let's build ourselves a nest) or his zippy *Ganz ohne Weiber geht die Chose nicht / Ganz ohne Dornen blüht die Rose nicht* (Quite without women we can't get along / Quite without thorns the rose just will not bloom). Singing the praises of Leo Fall's Kondja Gül – 'Rose of Istanbul, none but you / Shall be Scheherazade to me' – cheerful and insouciant the young hussars and dragoons went to their deaths in the Ukraine and the Dolomite mountains.

In January 1916 a hybrid was born which perfectly suited the taste of musical lowbrows but incensed earnest music-lovers as no other operetta kitsch had ever done. This was a *Singspiel* called *Das Dreimäderlhaus* (The House of Three Maidens), fashioned from Schubert's own works by one Heinrich Berté and woven around the composer's life and unhappy love for Hannerl Tschöll, the youngest of a glazier's three daughters. The novel by R.H. Bartsch on which it was based, entitled *Schwammerl* (Mushroom), which was Schubert's unflattering nickname, drew a tender but rather unfortunate picture of him as a short, stocky and bespectacled young musician too shy and awkward to win the lasting affections of the girl he wanted to marry. All this looked far worse on a stage designed in sugary Biedermeier style than it had done on paper. Moreover, the artless plot about a Baron Schober capturing Hannerl for himself, rather than for his friend the composer, by singing to her *Ich schnitt es gern in alle Rinden ein* (I carved it gladly on all the trees), usurped Schubert's loveliest musical passages from his impromptus, his chamber music and his *Lieder*. Many people who would never have entered a concert hall now heard them as the accompaniment to a soppylittle story.

Would Schubert himself have disdained this kind of popularity? Perhaps not, being himself 'a man of modest origin', a son of the simple folk. We know from one of Mozart's letters how delighted the composer of *The Marriage of Figaro* was when he heard the tunes of his opera played in a Prague ballroom. 'I did not dance because I was too tired. But I watched with pleasure how all these people hopped about with such ardent joy to the music of my *Figaro*, all turned into *contredanses* and German dances. For here there is no other talk than of *Figaro*, nothing played, blown, sung or whistled but *Figaro*.' His posthumous blessing of the *Dreimäderlhaus* being impossible, we can only guess that Schubert might not have found fault where Mozart did not object. The purism of people who are not themselves creative is seldom shared by those they mean to defend.

It was thus that great composers like Wagner, Brahms and Mahler had the deepest admiration for Johann Strauss, whose musical genius they rated as highly, if not more so, than their own. In Vienna especially, light music of some quality was adored by the most fastidious members of the intelligentsia. It has been recounted how at the Café Griensteidl Hofmannsthal's friends amused themselves by singing his poem *Lebenslied* (Song of Life) to the tune of Pick's *Fiakerlied*. These most hermetic and esoteric verses, beginning with the lines *Den Erben laß verschwenden | An Adler, Lamm und Pfau* (Let the heir squander his bequest on eagle, lamb and peacock), indeed fits the rhythm perfectly. The borderline between the lofty and the lowly was often crossed in both directions, as we have seen. If Oscar Straus misbehaved at a concert of the Vienna School while Lehár, without professing to 'understand' their music, assured its members of his support, it was due rather to the personal insult Straus had suffered from Schönberg than to a lack of professional solidarity. Schönberg, as well as most of his early pupils, had conducted light music in his youth. At a concert arranged by an 'Association for Private Music Performances' founded by him in 1918, four waltzes by Johann Strauss were played in an adaptation by Schönberg, Berg and Webern. According to Berg, 'frenetic applause' was their reward.

In one respect composers of *Wienerlieder*, waltzes and operettas were favoured far above any other musicians or even writers and artists – they knew, and daily had proof of it, that they filled the needs of the genuine feelings of the people of Vienna, and gave expression to them; indeed, that they were the city's *vox populi*. As Eduard Kremser consoled his readers, and Gustav Pick showed so convincingly, anyone, whatever his antecedents, who lived within Vienna's walls and became absorbed by its aura could turn into such a voice. Robert Stolz, the twelfth son of a music teacher, was born in his father's *conservatoire* at Graz, the provincial capital of Styria. When, after conducting orchestras at Marburg, Salzburg and Brünn, he reached Vienna at the age of twenty-five, he was fortunate enough to be entrusted with the first night and subsequent performances of *The Merry Widow*. Within a few years, Stolz was able to write *Wienerlieder* of true local feeling, from *Servus Du ...* (Goodbye, you ...), a sweet farewell that could have been sung by any of Schnitzler's little seamstresses or chorus girls, to *Wien wird bei Nacht erst schön* (Vienna grows more beautiful at night), *Im Prater blüh'n wieder die Bäume* (The trees of the Prater are in bloom again), and the world-famous *Zwei Herzen im 3/4 Takt* (Two hearts in three-four time).

The same applies to Hermann Kohn, born in the workers' suburb of Meidling, who under the pseudonym Hermann Leopoldi eulogized many of the city's districts in little songs of the utmost charm. One of them, about two lovers in a small coffee-house at Hernals, successfully crossed the Atlantic – as would its composer under less pleasant circumstances in 1938 – under the title 'A Little Café Down the Street'. (Like Leopoldi, the racially unencumbered Stolz preferred to seek refuge in the States rather than stay on in Hitler's Vienna, from which all his librettists had been driven into exile or death.) Quite often the writers of *Wienerlieder* anticipated or even aroused a popular feeling instead of waiting for it to emerge. In the second year of the war, when the eighty-five-year-old Emperor Franz Joseph was in declining health and plagued by the realization that the hostilities would not end as soon as had been assumed at the outset and might even mean the end of his dynasty's reign, a song was heard one night in the smoke-filled cellar cabaret Simplicissimus. The singer was a small, slim redhead called Josma Selim, and the words and music had been written by her husband Ralph Benatzky. Out there in the park of Castle Schönbrunn, it said, sits an old gentleman in a troubled mood: 'Dear good old Sir, don't have a heavy heart, Vienna is happy to have an emperor like you.'

Draußen im Schönbrunner Park was soon taken up by the newspaper sellers, the cooks and washerwomen singing in their courtyards, the street-musicians and *Heurigen* bards. Until the dear old gentleman on the throne breathed his last in November 1916 this song did the rounds in the city and reached out into the realm wherever German was spoken. It was the last fervent display of loyalty to the house of Habsburg in the imperial residence and beyond. In the middle of the First Republic its author was to create the now world-famous operetta *The White Horse Inn*. And in the Second Republic, having returned from his American exile (into which he too had been forced by his descent) and settled cautiously in Switzerland, he regularly acted as a stand-in for Franz Joseph I, whom he had eulogized so long before. During a few August weeks at the original White Horse Inn at the small Austrian summer resort of St Wolfgang, whenever his tunes were played by bands floating past on rowing boats in the annual fête on the lake, he was asked to step onto the terrace and acknowledge the homage of the crowd – just like the emperor in the last scene of the operetta. After that Ralph Benatzky and his lovely last wife Kirschi went back to their home in Zurich, where they felt entirely safe.

12

CONFLAGRATION AND AFTERGLOW

In the course of the year 1913 the Austrian artist Oskar Kokoschka began painting his masterpiece, a wild and wonderful composition showing a couple adrift on a turbulent sea. Not yet 'the greatest living British painter' (by passport only), as he was to be called in the early sixties when his first London retrospective opened at the Tate Gallery, Kokoschka here expressed the microcosm of his innermost turmoil in a picture which seemed to mirror the macrocosm of outside events at the time.

During the preceding winter he had met and fallen in love with the beautiful widow of Gustav Mahler. Alma, finding herself able for neither the first nor the last time to inspire a man of genius, entered into a stormy relationship with young Kokoschka. After months of bliss, spent partly in Italy, it began to disintegrate. The painting of two lovers basking, happily entwined, in a bark on the waters, induced by a dream Kokoschka had one night in Naples, accordingly took on a different meaning. Now it exposed the man's doubts and anguish, of which his sleeping lover was still unaware, and the bark seemed no longer to glide along, but to have been shipwrecked. 'The boat in which we two are being tossed about, as on the ocean, is a house big enough for the whole world of pain which we have gone through together,' Kokoschka wrote in 1914 to his friend, the writer Albert Ehrenstein. 'And I am going to the war, secretly. After the red picture I should really go under.'

The 'red picture', called *Die Windsbraut* (or *The Tempest*) and in fact painted in glowing greens and blues and yellows as well as reds, intense as Bengal lights, has been interpreted in our day as a potent metaphor of 'collapse, dissolution, *Finis Austriae*, the end of time'. There is an ironic significance in the fact that with the money a Hamburg chemist paid for *The Tempest* Kokoschka bought the half-breed horse he needed to take up an officer's commission in the empire's most aristocratic cavalry regiment – an honour he owed to his friend Adolf Loos who had procured some high-ranking patronage. It was not merely panache which made him volunteer before his call-up was due, nor did he enter into the fray with quite the insouciance that his fellow officers felt or at least displayed. He did it mainly because he was on the rebound from his unhappy affair with Alma (possibly even having been urged by her to sign up), but nevertheless he seemed to have enjoyed donning the flamboyant uniform of the dragoons – light blue jacket with white revers, red breeches and a shiny golden helmet, 'a wonderful target', as later he recalled – and suddenly becoming part of an élite to which otherwise he would never have been admitted. The *Oberwildling* (super-rowdy) of former days, the expressionist *épateur* of the bourgeoisie and, in their eyes, an utter immoralist, rode to war masquerading as an operetta hero. It was also symbolic of what could now indeed be called a 'joyful apocalypse' that after several skirmishes on the Ukrainian front Oskar Kokoschka was shot in the head and, lying half-conscious on his dead horse, was bayoneted, but even then not killed, by a Russian soldier.

When the conflagration broke out after nearly fifty years of relative peace it seemed so unreal that at first nobody seemed to grasp its full implications, not even the statesmen, politicians and generals who had launched it. The causes were manifold and, to some extent, buried in the recesses of time. The basis of the age-old grudge of the northern Slavs against the dynasty could be traced back as far as the burning at the stake of Johann Hus, the Czech religious reformer, in the fifteenth century, ordered by the church but condoned by the Habsburg Emperor Sigismund; or the Battle on the White Mountain near Prague in 1620, won by the imperial troops of His Most Catholic Majesty Ferdinand II against the Protestant Bohemians, after which the native nobles were either beheaded or dispossessed, and 120,000 Bohemians and Moravians had to leave their country. When the Hungarians, humbled, if less drastically, after their rebellion in 1848, not quite two decades later achieved equality with Austria, resulting in the change to a 'Dual Monarchy', the Czechs' grievance flared up again. The annulment in 1897 (following hysterical outbursts against it by Pan-German extremists) of a decree issued by Prime Minister Count Badeni ordering bilingual administration in Bohemia and Moravia, enraged them once more, although they had thought it less than perfect.

The southern Slavs – whose anger finally triggered off the war – had no fewer reasons to complain. There were differences in their attitude towards the rulers of the realm. The Slovenes and Croats on the whole felt loyal to the Habsburgs, but Bosnia and Herzegovina, which had been occupied by Austria from 1878 and were finally annexed in 1908, were set on rebellion. To them it seemed that they had exchanged near-serfdom under the Turks not for complete freedom – as the Serbs had done after the Peace of San Stefano in 1878 – but merely for a lighter yoke. True, the German-speaking 'master race' in Vienna treated them considerably better than the Magyár 'master race' in Budapest treated the Slovaks and Romanians under their jurisdiction. Yet the Slavs in the Dual Monarchy were on the whole considered inferior to the other member nations – 'a people without history', as the German Socialist Friedrich Engels slightingly called them – and mainly fit to serve as tailors, cobblers and domestic servants, as, indeed, did many of those Czechs who made up thirty per cent of the citizens of Vienna.

Again and again the pride of Bohemians was especially wounded. Their magnificent city, golden Prague, had housed many monarchs of the Holy Roman Empire and was still considered the outstanding 'baroque wonder' north of Italy. In 1848 the Czech historian Frantisek Palácky had made his famous remark: 'Truly, if the Austrian state had not existed for a long time, in the interests of Europe, in the interests of *humanitas* itself one should hasten to create it.' Now, towards the end of the century, forces within and without were hastening to destroy it. Nationalism, the scourge of the age, spurred on the pan-Germans, the pan-Slavs and the Italian irredentists to tear the Habsburg monarchy apart. Moreover, within the crown lands and especially in Vienna the mutually hostile factions of Marxist Socialists, Christian Socialists and the liberal bourgeoisie defended their aims ever more vigorously. Most of the Liberals – from which the bureaucracy was recruited – retained their belief in German-Austrian superiority; the Christian Socialists, under Vienna's Mayor Lueger, looked after the upwardly mobile lower middle classes; and the Socialists tried to ameliorate the plight of the workers, whose families, in the wealthy capital of an empire of fifty-one million people, often lived in abject poverty and appalling conditions – the overcrowded and damp tenements breeding tuberculosis, the 'Viennese disease'.

High above all these frictions and conflicts sat the great father-figure of Franz Joseph – not on a throne, but at his desk, the first civil servant in his realm and at the same time, by divine right, its indisputable sovereign. The tragedies he had suffered – the suicide of his only son and heir, the execution of his brother Maximilian in Mexico, the assassination of his empress at Geneva – had rendered him, if possible, even less emotional and more dutiful than he was by nature. He was the only man in the Dual Monarchy who could still hold it together. Yet the conviction handed down to him by six centuries of Habsburg ancestry that he was 'a German prince', had led him or his government to enter into a treaty with the German Reich whose Prussian masters had defeated his armies but thirteen years earlier. From 1879, Austria-Hungary was inextricably bound to the

Reich of the last Hohenzollerns – a fact which is considered by some the crucial catalyst of the Habsburg empire's downfall. Although Austria sparked off the First World War, the German wish for expansion also played a decisive part. The 'brotherhood in arms' was to drag both countries into the disaster which lay in store, and to prevent any moves towards a separate peace treaty with the *Entente* powers (Russia, France, Great Britain) such as were attempted by Austria after the old emperor's death in 1916.

Among the last Habsburgs the most ambiguous figure was without doubt Franz Ferdinand, heir apparent after the deaths of Crown Prince Rudolf and his own father, the Archduke Karl Ludwig. No thumbnail sketch, which is all that is possible here, can do justice to his character. The eldest son of Franz Joseph's eldest brother, he was in his youth a victim of tuberculosis – which sometimes struck the royal family in their dark and dank castles just as easily as the lower orders in their crammed lodgings. Having overcome the disease with great self-discipline he fell in love with a Countess Chotek who, although of age-old Czech nobility, was still considered unfit, according to dynastic law, to become his empress. In 1900 a morganatic marriage took place. Franz Ferdinand is credited by most historians with having favoured a policy of 'trialism', which should have given the Slavs equality with the German–Austrians and the Hungarians in the monarchy, and which is ascribed to the influence of his wife Sophie – later raised to the rank of Duchess of Hohenberg. More recently, the Bosnian politician and writer Vladimir Dedijer has disputed this view. In his opinion Franz Ferdinand early on abandoned the idea of 'trialism' except as a stick with which to beat the Magyárs. Since it was in the Bosnian capital, however, that young Gavrilo Prinčip murdered the heir apparent and his wife in June 1914, Dedijer may not be without prejudice in the matter.

Franz Ferdinand, who in the last decade of Habsburg rule formed his own coterie opposed to the thoughts and acts of the emperor at his residence, the Castle Belvedere, was certainly a bundle of contradictions. To some he appeared lazy, narrow-minded, unrefined. (He hated modern art, despised Otto Wagner's new church at Steinhof, and wished that somebody 'would break every bone in Kokoschka's body'.) Others held him to be a far-sighted statesman, and not without reason, for he condemned the treaty with the German Reich and aimed at a rapprochement with Russia as a better guarantee of peace.

'A war between Austria and Russia', he rightly foretold in 1913, 'would end either with the overthrow of the Romanovs or with that of the Habsburgs, perhaps with both.' At the same time he was known to be fickle, mean, tactless and a brutal huntsman. His uncle the emperor disbelieved in him utterly. 'I feel tired,' he once said, 'I would like to abdicate if I had a son whom I could trust, but never in favour of this dangerous fool.' Karl Kraus on the other hand, notoriously unstable and often wrong in his political judgements, was to write in his obituary of the archduke: 'In an epoch of general human misery, which in the Austrian experimental station for the end of the world takes on the grimace of a gently lingering illness, Franz Ferdinand seems to have had the stature of a man.'

On 17 June 1914, the heir apparent shot 2,763 ring-doves, having bagged his five-thousandth stag some time earlier. On 21 June Bertha von Suttner, the apostle of peace, died. On 28 June Franz Ferdinand and his wife Sophie, having gone to inspect manoeuvres in Bosnia despite threats to their lives, were assassinated in Sarajevo by Gavrilo Prinčip, a youth of less than twenty years. When the news reached Vienna people were stunned at first. Yet two hours later, according to the memoirs of the writer Stefan Zweig,

no more signs of real grief were noticeable. People chatted and laughed, late at night music was played again in all the amusement places. There were many on this day in Austria who secretly heaved a sigh of relief, because this heir of the old emperor had been done away with in favour of the very much better-liked young Archduke Charles.

Six weeks later Austria was at war. On the joint initiative of the imperial and royal foreign minister Count Berchtold, a wayward and mediocre playboy happier in the *chambres séparées* of the Hotel Sacher than in his office, and the ambitious chief of staff Count Conrad von Hötzendorf, an ultimatum had been served on Serbia, which was rightly assumed to have plotted the assassination. To be fair, it must be stressed that the Magyárs, often called the 'gravediggers of the monarchy', tried to stem the tide of disaster. Their prime minister Count Tisza warned Vienna of 'a dreadful calamity'. But the ultimatum went off, so worded as to be unacceptable. And rejected it was. At his summer residence in Ischl the emperor in utter dismay signed a War Manifesto *To my Peoples*, which may or may not have been drafted for him by one Maurus Block, editor of the Prague German paper *Union*. The subversive activities of a hateful opponent, it said, had forced him, in order to guard the honour of his monarchy, 'to protect its prestige and its predominance, and to safeguard its possessory rights after long years of peace, to take up the sword'. The penultimate sentence, often quoted against him later, was: 'I have studied and considered everything [*Ich habe alles geprüft und erwogen*].'

The culprits in the capital had been convinced: 'Serbia will be dealt with in four weeks'. But on 3 August Germany declared war on France, on the following day England declared war on Germany, on 6 August Austria-Hungary declared war on Russia. Waves of patriotism swept all Europe, including the Habsburg realm, which by then was deemed by many to be a 'Peoples' Prison' (*Völkerkerker*). The term, coined by Lenin for Tsarist Russia, is supposed to have been taken over and applied to Austria-Hungary by the later president of the first Czech Republic, Thomas Garrigue Masaryk. Yet it was not only the two 'master-races' in the monarchy who went to war with enthusiasm. At first, a great number even among the twenty-nine million Slavs and Italians (as against the twelve million German-Austrians and ten million Magyárs) who were dissatisfied with their status in the empire must also have been roused by a sense of adventure after so many tranquil decades. The fatal nature of the ultimatum to Serbia was not generally recognized as such, while the bloody deed of Sarajevo was blatant. It was therefore possible even for artists and intellectuals, cosmopolitans, socialists and those who were fundamentally pacifists to believe that the Austrian case was just.

Not merely the leading Liberal paper devoted to German culture, *Neue Freie Presse*, but also the Labour daily *Arbeiterzeitung* supported the war in more or less hysterical terms. Most of the well-known writers, with the exception of Karl Kraus and Arthur Schnitzler, now voiced their fervent loyalty to emperor and country and their readiness to help the effort in one way or another. In September 1914 Hofmannsthal wrote a poem called 'Austria's Answer', devised as a reply to the German classicist poet Rudolf Alexander Schroeder's lyrical 'German Field-Post Greeting', and paraphrasing a piously patriotic poem by Grillparzer which had been woven around the first words of the national anthem: 'God preserve our Emperor'. Its preamble was: 'Peoples motley at the front / Will the fire weld them? / Austria, manifold soil / Will she brave the dangers?' Hofmannsthal's reply was this: 'Answer in the field will give / Our fist clenched tightly / Answer will be just two words / Those of "God preserve".' When he went on to talk of fighters joining with worshippers, of people standing by people 'breast to breast' to shout their 'God preserve', of 'heroes becoming like children and children turning into heroes', of the 'holy old' tradition inspiring them all, the morbid and melancholy young Loris himself seemed to have turned into an Austrian jingo.

Others of coarser grain, like the Styrian Ottokar Kernstock (a priest to boot), soon produced worse poetry and deadlier sentiments. There is no need in this context to denounce them all, but merely to point out that at first there were very few who abstained from militant approval. Arnold Schönberg, having joined Vienna's own regiment, 'Hoch und Deutschmeister', but been found unfit for the front, was in such patriotic mood that he wrote military marches and choral works for his comrades. Soon however he changed his mind, and was by no means unhappy when friends tried to obtain his release from military service. Kokoschka, too, once his pride in his colourful uniform and elevated company in the dragoons had worn off and the four-week spree had expanded into a worldwide conflagration, wished for nothing so much as a return to civil life. 'I urgently need money and quiet,' he wrote to Albert Ehrenstein and, addressing himself to nobody in particular, 'Please stop the war, I want to work.' By then it was the end of 1915 and no end to the war was in sight.

In this concluding chapter the historical background to the further cultural developments in Austria must inevitably play a larger part than before. In order to understand the afterglow of Vienna's 'golden autumn', the reader should have at least an idea of the intelligentsia's attitude to the ever more senseless slaughter, and of the way in which they faced the cataclysm of 1918, tried to overcome it and attempted to make themselves at home in the First Republic. Again, Hofmannsthal may serve as an example. He too had been drafted into service, as a 'reserve lieutenant', first behind the front, then in the capital. Later to be occupied with 'psychological warfare', he was employed until April 1915 in the welfare department of the War Ministry.

Though usually thought to have been unconcerned with social problems and the plight of the lower orders, Hofmannsthal became aware of the danger of unemployment threatening workers outside the war effort. He arranged for a meeting with the Labour leader Victor Adler, then with Prince Liechtenstein at the Ministry of the Interior, and – as he wrote in a hitherto unknown letter to his wife – sought 'to establish permanent contacts between exponents of the employers' viewpoint and that of the workers'. It is not recorded whether he was successful. But the idea was institutionalized in the Second Austrian Republic under the name of the Parity Commission, a benefit to industrial relations and the envy of the free world.

Other writers, among them Rainer Maria Rilke, Franz Werfel and the great reporter Egon Erwin Kisch from Prague, Alfred Polgar, Felix Braun, Franz Theodor Csokor, Hans Müller and Emil Lucka, sooner or later found refuge either in the Imperial and Royal War Archives or in the Military Press department at Stiftskaserne, a barracks in the Viennese district of Mariahilf. Hofmannsthal went on goodwill tours to neutral countries, lecturing on 'Austria in the Mirror of her Literature'. Stefan Zweig, a convinced pacifist who managed to move to Switzerland in 1917, had also been recruited for a while to the War Archives, where he is now known to have concocted, together with K.F. Ginzkey and R.H. Bartsch, a gruesome account of 'The Russian Invasion of Galicia'. His writer colleagues, as reported by him in his memoirs, were unwilling to support a plan he had devised for an international conference in Zurich of intellectuals from all Europe, in order to bring about at least a 'spiritual peace'. Rilke, he recalled, 'on principle avoided any kind of official and common action'. Hofmannsthal and Jakob Wassermann, as he knew from private conversations, 'could not be counted upon'. During the first years of the war no attempt was made by Austrian men of letters, artists, musicians or scholars to denounce the bloodshed. Nor did a single work of art foster pacifist ideas, apart from Stefan Zweig's own drama *Jeremias*, performed in Switzerland in 1918.

Karl Kraus went as far as he could in his *Fackel*, even publishing the occasional fairly harmless excerpt from his *Last Days of Mankind* – the most powerful indictment of the First World War to emerge in the immediate aftermath. Although Kraus wrote most of it between 1915 and 1917, the first version appeared in print as a special edition of *Die Fackel* dated 1918–19, and a more or less final one was published as a book only in 1922. The play, 'unperformable except at a theatre on Mars', as Kraus himself predicted, ranged from scenes of crude satire and parody, merciless towards individuals in every stratum of military and civilian life (especially those journalists, speculators and social climbers of Jewish extraction for whom he had the most contempt), to brilliant analyses of the progress and morals of the war, and poetry that was both biting and gripping. The great dialogues between the *Nörgler* ('grumbler' or 'grouser' in existing English translations) and the Optimist were developed from regular meetings Kraus had with his friend Loos, though during the nocturnal hours at Kraus's desk they certainly acquired their own dialectic. While, as in Kraus's every utterance, many allusions, paraphrases, references to contemporary personalities and events must remain forever inaccessible to a non-Viennese and even to late-born native readers, *The Last Days of Mankind* conveys as no other literary document the authentic climate of the Dual Monarchy's decline and fall.

In November 1918 a dynasty tumbled that had reigned uninterruptedly in Europe, and at times overseas, for nearly seven and a half centuries. Yet its fate had been sealed almost exactly two years earlier, when the old emperor breathed his last at Castle Schönbrunn. To those who were children at the time his obsequies were the most memorable event in their earliest recollection – Chancellor Bruno Kreisky, the author Manès Sperber and the present writer have testified to that effect. The funeral procession slowly moving along the Ring, with uniformed riders and black and white horses decked out with all the *pompes funèbres* that the Viennese love of macabre pageantry was able to muster, seemed to be accompanying the monarchy itself to the grave. Bells tolled the finale not of an era, but of the longest continuous chapter in modern history. What remained was palpably, even visibly, no more than an aftermath. Young Archduke Charles, who had formerly plastered his work-room with illustrations from the comic paper *Die Muskete* (The Musket), a well-meaning young man married to the French- and Italian-educated Princess Zita of Bourbon-Parma, became emperor. (The Viennese were especially touched by his generosity in leading Franz Joseph's *amie amoureuse* Katharina Schratt to his bier among the family mourners, when it became known). From the first he sensed the impending disaster and harboured hopes of a separate peace with the *Entente* powers. He soon dismissed his warlord Conrad von Hötzendorf, reconvened Parliament, which had been sent home in 1914, and decreed an amnesty for the Slavs – but all in vain. His realm and throne were doomed.

Two moves towards a separate peace were initiated in the early months of 1917, but both were destined to do more harm than good. One was undertaken privately by Berta Zuckerkandl, who has made a brief appearance here before as the muse of *art nouveau*, and in whose salon the Secessionists planned their schism from the Künstlerhaus. This outstanding woman was the daughter of Moritz Szeps, a native of Galicia who had made a brilliant career in Vienna as a political journalist, founder and editor of the influential *Neue Wiener Tagblatt*. For ten years, up to the suicide of Crown Prince Rudolf, Szeps – an unconverted though non-observant Jew – had been a friend and chief adviser to that unhappy, enlightened heir to the throne. In his palais in the ninth district, a splendid building which is now the Swedish Embassy, he had received many international statesmen, among them Georges Clemenceau, who took a fancy to his charming younger daughter, Berta. (So, incidentally, had Disraeli some time earlier, when the child had accompanied her father to the Congress of Berlin in 1878). In due course, on a visit to Paris by Berta and her elder sister, Georges Clemenceau's brother Paul fell in love with Sophie. He married her not long after Berta had found her own husband in handsome Emil Zuckerkandl, a promising anatomist.

Once separated by the war the sisters, who were deeply attached to each other, corresponded via Switzerland and plotted for a French-Austrian *rapprochement*. The moment seemed ripe when the young emperor himself was rumoured to have similar aspirations, supported by his new foreign minister Count Ottokar Czernin. With the help of Hofmannsthal – who

Above *Archduke Franz Ferdinand, heir apparent, in about 1910.*

Above left *Franz Joseph in the last years before the outbreak of the First World War.*

Left *Baron Georg (later Sir George) Franckenstein as the Emperor Maximilian 1 in the jubilee procession of 1908.*

Opposite above *Austrian army officers and their wives in a Moravian garrison, 1916.*

Opposite below *A pre-worded multilingual postcard from the front in the First World War.*

Ich bin gesund und es geht mir gut.
Egészséges vagyok és jól érzem magamat.
Jsem zdráv a daří se mně dobře.
Jestem zdrów i powodzi mi się dobrze.
Я є здоров і менї веде ся добре.
Sono sano e sto bene.
Jaz sem zdrav in se mi dobro godi.
Zdrav sam i dobro mi je.
Sunt sănătos şi îmi merge bine.

Lidová hymna

Zachovej nám, Hospodine,
Císaře a naši zem!
Dej, ať z víry moc Mu plyne,
Ať je moudrým vladařem!
Hajme věrně trůnu Jeho
Proti nepřátelům všem;
Osud trůnu Habsburgského
Rakouska jest osudem!

Néphymnus

Tartsa Isten, óvja Isten
Császárunk s a közhazát!
Erőt lelve a szent hitben
Ossza bölcs parancsszavát
Hadd védnünk ős koroná
Bárhonnét fenyitse vész!
Ausztriával Habsburg tró
Egyesitse égi kéz!

Német eredeti szöveg: Johann Gabrie
Zene: Joseph Haydn

*Multilingual postcards of Franz
Joseph I and the old Austrian
anthem, issued recently.*

Right *The funeral of Franz
Joseph I.*

Imnul împěrătesc.

Doamne sânte, întăresce
Pra al nostru Împêrat!
Să domnească 'nțelepțesce
Pe dreptate răzimat!
Părintescile-i coroane
Credincios să-i apěrăm:
De-a Habsburgei nalte troane
Soartea noastră s' o legăm!

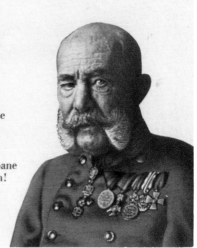

would not have lent his weight to her wish to break up the Austrian-German 'blood-brotherhood' had he known about it – Berta was authorized by Psychological Warfare to go on a mission as 'cultural apostle' to Switzerland. Once there, she easily made contact with her sister, who was thought to have Georges Clemenceau's ear. The whole conspiracy would deserve a chapter of its own. Suffice it to say that Berta's endeavours were spoiled by none other than the German aesthete Count Harry Kessler (a friend of Hofmannsthal, with whom he had written the ballet *Josephslegende* for Diaghilev), who reported her every move to the foreign office in Berlin; and that Georges Clemenceau, prime minister once again at the end of 1917, decided for 'war until final victory'.

The other move, in which Berta Zuckerkandl was wrongly suspected of having been involved, was initiated by the emperor himself. In January 1917 Prince Sixtus of Parma, who with his brother Xavier served in the Belgian army, received word from his sister, the Empress Zita, that she would be grateful to him if he would assist the emperor in his wish for peace. The French president Poincaré was informed, and in March the two Princes of Parma undertook a secret journey to Vienna, where they met with the imperial couple. Charles handed his elder brother-in-law the famous 'Sixtus letter', the content of which is now known. In it he stressed his sympathies for the 'valour' of the French army and the 'sacrificial spirit' of the whole French people. He promised to use his influence with his allies to support French demands for the return of Alsace-Lorraine, alluded to other peace terms and then begged Sixtus to sound out both France and England as a basis for speedy negotiations.

'In the hope', he concluded, 'that we may together put an end to the sufferings of so many millions of people and so many families living in grief and fear, I beg you to believe in my ardent brotherly affection.' The letter was taken by Sixtus to Poincaré, and Lloyd George was informed of its contents. Implored to prevent the monarchy's downfall by a descendant of the very same Hungarian Count Battyány who with Franz Joseph's consent had been executed in 1849; put under constant duress by the German Emperor Wilhelm; hampered by the blunders of his hapless foreign minister Count Czernin, and finally left in the lurch by Clemenceau, Charles went on striving for peace. But his hopes were dashed. The war took its course towards defeat. On 11 November 1918, Charles abdicated his throne, the next day the Republic was proclaimed and on 23 March 1919 the last Habsburg emperor left Austria.

At this point, I must abandon the attempt to outline official events in the questionable manner of potted history. The breakaway, and setting-up of independent new states or amalgamation with existing foreign ones, by all nations except for the German-speaking Austrians; the Peace Treaty of St Germain which deprived the helpless mutilated rump of such vital necessities as a true identity, a sound economic basis and an outlet to the sea – these cannot be dealt with here, though a few political milestones on the path of the First Republic will have to be mentioned. What should be made clear, however, before cultural life in Vienna up to the Anschluss can be summed up, is the mode of feeling, the existential mood that prevailed among the citizens of 'German-Austria' after the traumatic collapse. They had experienced, according to the historian Norbert Leser, a 'reduction shock'. In his view their state of mind resembled that of 'a family, unexpectedly evicted from a roomy apartment, who are forced all of a sudden to go on living under impossibly cramped conditions.' It could also be compared to the feeling after the loss of an arm or a leg, which yet goes on hurting as though it still existed. Bereft of the surrounding expanse of an empire, left on its own, cold and trembling, amid 'successor states' that had turned from being close, if sullen, relations into foreign and unfriendly neighbours, German-Austria was looking for another, wider context, a larger apartment inhabited by people who would give them shelter and adopt them into their own family.

This context could have been provided by Germany – by now rid of her ruler as well, and a democratic state whose protective embrace need not be shunned or feared. But an Anschluss, desired by the founders of the First Republic and laid down in the second article of its charter ('German-Austria is part of the German Republic'), had been forbidden by the *Entente*. It was especially desired by the Austrian Socialists, whose belief in international or supranational structures had formerly allowed them to be most fervent supporters of the multi-ethnic monarchy. Now their wish for a union with the Weimar Republic was anchored, up to 1933 and the advent of Hitler, in their party programme. Some Liberals, still pan-Germanic, and all right-wingers yearned to join the second German Reich. It was the Christian Socialists, now guided by the shrewd prelate Ignaz Seipel, as well as the few monarchists still about, who in the First Republic kept alive the spirit and traditions of Franz I's Austrian Empire. Much later, in the Second Republic, when the overwhelming majority had accepted this separate identity, the Swiss writer François Bondy felicitously defined 'Austrianness' as 'the smile of the Cheshire Cat left over from the old monarchy'. Most Austrians would subscribe to this today.

The first decade and a half of German-Austria were marked by a dualism of a different kind. After a coalition of the conservative and workers' parties which lasted but two years, the country's government was firmly in Christian Socialist hands, while at the capital's town hall, with all its administrative and cultural functions, the Social Democrats were immovably entrenched. It was 'Red Vienna' which dominated all efforts, in an entirely impoverished and hopelessly overcrowded city, to provide adequate housing, sufficient schooling, and health and welfare services more efficient and just than those which had existed in the prosperous imperial residence. Moreover, it had to lend support, with whatever meagre means were at its disposal, to a re-awakening of the arts and the spreading of their achievements among the lower classes (who up to now had been deprived, for lack of time and means as well of education). Thereby it would spread the benefits of the wealth of talent that Vienna had produced during the preceding era of greatness and, it was hoped, would produce again.

This endeavour was first and most successfully undertaken in the field of music. 'Workers' Symphony Concerts', after all, had existed since 1905. Now the head of the newly established Social Democratic Agency for the Arts (*Sozialdemokratische Kunststelle*), David Josef Bach (unlike his famous namesakes neither a Protestant nor even a Christian), appointed Anton Webern as its new director and conductor. Webern also took over the active Workers' Choir, *Freie Typographie* (Free Typography), later to be replaced by Erwin Stein. By the time all this happened Schönberg's 'Association for Private Music Performances', founded in 1908, had already expired. But at the school of Dr Eugenie Schwarzwald, in whose festival hall the famous waltz concert had taken place in May 1921 – with Schönberg and Kolisch playing the first violins, Webern the cello, Berg the harmonium, Eduard Steuermann the piano and Karl Rankl one of the second violins – pieces by modern composers were occasionally performed in the twenties and thirties on a similar basis.

Like Schönberg, the close members of his circle had gone to war with patriotic feelings for emperor and country, but were soon disillusioned and glad to be out of uniform again. They all greeted the departure into a new, democratic age with great hopes and elation, and *Music Sheets of Departure (Musikblätter des Anbruchs)* was the name of the most important periodical to cover the contemporary scene from 1919. In February 1923, as we have seen, Schönberg had disclosed to his disciples the new twelve-tone method he had secretly evolved. From the end of the war Mödling, his residence near Vienna, had become a regular meeting-place for his growing number of adherents. Beside his early ones they now included Hanns Eisler, H.E. Apostel and Roberto Gerhard, as well as the conductors Swarowsky, Rankl and Erwin Stein, the pianists Serkin and Steuermann, the writers and musicologists D.J. Bach, Paul A. Pisk, Paul Stefan and Josef

Rufer, and the physician Marie Pappenheim, his librettist in *Erwartung*.

The departure had been promising, but the arrival took a long time. At the Workers' Symphony Concerts fragments from Berg's opera *Wozzeck*, completed in 1921 and published with financial help from Alma Mahler, were brought before the Vienna public, but the first performance was in Berlin in 1925. Schönberg's *Verklärte Nacht* was played twice by the Vienna Philharmonic, but it was not at the State Opera (as it was now called), rather at the far less coveted *Volksoper*, that his monodrama *Erwartung* and *Die glückliche Hand* were at last shown in 1924. In that same year Webern's *Fünf sakrale Lieder* (Five Sacred Songs) reached a Vienna concert hall, as did his *String Trio*, op. 20, in 1927, but such occasions were rare and he was known mainly as a conductor. Egon Wellesz fared better than his friends in one respect. His opera *Alkestis*, the outcome of a deep and lasting friendship with Hofmannsthal (who had written the verse play after Euripides in his youth), was staged at Mannheim and elsewhere in Germany but has not been seen in his native city to this day. However, he was actually awarded a premiere at the State Opera. In 1930, during his short directorship, Clemens Krauss had brought *Wozzeck* to Vienna. The following year he played and conducted *Die Bakchantinnen* (The Bacchantes), by Wellesz. He even decreed for it sixty choir and twenty orchestra rehearsals. 'We shall perform this work only when it is as firmly anchored as *Die Meistersinger*,' said Krauss.

Of all the more recent disciples of Schönberg, Hanns Eisler might be called the most interesting and, in his later career, the most original. The only truly political composer Austria ever had, Eisler began by writing one of the first twelve-tone works not by Schönberg, *Palmström*, in 1924 (*Lieder* after poems by the German Christian Morgenstern), and some equally witty pieces for chamber orchestra and singers based on his own texts and collages – *Tagebuch* (Diary) and *Zeitungsausschnitte* (Newspaper Cuttings). But even before he removed himself to Berlin in 1926, there to set to music Bertolt Brecht's most radical songs, he wrote choral pieces for Webern's 'Free Typography' which, in the highly strung, ideologically polarized atmosphere of the First Republic, emphatically put the case for the underdog. In several 'suites' for a small orchestra without strings, Eisler introduced forms of jazz music, which by now had filtered into Europe. Soon an opera written in the late twenties entirely in that idiom by the most protean composer of his time, Ernst Krenek, became the rage in Vienna – if only for a strictly limited span.

Jonny spielt auf (Jonny Strikes Up), eight years before *Porgy and Bess*, made use of jazz, not in the realm of operetta as Gershwin had done earlier in *Lady Be Good*, but in that of serious musical drama. Krenek had tried and was to go on trying all the styles and techniques brought forth by his epoch: expressionism, atonality, twelve-tone and other serial, even electronic music. Alma Mahler, to whose daughter Anna he was married briefly, called him 'one of my seven plagues'. The pianist Glenn Gould thought that this reserved, sometimes crotchety, always uncompromising man was 'one of the least understood musical figures of our time'. Krenek's rigidity, moral and aesthetic, can most probably be explained by his lifelong admiration for Karl Kraus, who had a way of instilling this quality into his initiates. His large and complicated oeuvre is still under review. His character remains unchanged. When a newly appointed director removed his *Charles* v from the repertoire of the State Opera, this 'honorary citizen' of Vienna, in permanent exile at Palm Springs, vowed never to set foot on his native soil again.

Musical life in the Austrian capital had not drastically altered in fact since the hiatus. After 1918, as before, the emphasis lay on tradition. The Socialists, relying in their cultural policy on well-informed intellectuals such as D.J. Bach, might do as much as they could to foster the musical avant-garde. The public's taste, on the whole, stayed conservative. The composers mentioned above, to whom must be added Schreker and Zemlinsky, still lagged far behind eighteenth- and nineteenth-century music in general favour. Opera on the other hand was dominated by the works of Richard Strauss, who was co-director for a while and had moved to Vienna. The only contemporary writer of musical drama to match his success, in one instance, was Erich Wolfgang Korngold. The son of Julius Korngold – music critic of *Neue Freie Presse* and as influential, indeed powerful, as his predecessor Hanslick had been – he began to compose at the age of seven, learnt counterpoint at nine, played Mahler his cantata *Gold* in 1907 when he was ten, and was sent by him to Zemlinsky for further study. After seeing his ballet pantomime *Der Schneemann* (The Snowman), which the child prodigy had written at eleven performed at the Court Opera, and creating some operatic works which were put on at Munich under Bruno Walter, young Korngold was called up. He spent the last two years of the war conducting the band of an infantry regiment and working on *Die tote Stadt* (The Dead City) after Georges Rodenbach's novel *Bruges la Morte*. First staged at Cologne in 1920, it had a triumphant Vienna premiere the following year, with Maria Jeritza in the double role of the ghostly Marie and the very much alive Marietta. The theme song of this brilliantly inventive and headily macabre example of early art deco kitsch swept the city and at a moment's notice can still be sung with nostalgic gusto by survivors of the period, like any operetta hit.

There were other composers who carried on in the late–romantic, impressionist vein respectably enough, and never ventured into atonality or serialism. Among them were Joseph Marx, still remembered for his *Lieder*, and Wilhelm Kienzl, who wrote an opera, *Der Evangelimann* (The Evangelist), as well as the first national anthem of the Republic – in use until 1929 when it was replaced by the old Haydn tune. Franz Schmidt, composer of the oratorio *Das Buch mit sieben Siegeln* (The Book with Seven Seals), has been called 'the most important Austrian master of the symphonic style after Bruckner'. Other young talents, whose origins were less acceptable to the powers that be, were pushed off the path of a promising career and lost touch with the age-old inspirational legacy of Viennese music, to which they became an irretrievable loss. One who may serve as an example was Erich Zeisl, born in 1905 into a lower-class Jewish family. His father owned a coffee-house near the Northern Railway Station in the Leopoldstadt, where during and after the war a great number of co-religionist fugitives from Russian-occupied Galicia arrived. Yet in his early work, until he had to flee from Austria himself, young Zeisl encompassed and even embodied all the melodic, orchestral and expressive traditions of Austro-German romanticism. In 1934 Paul Pisk, Schönberg's friend and pupil, stressed that 'among Viennese composers under thirty', Erich Zeisl was 'one of the strongest personalities'.

Between 1920 and 1938 Zeisl wrote almost a hundred art songs – some, like Mahler's, from *Des Knaben Wunderhorn*; several choral works based on texts from the Bible, classical antiquity and – using some forms of jazz as well – black American poetry; instrumental music; and four dramatic works. Four years before he was driven into exile he won the Austrian State Prize for his large-scale *Requiem Concertante*. A performance of his *Singspiel*, *Leonce und Lena* – after the comedy by Georg Büchner, whose drama *Woyzeck* had inspired Alban Berg – was scheduled at the small baroque theatre of Castle Schönbrunn, but was cancelled when Hitler marched in. Zeisl found his way to Paris and eventually to the United States, where he went on writing beautiful music, but never again a *Lied*. *Leonce und Lena* was later staged by the Los Angeles City College Opera Workshop. His music drama *Hiob* (Job), however, was never completed. For some time, he had to earn his living by providing the accompaniment to *Fitzpatrick's Travelogues*. He, who had written a Christian Mass and Requiem in his youth, now dedicated a *Requiem Ebraico* to 'the memory of my father and countless other victims of the Jewish tragedy in Europe'. The fact that a son of Viennese-born Arnold Schönberg married the only daughter of Viennese-born Erich Zeisl in far-off California – after both composers had died – may be irrelevant, but it is none the less significant.

Music and architecture, as we have seen, were the first arts to have been promoted officially in the Austrian capital, especially by the three 'baroque emperors', who had introduced opera from Venice and Naples to their own city (as well as occasionally composing musical works themselves) and paid builders to create the great palaces and churches still standing today. Likewise, after setting up an art agency to foster and find a public for contemporary compositions, the town councillors of 'Red Vienna' next turned to the city's most urgent need: the relief of its housing shortage. An influx not only of Galician Jews fleeing from the Russian soldiers (from whose hands they had suffered bloody pogroms often before), but of many German-speaking nationals of the new 'successor-states', had swelled the numbers of the city's inhabitants. As has been pointed out before, during Vienna's industrial growth many splendid palais and apartment houses had gone up in town, but few decent tenements for the working classes. Now the situation became intolerable. So, by means of a severe system of taxation devised by Councillor Hugo Breitner, money was raised for the building of the famous council houses that were soon to impress the world.

The new Housing Tax, as painful to those rich people who were left as to the better-off middle classes who were already bemoaning their loss of capital and property due to the war, turned out to be the town council's most contentious measure. While it enabled the city fathers to provide about 64,000 cheap apartments in the decade between 1923 and 1933, it also increased the anti-Semitism already rife among the Christian Socialists and pan-Germanic parties. Jews had not merely helped to found the Social Democratic movement but, in response to the hostile attitude of the others and even more because of their own progressive beliefs, had also become increasingly active in it. Now they found the hatred aroused by it mainly directed against themselves. The right accused them of being 'Bolshies' and the left of being 'capitalist bloodsuckers'. In fact, during the post-war period of inflation even their own Social Democratic Party produced posters bearing repellent caricatures of profiteers with Semitic features.

Undaunted, the town councillors responsible for finance (Breitner), and for public health and welfare (Julius Tandler), carried on their beneficial work. The names of those who actually built the great new *Volks-wohnungspaläste* (People's Palaces), sometimes inspired by the example of Otto Wagner, are now largely forgotten. One of them, Josef Frank, has been restored to the public memory as the guiding spirit of a smaller and more élitist 'model settlement', the *Werkbundsiedlung* of about fifty smaller houses, designed by various architects such as Josef Hoffmann, Adolf Loos and Richard Neutra in Lainz near Vienna in about 1932. But who remembers now that the great, sprawling tenements of Reumannhof in the fifth district were erected by Hubert Gessner; that Winarskyhof in the twentieth had no fewer than five architects (Josef Hoffmann, Josef Frank, Oskar Strnad, Oskar Wlach and Peter Behrens); or that the pride of them all, Karl Marx-Hof in the nineteenth, was planned by only one, Karl Ehn? This was a building containing 1,600 apartments, with a façade nearly 1,200 metres long; yet it was only three storeys high with large inner courts, each flat giving onto one of them and furnished with a loggia. The allegation soon to be heard that this and the other superb examples of social housing were at the same time 'fortresses' where the final workers' revolution was being prepared, provoked Christian Socialists in February 1934 to try to blow them all up – of which more will be said later in this chapter.

Painters, sculptors and graphic artists mostly had to look after themselves. Neither the state nor the city nor potential private patrons had sufficient funds, in those meagre years, to commission or collect works of art in adequate numbers to provide for their creators' basic requirements. A small percentage of the building costs of the council houses was reserved for their adornment or for statues to be placed in their courtyards and gardens. Georg Ehrlich, one of the finest draughtsmen and sculptors of the First Republic – who was to receive full recognition only in his English exile – once or twice profited from this policy. It was hard, unimaginably so to artists nowadays whose products have become highly marketable investments, to make a living from their work. Young painters and their like were poor, often had to frequent coffee-houses because they could neither pay for decent studios nor heat them properly, and went round hawking their pictures, often for recompense in kind, to slightly more moneyed friends.

Even so, as at the time of the Secessionists, groups were formed and new exhibition halls discovered. The motto carved in stone on Olbrich's building could still be read: *Der Zeit ihre Kunst – der Kunst ihre Freiheit* (To the times their art – to art its freedom). Now, in these socially conscious days, the slogan was: *Der Kunst ihre Pflicht – der Zeit ihre Kunst* (To art its duty – to the times their art). This was not engraved anywhere, but an appropriate site would have been the building where the artists' association *Hagenbund* held its shows. No uniform pattern such as had existed in the era of *Jugendstil* can be said to have dominated the visual arts. Secessionism, it is true, had given way to expressionist forms as early as 1908. But they went on co-existing with ventures into cubism, surrealism, constructivism and abstract art. Moreover, an Austrian variant of *Neue Sachlichkeit*, the extremely realistic school which had come into fashion in both art and literature in Dresden and Berlin, was represented by a few remarkable artists – among them Rudolf Wacker and Otto Rudolf Schatz.

Others followed a whole range of influences: verism and the German *Blaue Reiter* group, futurism from neighbouring Italy, and the remnants of cubism and expressionism. One artist indebted to all these was the painter and draughtsman Carry Hauser, who lived into the mid-eighties and in his old age, after a long period of fairly conventional work, returned to the dream-like visions and inspired techniques of his youth. In the Vienna of the First Republic he and other artists, having explored multifarious paths, in the end developed their personal style: Anton Kolig and Herbert Boeckl a forceful, often eruptive one; Franz Wiegele softer and more poetic forms; Fritz von Herzmanovsky-Orlando and Paris Gütersloh a baroque playfulness, as in their writings; Georg Merkel and Felix A. Harta a kind of mythological realism; and Alescha (Theodor Allesch) a beautifully structured view of townscapes and craggy mountains, the motifs for which he found while roaming all over Europe. One of the most lovable painters until well into the fifties was Josef Dobrowsky. His portraits and landscapes, realistic but often illumined as if by an inner magic, are among the most remarkable achievements in Austrian art between the wars.

Some of the greatest talents in those years avoided the hopelessness of the capital by either moving to the country, staying in the provinces if they were born there, or seeking out the more vital intellectual and artistic centres of Frankfurt, Dresden and Berlin. Oskar Kokoschka, the only giant left over from Vienna's most fruitful epoch, was usually abroad: he turned up briefly now and again to be with his beloved mother and brother, painted his view of the city from Wilhelminenberg during a whole year's stay in 1931, and in 1933, when he saw Austria tottering towards Fascism, left for Prague – as he thought for good. Alfred Kubin, a demonic draughtsman and author, lived in a derelict castle many hours' journey from the metropolis. Anton Faistauer had gone to Salzburg, Wiegele and Boeckl to Carinthia, and Wilhelm Thöny, co-founder of the Graz Secession, to Paris and later New York.

One painter who first made her mark in the mid-twenties had to wait until she was nearly eighty before she was spectacularly 'discovered' by the international art world during her retrospective at London's Goethe Institute. Marie-Louise von Motesitzky (a great-granddaughter of the Baroness Sophie Todesco, whom we have often met before), was a student of Max Beckmann in her early years, and in her English exile a friend of Kokoschka. Now she is rightly being linked with both these geniuses and praised for the 'intensity of feeling', the 'clarity of light and vision', the 'fluid brushwork' and 'incandescent colour' of her work. Beckmann's prophecy that one day this artist of purely Viennese background, upbringing and nature might be considered as 'Germany's greatest woman painter', a successor to Paula Modersohn-Becker, seems at last fulfilled.

Since this concluding chapter must not grow out of all proportion, far too little space is left for the most exciting aspect of cultural life in Vienna after 1918: its literature. The wealth and variety of writing in those two decades alone belie T.S. Eliot's well-known lines about 'Twenty years largely wasted, the years of *l'entre deux guerres*'. To the Café Griensteidl generation, to put it flippantly, a Café Central and a Café Herrenhof generation had been added. While the first was still producing some late masterpieces, the other two were desperately hampered by the lack of generous publishers, of well-paid newspaper work, of a readership able to buy, not merely borrow, books, and of lucrative new media and literary prizes such as now sustain a good many authors. They plodded on as best they could, on their way to local or even international fame.

Many, having whiled away their hours dozing, scribbling or exchanging futile schemes with like-minded friends around the marble-topped table of their favourite coffee-house home, one day gave up and went out to look for a job, even a menial one, to make some sort of a living. When one child of the Herrenhof, Friedrich Torberg, at the age of twenty-two found his first novel being published by the highly regarded Paul Zsolnay Verlag, and even rewarded with the modest Emil Reich Prize (the only one Vienna had to offer), older and wiser men blanched and the young ones' hopes were raised again. When three years later a woman at the same age repeated the feat, the Café Herrenhof appeared to have scored a double hit.

No more, then, can be undertaken in this context than an attempt to distinguish at least the most notable writers of the period and place them according to their rank – not in the eyes of their contemporaries, but in those of posterity. Some of them can be mentioned merely *hors concours*, as it were, for what I believe is a valid reason. Franz Kafka spent most of his life in the Dual Monarchy, and even worked in its civil service. Rainer Maria Rilke, born like him in Prague, was certainly an Austrian. But neither of them would have written as he did had he been Viennese. Even those authors who having grown up in the Bohemian capital sooner or later settled in Vienna (among them Franz Werfel and Leo Perutz), never shed the mystical, metaphorical bent they had acquired in their youth. The Viennese were sceptical, urbane and polished, capable even in their decadent melancholy of slipping at any moment into frivolity. The writers of Prague were doubters and visionaries, concerned with *Weltanschauung*.

*Dear Gespielin
With my best wishes and
compliments of the season 1946,
yours OttoKokoschka*

Left *Oskar Kokoschka in the
early 1920s.*

Above *Oskar Kokoschka's
Christmas card to the author in
1946.*

Opposite *Hans Flesch (Edler)
von Brunningen, the author's
husband: drawing by Egon
Schiele, 1914.*

Above *Alexander Lernet-Holenia.*
Above left *Joseph Roth.*
Left *Robert (Edler von) Musil.*

Above *Ernst Krenek.*
Right *Erich Zeisl.*

Above *Alma Mahler, wearing a Jugendstil choker.*

Above right *Eugenie Schwarzwald.*

Right *Ignaz Seipel, high cleric and Chancellor of Austria in the First Republic.*

Opposite *Berta Zuckerkandl.*

Above *Gottfried Kunwald, banker and financial adviser to Chancellor Seipel.*

Left *Hugo Breitner, town councillor for finance in the First Republic.*

Below *Otto Bauer, Socialist leader.*

*Das Denkmal der Republik,
Wien, 13. II. 1934.*

The monument erected to the founders of the First Republic, covered in
February 1934 by Kruckenkrenz flags.

Instead of delving into the microcosm of their own subtle feelings, they searched for the meaning of existence and for transcendental truth. Their deep earnestness, their religious fervour or their equally fervent denial of a higher being sprang from the same historic and geographical source.

Rilke and Werfel, Kafka and Brod, Urzidil and Perutz, though not brought up in the same faith, were all wrestlers with the angel, dreamers of age-old myths, disdainful of Viennese mundanity. All their lives they remained rooted in the medieval occultism of Prague, a city where Jesuits, Jews and Utraquists had quested for God as had the alchemists for gold and the philosophers for their stone; where Johannes Kepler and Wallenstein watched the stars for different reasons; and where both the emperor Rudolf II and the 'high rabbi' Löw – whom he held in much esteem – tried to fashion a human being, the *Golem*, from clay. In his most touching book, *Nachts unter der steinernen Brücke* (At Night under the Stone Bridge) Leo Perutz, having finally landed in Tel Aviv, told of an imaginary love affair between the emperor and the rabbi's daughter. Wherever Perutz lived, he was surrounded by the shades of Bohemia's past.

Even Rilke, having left his native city soon after childhood, was for ever caught in its aura, just like Franz Werfel, whose early poetry he had admired and whose *fausse mentalité juive* he later mocked. Rilke's some-what sugary conception of the Holy Virgin as expressed in his lyrical volume *Marienleben* (Life of Mary) had its counterpart in Werfel's *Das Lied von Bernadette* (Song of Bernadette) – a relic of the same naïve piety that had been passed on to Rilke by his mother and to Werfel by his nanny Bábi. As for Franz Kafka, although the Austrian bureaucracy he knew so well found its way into *The Trial* and *The Castle*, the parabolic eschatology he pursued in all his prose was far from anything written in Vienna during his lifetime. The facts that he died in its immediate vicinity, at a nursing home in Lower-Austrian Kierling, and that under his influence young Viennese writers after the Second World War would turn to his subjects and use his style, are merely due to the vagaries of fate.

Those of the 'Prague Circle' – as the German-language authors in that city came to be called – who sooner or later settled in Vienna, and joined in its literary life, must of course be counted among the locals. Not so, to my mind, a man from Fürth near Nuremberg who in 1898, when in his early twenties, took up residence in Austria, first in the capital and after the war in Alt-Aussee. He was twice married to Viennese women and became a dear friend of Hofmannsthal and Schnitzler, Beer-Hofmann and Andrian. Yet the great novelist Jakob Wassermann, a most imagina-tive writer, endowed – according to Thomas Mann's well-meant but unfortunate analogy – with an 'oriental gift for spinning yarns' like 'a story-teller in a Levantine market-place', was not, and could not be, part of *Jung-Wien*.

All his life Jakob Wassermann, a Jew and a German who suffered from this double loyalty as no Austrian writer ever did, remained a foreigner in their midst. Although his friends admired and even loved him, met with him regularly in town and (when he had taken over Andrian's house in their favourite lakeside village) also in Alt-Aussee, they did not think of him as one of them, and he never felt accepted. To the end Wassermann retained his Franconian accent, and his novels, stories and essays were concerned with German or German-Jewish characters and problems. So was the epic trilogy *Die Schlafwandler* (The Sleepwalkers) by Hermann Broch, who at some point had also moved to Alt-Aussee from Vienna. But Broch, unlike Wassermann, belonged.

When the First Republic set in, *Jung-Wien*, though no longer young, was certainly not in its dotage. Schnitzler was under sixty when two scandals erupted in connection with his *Reigen*: one in 1920, at the Berlin premiere, followed by a court case which he won; the other, a year later, at the Viennese theatre Kammerspiele. When the play had first appeared in print in 1903 it had been attacked as a *cochonnerie*. Now a judge in the progressive Weimar Republic found that it had sought to fulfil a moral purpose by showing up the false and shallow nature of contemporary love-lives. The Viennese public was less enlightened. But Schnitzler took it calmly. He had undergone the transition from the Dual Monarchy to little German-Austria with perfect ease, and had accepted as quite natural a system of government in keeping with his own ideas of justice and equality. Even so, like Hofmannsthal he never wrote a play or prose-work set in the new age.

What Schnitzler did write, besides more comedies and stories, was the novella *Fräulein Else*, his second attempt at 'interior monologue'. 'Well-told as *Leutnant Gustl* is,' wrote Hofmannsthal in a letter, '*Fräulein Else* beats it any time. What you have created is a genre in its own right within German literature'. One may be allowed to rank Schnitzler's *Traumnovelle* even higher, however. Published in 1926, it contains not the slightest allusion to contemporary politics, but – though first drafted nineteen years earlier – in its description of an unrestrained, hectically promiscuous party at a private villa it exactly mirrors post-war Viennese society, which took pleasure in breaking every hitherto respected taboo. The story also exposes the underworld of unconscious drives in the human soul, as exposed by Freud in his study *Das Ich und das Es* (The Ego and the Id) – which came out in 1923, the year in which Schnitzler resumed work on *Traumnovelle*. Though showing no trace of being set in the present, his last novel,

Therese, whose heroine, the daughter of an army officer, sinks down the social scale until she is murdered by her illegitimate son, reveals a deep concern for the life of the underprivileged, engendered, no doubt, by the spirit of the time.

Schnitzler died in 1932. Three years earlier Hofmannsthal had been laid to rest at the age of fifty-five. The suicide of his elder son Franz a few days before had shaken him to the core. He was struck down by a heart attack as he was setting out for the funeral. It had been harder for him than for Schnitzler to adapt to a state lacking the breadth and variety, the *concordia discors*, of the monarchy in which he had felt entirely at home. His delightful comedies *The Difficult Man* and *The Incorruptible* were both set in an aristocratic and upper-class world which no longer existed in this form or – in the First Republic – had withdrawn from view. While providing Richard Strauss with two more superb libretti, *Die Frau ohne Schatten* and *Arabella*, he devoted his time mainly to writing for, planning, and running the Salzburg Summer Festival which, together with the great theatre director Max Reinhardt, he had founded in 1918. The work on his drama *The Tower* must have overshadowed his last decade, since with every new version he wrote it became clearer to him that its soaring ambitions could not be fulfilled.

Hofmannsthal's ambiguous attitude towards German-Austria should at least be touched upon, as it was the ultimate result of an age-old conflict. In 1938 Thomas Mann would point out that 'Austria had never belonged to Germany, but rather Germany to Austria.' The heritage of the Holy Roman Empire which ages ago had passed to the German people, replaced though it had been by the Austrian Empire in 1804, would still haunt both Germans and Austrians. It even served as an excuse for intellectuals temporarily seduced by National Socialism, who later claimed that they had confused the Third Reich with the Holy Roman one. Although Hofmannsthal neither could nor would ever have sided with the Nazis, and despite his deep love for Austria in whatever form it survived, in his later years he fell victim to the general idea of a German nation encompassing the Austrians. Influenced by the literary historian Josef Nadler – soon to be *persona grata* during the Hitler regime – when lecturing in 1927 at Munich University on *Das Schrifttum als geistiger Raum der Nation* (Literature as the spiritual realm of the nation), Hofmannsthal demanded a 'conservative revolution' whose goal would be 'a new German reality in which the whole nation can take part'.

It is thus, gripped by the same obsession with 'Germanness' that had held the last Habsburg emperors in its sway, that Austria's most proto-typical writer came to deny a separate Austrian identity and a separate

Austrian literature, thereby negating his own *raison d'être*. On an entirely different level this paradox was echoed by Josef Weinheber. A man of simple birth, yet endowed with a mastery of language which owed less to his schooling at a minor high school at Mödling than to his – frequently admitted – devotion to Karl Kraus, he grew to be the new bard of Vienna, and took pride in being its poet *par excellence*. While he fashioned his more elevated lyrical work after Hölderlin and Rilke, his verses in the vernacular were unique – praising his city, its inhabitants, their customs and manners in the most loving and poignant way.

The Vienna he knew when he began to write in the twenties was now, in its ethnic diversity, an exact microcosm of the lost Habsburg empire; and the character of the people he portrayed so differed from that of the neighbouring Reich Germans that Weinheber should have been the last person on earth to assist in bringing them into line and subjugating the *genius loci* under Hitler's heel. Yet that is exactly what he did when he became an illegal National Socialist party member and later *poeta laureatus* of the *Ostmark*, while Austria was so called. However, he lived to regret this decision and died atoning for it, in 1945, by his own hand. After he had bought a house in Weinheber's village, W.H. Auden wrote a moving poem to the 'categorized enemy of twenty years ago' in which he paid his respects to his 'neighbour and colleague':

> For even my English ear
> Gets in your German
> The workmanship and the note
> Of one who was graced
> To hear the viols playing
> On the impaled green.

The Griensteidl generation had been the first to introduce writers of Jewish origin to Viennese literature. They added so much to its mainstream that in the following decades it kept on swelling and branching out in all directions, until in the twenties and thirties of the new century an estuary had formed which it is impossible to explore sufficiently within the scope of this book. What must be stressed is that where Jews and non-Jews are grouped together according to their outlook, choice of themes and even manner of style, no fundamental distinctions between them can be discerned. In their nostalgic loyalty to the monarchy and the house of Habsburg, writers like Joseph Roth and Alexander Lernet-Holenia hardly differ. When Roth was at work on his beautiful swansong of Austria-Hungary, the novel *Radetzkymarsch*, Lernet-Holenia – whose own touching dirge *Die Standarte* (The Standard) would appear just two years later in 1934 – helped his friend from Galician Brody with the correct descriptions of regimental colours and uniforms.

Lernet-Holenia in turn owed much to the example of his friend Leo Perutz from Prague when, after publishing some volumes of sublime poetry, he conceived a host of colourful fantasies and adventure stories which by virtue of their flawless prose achieved literary distinction. In their precise psychological insights, their philosophical bent, the sharpness of their social criticism and their interest in the great sweep of history, Robert Musil and Hermann Broch display affinities and even similarities. Although Musil's epoch-making novel *The Man without Qualities* is concerned with the land he calls *Kakanien* (derived from the initials of *kaiserlich* and *königlich* – imperial and royal) while Broch's *Sleepwalkers* is set entirely in Germany, both deal with a disintegrating society, disintegrating values, and the conflict between the rational and the irrational.

The names mentioned so far are among those paramount in the First Republic. To them must be added that of Stefan Zweig, who towered above them all in popularity and worldwide acclaim, though not necessarily in quality. Of his large and uneven *oeuvre*, comprising poetry, drama, novels, novellas, essays, biographies and translations, three books may be taken as representative: the volume of essays *Der Kampf mit dem Dämon* (1925, on Hölderlin, Kleist and Nietzsche, published in English as *Master Builders*), the collected stories entitled *Verwirrung der Gefühle* (1922, translated into English as *Conflicts*), typical of Zweig's almost feminine sensitivity, and the monograph *Castellio gegen Calvin*, a patient unravelling of one of the most gruesome chapters of religious persecution – the lonely fight of a Protestant humanist against Calvin's theocratic dictatorship at Geneva, ending with Castellio's death. Written in 1936, after Zweig had left his post-war Salzburg domicile and gone into premature exile in London, this fine book draws a wistful parallel with the Hitler era which by now had set in: 'Posterity will not be able to grasp that we should again have had to live in such deep darknesses, after the light had already appeared once before.'

Franz Werfel has been mentioned as a native of Prague. He came to Vienna in 1917, after some active war service, having also been directed to the military press department at Stiftkaserne. Werfel had stood out from the early Austrian expressionists – Kokoschka (in his writings); Albert Ehrenstein; Georg Trakl in Salzburg; Heinrich Nowak; Hans Flesch von Brunningen; Berthold Viertel, one day to be the model for the endearing Dr Bergmann in Christopher Isherwood's *Prater Violet*; and Hugo Sonnenschein, who liked to be called 'Brother Sonka' – as the author of the most ecstatic volume of poetry, *Der Weltfreund* (Friend of the World), published in 1911. Soon after arriving in the capital he started an affair with Alma Mahler, then married to the architect Gropius, and in her husband's absence was received into the literary and artistic élite of her salon. Yet Werfel could hardly wait for the end of the war and the outbreak of a revolution – which, however, never came. Despite their 'verbal radicalism', the Austrian Marxists in practice behaved more like Fabians, quietly ushering in the republic and, at first at least, sharing governmental power with the Christian Socialists. In the course of his life with Alma, whom eventually he married, Werfel was to turn more and more into a moderate liberal with a wide degree of tolerance for authoritarians, as his acquiescence in the Austro-Fascist regime and friendship with its leader Schuschnigg was to prove.

Meanwhile in the twenties he was almost as prolific as Stefan Zweig, producing plays and prose works, among them a biography of Verdi subtitled *A Novel about Opera*, and the long saga *Barbara oder die Frömmigkeit* (Barbara or Piety), woven around his Bohemian nanny but containing descriptions both of his own war experiences and the 'shadow realm' of the Café Central, whose most important chronicler he thus became. All his books were published by the new firm set up by his stepson-in-law Paul (von) Zsolnay, then the second though not last husband of Anna Mahler. Apart from the seven Hitler years, Zsolnay Verlag remained until well into our day Vienna's only distinguished publishing house of *belles-lettres*. Like all the Griensteidl generation – excepting of course the adversary in their midst, Karl Kraus – and many of the Café Central generation, after his short revolutionary phase Franz Werfel took little interest in politics or current affairs. He did not write a novel about the First Republic, but an epic about the plight of the Albanians under the Turkish yoke, *Die vierzig Tage des Musa Dagh* (The Forty Days of Musa Dagh), which elevated him almost to sainthood in the eyes of that people.

There were political writers, however, among the Café Herrenhof generation, though few of them were seen at this coffee-house which had replaced the Central as a home for literati after 1918. Some of them belonged to the Socialist movement or thought of themselves as its representatives. Most remarkable among them was Alfons Petzold, whose novel *Das rauhe Leben* (The Rough Life, 1920), as well as his poetry, were an expression of 'proletarian' (a term then proudly used by the workers) issues and grievances which his party hoped to put right. Another 'Labour poet' was Josef Luitpold (Stern), the son of a lathe-turner and unlike Petzold of Jewish extraction, who rose to administer the party organ *Arbeiterzeitung*.

Luitpold, well-educated and a great educator himself, somewhat idealized the class he came from, which at least helped to give its members self-confidence. Rudolf Brunngraber, also an advocate of the little man in a number of novels dealing with the industrial and economic aspects of his time, was more pessimistic. The poetry of Ernst Waldinger, and even more the recently rediscovered work of Theodor Kramer (one later to be exiled in the States, the other in England), conveyed the authentic feel of what it was like to be a peasant, a charcoal-burner, a glass-blower, a day-labourer, a distiller or a soldier lying in the marshes of Volhynia during the war. Jura Soyfer, a most remarkable talent to emerge from the little cellar cabarets that sprang up after 1933, and one of the few whose family had come from a Jewish quarter in Russia, wrote the most directly political verse. The last composition of his tragic life was the *Dachaulied* (Song of Dachau), after which he died, aged twenty-six, in Buchenwald.

The work of others who were drawn to the left but were not necessarily members of any party reflected the happenings of their troubled time. These events must be sketched, if only briefly, not merely in order to provide the background to their writings, but also to bring Austrian history up to the closing date of this book. Four or five milestones should be recorded. The first, and from the point of view of literature the most important, is 15 July 1927, when the workers of Vienna, caught up with an uncontrollable mob, tried to burn down the Palace of Justice in revenge for a judicial outrage: the acquittal of three *Frontkämpfer* (ex-servicemen) who, in a tussle with the left-wing paramilitary organization *Schutzbund*, had shot two innocents, a war cripple and a child. By the time this happened, bitter enmity already existed between the Social Democrats and the Christian Socialists, quite apart from the German-Nationalists or, by now, National Socialists, who took advantage of any strife within the capital to further their own ends.

Otto Bauer, 'red' ideologist and Labour's chief spokesman, was locked in constant rhetorical battle with the 'black' Ignaz Seipel, 'the prelate without mercy', who – intermittently as Chancellor of the republic – represented the Christian Socialists. Private armies like the right-wing *Heimwehr* (Home Defence), founded as early as 1919 and now led by a veritable prince, Rüdiger von Starhemberg, and the *Republikanischer Schutzbund* (Safeguard Alliance), called together by the Social Democrats in 1923 to counter the *Heimwehr*'s threat, were ready to turn the battle of words into action at any time. July 1927 was the first occasion. The workers had spontaneously marched against the seat of Austria's jurisdiction and set it alight. The 'black' Police President Schober, against the wishes of 'red' Burgomaster Seitz, but with the consent of Chancellor Seipel, ordered his men to shoot. In the resulting bloodbath eighty-nine people died and many more were injured.

After that, reconciliation between the two main camps in Austria was hopeless. When, under economic pressure and the need to stabilize the currency, tentative moves were made in 1931 to form another coalition, it was the Social Democrats who in the end refused. The next fatal date was 7 March 1933, when Chancellor Dollfuss, in power for less than a year, made use of a technical crisis in Parliament to abolish its function. While Hitler was taking over in Germany next door, in Austria democracy by representation came to an end. Along with neighbouring Italy under Mussolini and, to some extent, Hungary under Admiral Horthy, it had now become a quasi-Fascist corporate state, matching Germany's swastika with its own *Kruckenkrenz*. Within less than a year the Socialists, and with them 'Red Vienna', had been utterly crushed. On 12 February 1934, provoked beyond endurance, the *Schutzbund* – or rather its commander at the provincial town of Linz, and again without orders from above – began the rising that had been simmering for some time. A general strike was thereupon called by the party leadership in Vienna. In the afternoon of that day the government mounted howitzers aimed at all the major blocks of council houses – including one, allegedly, in Alma Mahler-Werfel's garden high above and opposite the Karl Marx-Hof – and gave orders to fire. The battles spread to some of the industrial centres in the country and lasted three and a half days. By then Dollfuss had won.

The 'pocket dictator' now had but five months to live: 25 July in that same year is the fourth date to remember. During a short Nazi putsch Dollfuss was shot dead in his chancellery. Mussolini sent troops to protect her border, and for the moment Austria was saved from Hitler's entry. In the summer of 1936 Dollfuss's successor, Kurt (von) Schuschnigg struck a deal with Hitler, hoping in vain thereby to ward off his menace. When on 12 March 1938 Big Brother did march in after his troops had crossed into Austria during the night, Mussolini no longer supported his Austrian friends. The Anschluss was complete. This was probably the first date to impinge on a number of foreign statesmen who for a long while had known next to nothing of what was going on in that far-away little country, German-Austria.

Remarkably enough none of these events was to give rise to a major work of Austrian fiction, except the first ominous confrontation in 1927 with its spectacular climax of the Justizpalast going up in flames. A young author sitting down some years later to write a novel which was finally to bear the Dostoevskian title *The Demons* studied all the relevant documents carefully, then turned the events of 15 July into the central theme of his

book. Though he published at least two novels before the Anschluss –
Das Geheimnis des Reichs (The Mystery of the Realm) and *Ein Mord, den
jeder begeht* (A Murder Everyone Commits) – Heimito von Doderer did
not finish *Die Dämonen* (The Demons) until the mid-fifties, for which
reason we cannot deal with it here. However, another work which made
use of the July happenings, albeit allegorically, was Elias Canetti's *Die
Blendung* (*Auto Da Fé*). As the English title suggests, the burning of its
hero Kien's library was not merely the pivot of the book but also a
reflection of the arson at the Palace of Justice – which the author witnessed
and which was also to inspire his voluminous treatise *Crowds and Power*,
his most ambitious work.

Anton Wildgans, who has been mentioned earlier on as a playwright,
expressed his belief in the First Republic with the help of an archaic form.
His benign satire *Kirbisch*, couched in hexameter verse, described a rural
community on the way to a brighter future. A far more direct approach
to the contemporary scene with all its social, economic and political
ramifications was undertaken by Robert Neumann, who had first attracted
attention in 1927 with his supremely funny and deadly accurate parodies.
The art of lampooning fellow writers had already been practised by Franz
Blei in his *Bestiarium Literaricum* (Bestiary of Literature, 1920), to which
Musil lent a helping hand.

Neumann's *Mit fremden Federn* (With Foreign Quills – an untranslatable
pun) was a resounding success. Before repeating their achievement with
a second volume *Unter falscher Flagge* (Under a False Flag) in 1932, he
published a vast novel *Die Sintflut* (The Flood), followed by another *Die
Macht* (Power), which together add up to the most vivid and informative
fictional account of the Viennese twenties written at the time. Neumann's
experience as a banker during the period of inflation helped him unravel
the intricate financial dealings in which Austrian statesmen were equally
involved. Many of his characters were taken straight from life – such as
Dr Lassalle in *Die Macht*, a portrait of the extraordinary Gottfried
Kunwald, the anti-Semitic Chancellor Seipel's Jewish adviser, the *éminence
grise* behind many of the government's economic measures, and a man of
great acumen who achieved all this despite severe physical handicap.

Vienna's last lustrum was a strange period, full of contrasts and contradictions. While Robert Neumann and Stefan Zweig had seen the
light and moved to England after the civil war of 1934, Austrian-born
intellectuals who had lived in Germany came back home to find refuge –
temporarily as it turned out. Ödön von Horváth, a child of the old
monarchy with a Hungarian passport who is nowadays considered to have
been a political playwright equal to Brecht, had done just this in 1933.

While Manès Sperber and Joseph Roth preferred the seemingly greater safety of Paris, others had followed Horváth's example, among them Robert Musil, Franz Blei, the dramatist Ferdinand Bruckner, Roda Roda, Alfred Polgar and Albert Ehrenstein. Karl Kraus uttered his famous quip: 'The rats are boarding the sinking ship.' Even Germans like Walter Mehring, Kurt Tucholsky, Fritz von Unruh and Bertolt Brecht himself, at least for a short while, took shelter in the capital of that sloppily Fascist state. After all Karl Kraus, who had sided with the Social Democrats for a long while and after 15 July printed large posters calling for the resignation of Police President Schober, had himself resigned, and in the face of the Nazi threat made his peace with 'the lesser evil' until his death in 1936.

On the surface cultural life went on undisturbed. In the Theater an der Josefstadt, taken over in 1924 by Max Reinhardt, run by him for a number of wonderful years and then deserted, Egon Friedell still occasionally took the stage. In the cellar cabarets that were now multiplying cautious fun was made of the authorities, who had enough sense of humour not to stop them. The three salons of Eugenie Schwarzwald, Berta Zuckerkandl and Alma Mahler-Werfel flourished – the last-named usually filled with members of the government and handsome *Heimwehr* officers, as Schuschnigg was an admirer of the lady of the house. (The circle of Dr Schwarzwald, on the other hand, included the young Count Helmuth James von Moltke, who was put to death not long after being involved in the German officers' rising against Hitler on 20 July 1944.) Under the benevolent eye of Schuschnigg's literary adviser Guido Zernatto, markedly Catholic authors by the names of Perkonig, Scheibelreiter, Waggerl, Mell, Henz and Heinrich Suso Waldeck flourished, some of them to turn into Nazis or at least to pay obeisance to the *Führer*. Others, like Bruno Brehm and Mirko Jelusich, did not hide their right-wing radicalism and were left in peace, along with young rebels in their cellar cabarets.

There was a further development. The 'Habsburg myth' – as it was called by the Italian Germanist and historian Claudio Magris, himself a native of the former Austrian port Trieste – reappeared in literature. Not only Lernet-Holenia, Joseph Roth and, in his more critical way, Robert Musil transported themselves in their imagination to the Dual Monarchy: a number of other writers liked to bask in its climate, which was milder, and often more scurrilous, than the prevailing one. The most attractive among them were the painters A.P. Gütersloh and Fritz von Herzmanovsky-Orlando. During the twenties Gütersloh was already working on his *chef d'œuvre*, a huge but never tedious, indeed utterly charming fable called *Sonne und Mond* (Sun and Moon). Like his friend Doderer's main opus it was published decades later, but must at least be mentioned here. Herzmanovsky-Orlando's *Der Gaulschreck im Rosennetz* (The old Horse's Nightmare in a Net of Roses) on the other hand, the most baroque, quaintly humorous and fanciful book to come out of the First Republic, soon found a small but fervent circle of devotees much like the early admirers of Tolkien's 'Lord of the Rings'.

One belated but touching account of the end of the war and the dispersal of the old Imperial and Royal Army was Franz Theodor Csokor's play *Der 3 November 1918*. Csokor had been an expressionist playwright in the early twenties who saw himself as a successor to Georg Büchner – a good and humane man who in his long life made friends the whole world over, yet on the whole was less successful as a writer than he deserved to be. His drama about a group of officers from all nations of the Austrian Empire recuperating in a military rest home high in the Karwendel mountains of southern Carinthia is the only one of his plays still performed – until recently – at Vienna's Burgtheater. Its premiere fell in the middle of the Schuschnigg era. He was honoured for it with the 'Burgtheater ring' and, having left Austria of his own free will in 1938, lived off the proceeds from its valuable diamond for a while in his Polish exile. A small but significant cut had been made in 1937 before his play could pass muster. After Colonel von Radosin has shot himself in grief over the Austrian downfall, he is buried by his fellow officers Orvanyi, Ludoltz, von Kaminski, Zierowitz, Sokal and Vanini. They each throw a shovelful of earth in his grave, saying 'Earth from Hungary', 'Earth from Poland', 'Earth from Carinthia', 'Slovenian earth', 'Czech earth', 'Roman earth', while they pay their respects to their dead colonel. Last of them is the Jewish military surgeon, Dr Grün. He hesitates for a moment, then throws in his shovelful, saying simply 'Earth from Austria'.

To remind a theatre audience of the special status accorded to the Jews of the monarchy – as a religious community, not a nation, they were under the direct protection of the emperor – was no longer permissible in Schuschnigg's corporate state, after his deal with Hitler. Franz Joseph, that questionable father figure, a basically narrow-minded man, given to erroneous judgements and wrong decisions, was all the same a true father-figure to his Jews. An episode in Joseph Roth's *Radetzkymarsch* has the emperor, on manoeuvres in Galicia near the Russian border, receiving the homage of some Jewish elders with 'coal black, flaming red and silver white beards'. One of them lifts up a Torah roll towards him and murmurs a blessing 'in his incomprehensible language'. The emperor thanks the elder, shakes his hand, mounts and rides off. Behind him he hears one of his aides tell the other: 'I didn't understand a word of what that Jew said.'

Whereupon the emperor turns round in the saddle and says: 'He was only speaking to me, after all, my dear Kaunitz,' upon which he rides on.

A well-told tale, and one that expresses the affection especially of eastern Jews for a ruler under whom they felt safe. Franz Joseph, hating all nationalist movements in his realm, also resented Zionism, which intended to remove some of his most loyal subjects to far-away Palestine. He would rather have had them adopt the way so many old Jewish families of his capital had gone in the past, from orthodoxy and the Leopoldstadt to assimilation, integration and the first district. He would gladly have ennobled all those who had made good as he had ennobled so many industrialists planting sugar beet in Moravia, brewing beer in Schwechat near Vienna or spinning textiles in the small town of Vöslau. Given another fifty years or so of untroubled peace, who knows what might have happened to the Jews of Austria? When writing his book *The Habsburg Monarchy*, the famous editor of the London *Times* Wickham Steed remarked that 'the Jews of Vienna would have ceased to be exposed to anti-Semitism were their ranks not swelled every year by thousands of newcomers from Galicia and Hungary'. This was true, and well known to those concerned.

Yet as these newcomers from the eastern parts of the monarchy settled down in the capital before and after the war, some among them, even within the span of one generation, were to enrich Austria's cultural, social and political life. So far their contribution was small compared to that of the 'western' Jews long established in Vienna. But a number of them, as shown by the example of the writer Joseph Roth, the painter Georg Merkel and the actress Elisabeth Bergner, made their mark without having to undergo a slow process of integration. After all, cities like Lemberg and Czernowitz, though far from the capital, had been centres of Austrian civilization just as much as Laibach or Trieste. People educated there were sometimes equal in erudition and aesthetic discernment to those brought up in the capital.

It is idle to speculate on what would have happened had the constant process of Jewish emancipation not been abruptly brought to an end. Perhaps if Hitler had not crystallized the prejudice and racial intolerance latent in the Austrians some acceptable solution would have been found. Jews who were willing quietly and gradually to merge with the Austrian population might have been able to do so, while those used to being part of an orthodox or exclusively Jewish community would have ended the diaspora and gone to Israel. Two examples may serve. In his autobiography the present Mayor of Jerusalem Teddy Kollek has explained his reasons for leaving Vienna in the mid-thirties: 'One generation more removed from mine might have been assimilated or indifferent [towards Judaism]. But for me the feeling of being Jewish and a part of the Jewish people and its history was a natural thing – not aggressive, but deeply rooted.' To Palestine he went, and became the most respected administrator in the country, perhaps the best and certainly the longest-serving burgomaster in the world. Even so, when filling in a questionnaire (originally devised by Proust) for a German magazine, he entered as his favourite flower the *Alpenveilchen* (an alpine variety of cyclamen). In his Californian exile another self-confessed Zionist, Friedrich Torberg, ended a nostalgic poem about Alt-Aussee with the mournful question: 'But the cyclamen – where are they?' At the first opportunity he went back to Austria.

There is no need to give in to the temptation of recalling the names of all the writers, artists, actors, musicians, philosophers and scientists who in 1938 were driven into exile or to their death. These should by now be familiar to readers of this book. When the exhibition 'Dream and Reality', presenting Vienna during the period with which we have here been concerned, moved from Vienna to Paris, a whole room was added to document their exodus – which nobody back home had particularly wanted to illustrate. '*Les gens pleuraient,*' was how a friend described the French visitors' reaction. Nobody cries for them in present-day Vienna. Nor, in the city they lived in for so many generations, is there left an awareness of the immense diversity of its former Jewish inhabitants. Just like the hierarchy of non-Jews, they had their social scale from the loftiest, most refined and worthy human beings down to the black sheep, the money-grabbers, sharks and criminals.

In writing this account of a great cultural epoch, I would have preferred not to have to point out which among the men and women who helped to create it were of Jewish descent. What they themselves would have wanted was to be accepted simply as Austrian poets, painters or composers. This was and still is a Utopian wish. For that reason one may do well to rouse the collective memory and stress the fact that it was due to a unique moment in history, to an unrepeatable symbiosis, that Vienna's great era came about. To profit from it in retrospect, as the city now does, would seem to oblige its inhabitants to pay more than lip-service to the memory of its banished or murdered Jews, and to respect those few left of the same faith who still trust them to the extent of once more living in their midst.

BIBLIOGRAPHY

Adorno, Theodor W., *Quasi una fantasia: musikalische Schriften II* (Suhrkamp Verlag, Frankfurt, 1963)

Adorno, Theodor W., *Alban Berg: der Meister des kleinen Übergangs*, Österreichische Komponisten des XX. Jahrhunderts, Vol. 15 (Verlag Elisabeth Lafite, Vienna/Österreichischer Bundesverlag, Vienna, 1968)

Adorno, Theodor W., *Versuch über Wagner* (Suhrkamp Verlag, Frankfurt, 1952)

Amann, Klaus, and Berger, Albert (eds), *Österreichische Literatur der dreissiger Jahre* (Böhlau, Vienna, 1985)

Andics, Hellmut, *Der Staat, den keiner wollte: Österreich 1918–1938* (Verlag Herder, Vienna, 1962)

Aspetsberger, Friedbert, and Stieg, Gerald (eds), *Elias Canetti: Blendung als Lebensform* (Athenäum Verlag, Königstein, 1985)

Ayer, A. J., Kneale, W. C., Paul, G. A., and Pears D. F., *The Revolution in Philosophy*. With an introduction by Gilbert Ryle. (Macmillan, London/St Martin's Press, New York, 1957)

Bahr, Hermann, *Wien* (Carl Krabbe Verlag, Stuttgart, 1906)

Berg, Erich Alban, *Als der Adler noch zwei Köpfe hatte: ein Florilegium 1898–1918* (Verlag Styria, Graz, 1980)

Berg, Erich Alban (ed.), *Alban Berg: Leben und Werk in Daten und Bildern* (Insel Taschenbuch 194, Frankfurt, 1976)

Blaukopf, Kurt, *Gustav Mahler, oder der Zeitgenosse der Zukunft* (Molden Verlag, Vienna, 1968)

Broch, Hermann, *Hofmannsthal und seine Zeit: eine Studie*. With a postscript by Hannah Arendt (R. Piper & Co., Munich, 1964)

Centro di Cultura di Palazzo Grassi, *Le arti a Vienna dalla secessione alla caduta dell'impero absburgico*, Exhibition catalogue (Edizioni La Biennale/Mazotta Editore, 1984)

Cole, Malcolm S., and Barclay, Barbara, *Armseelchen: the life and music of Eric Zeisl* (Greenwood Press, Westport, Connecticut, 1984)

Corti, Egon Caesar Conte, *Elisabeth: 'die seltsame Frau'* (Verlag Anton Pustet, Salzburg, 1934)

Csokor, Franz Theodor, and Rüther, Leopoldine, *Du silberne Dame du: Briefe von und an Lina Loos* (Paul Zsolnay, Vienna, 1966)

Elon, Amos, *Herzl* (Weidenfeld & Nicolson, London 1976; Schocken, New York, 1986)

Eschbach, Achim (ed.), *Bühler-Studien, Vols.* I and II (Suhrkamp Verlag, Frankfurt, 1984)

Flesch-Brunningen, Hans, *Die letzten Habsburger in Augenzeugenberichten* (Karl Rauch Verlag, Düsseldorf, 1967)

Fraenkel, Josef (ed.), *The Jews of Austria: Essays on their Life, History and Destruction*. Includes a contribution on 'Jewish women in Austrian culture' by Hilde Spiel (Valentine, Mitchell, London, 1967)

Freitag, Eberhard (ed.) *Arnold Schönberg in Selbstzeugnissen und Bilddokumenten* (Rowohlts Monographien, Reinbek bei Hamburg, 1973)

Freud, Sigmund, *Abriss der Psychoanalyse; Das Unbehagen in der Kultur*. Includes text of a talk by Thomas Mann as postscript (Fischer Bücherei, Frankfurt, 1953)

Friedländer, Otto, *Letzter Glanz der Märchenstadt: das war Wien um 1900* (Gardena Verlag, Vienna, 1969)

Fuchs, Albert, *Geistige Strömungen in Österreich 1867–1918* (Löcker Verlag, Vienna, 1978)

Gal, Hans, *Johannes Brahms: Werk und Persönlichkeit* (Fischer Bücherei, Frankfurt, 1961)

Grasberger, Franz, and Knessl, Lothar, *Hundert Jahre Goldener Saal: das Haus der Gesellschaft der Musikfreunde am Karlsplatz* (Gesellschaft der Musikfreunde, Vienna, 1970)

Hackermüller, Rotraut, *Einen Handkuß der Grädigsten/Roda Roda: Bildbiographie* (Herold Verlag, Vienna, 1986)

Haeusserman, Ernst, *Das Wiener Burgtheater* (Molden Verlag, Vienna, 1975)

Hautmann, Hans, and Kropf, Rudolf, *Die österreichische Arbeiterbewegung vom Vormärz bis 1945* (Europa Verlag, Vienna, 1974)

Hayman, Ronald (ed.) *The German Theatre: A Symposium*. Includes an essay by Hilde Spiel on the Austrian contribution (Oswald Wolff, London; Barnes & Noble Books, New York, 1975)

Herold, J. Christopher, *Mistress to an Age: A Life of Madame de Staël* (Hamish Hamilton, London 1959)

Herre, Franz, *Kaiser Franz Josef von Österreich: sein Leben – seine Zeit* (Kiepenheuer & Witsch, Cologne, 1978)

Historisches Museum der Stadt Wien, *Wien 1870–1930: Traum und Wirklichkeit*. Exhibition catalogue (Eigenverlag der Museen der Stadt Wien, 1985)

Hofmannsthal, Hugo von, *Briefe 1890–1901* (S. Fischer Verlag, Berlin, 1935)

Hofmannsthal, Hugo von, *Briefe 1900–1909* (Bermann-Fischer Verlag, Vienna, 1937)

Holm, Gustav, *Im Dreivierteltakt durch die Welt: ein Lebensbild des Komponisten Robert Stolz* (Ibis-Verlag, Linz, 1948)

Holzer, Rudolf, *Villa Wertheimstein: Haus der Genien und Dämonen* (Bergland-Verlag, Vienna, 1960)

Hubmann, Franz, *Das jüdische Familienalbum: die Welt von gestern in 375 alten Photographien*. Text by Janko Musulin (Fritz Molden Verlag, Vienna, 1974)

Hubmann, Franz, *K.u.K. Familienalbum: die Welt von gestern in alten Photographien*. With an introduction by Ernst Trost (Fritz Molden Verlag, Vienna, 1971)

Isherwood, Christopher, *Prater Violet* (Methuen & Co., London, 1946)

Jacob, H. E., *Johann Strauss: Vater und Sohn* (Rowohlt Taschenbuch Verlag, Hamburg, 1953)

Jäger-Sunstenau, Hanns, *Die geadelten Judenfamilien im vormärzlichen Wien* (Unpublished dissertation, Vienna University, 1950)

Jahoda, Marie, Lazarsfeld, Paul F., and Zeisel, Hans, *Die Arbeitslosen von Marienthal: ein soziographischer Versuch* (S. Hirsel, Leipzig, 1933)

Janik, Allan, and Toulmin, Stephen, *Wittgenstein's Vienna* (Simon and Schuster, New York, 1973)

Johnston, William M., *The Austrian Mind: An Intellectual and Social History 1848–1938* (University of California Press, Berkeley, 1972)

Jones, Ernest, *Sigmund Freud: Life and Work:* Vol. I: The young Freud, 1856–1900 (1953); Vol. II, Years of maturity, 1901–1919 (1955); Vol. III, The last phase, 1919–1939 (1957) (The Hogarth Press, London)

Kadrnoska, Franz (ed.), *Aufbruch und Untergang österreichischer Kultur zwischen 1919 und 1938,* (Europa Verlag, Vienna, 1981)

Kallir, Jane; *Arnold Schoenberg's Vienna*. Exhibition catalogue (Galerie St Etienne, New York, 1984)

Kampits, Peter, *Ludwig Wittgenstein: Wege und Umwege zu seinem Denken* (Styria Verlag, Graz, 1985)

Kann, Robert A., *Theodor Gomperz: ein Gelehrtenleben im Bürgertum der Franz-Josef-Zeit* (Verlag der österreichischen Akademie der Wissenschaften, Vienna, 1974)

Kaut, Josef, *Festpiele in Salzburg* (Residenz Verlag, Salzburg 1965)

Karlweis, Marta, *Jakob Wassermann: Bild, Kampf und Werk*. With a foreword by Thomas Mann (Querido Verlag, Amsterdam, 1935)

Kaus, Gina, *Und was für ein Leben …* (Albrecht Knaus Verlag, Hamburg, 1979)

Kokoschka, Oskar, *Mein Leben* (Bruckmann, Munich, 1971)

Kokoschka, Oskar, *Die Wahrheit ist unteilbar,* (Museum des 20. Jahrhunderts, Vienna, 1966)

Kollek, Teddy, and Kollek, Amos, *For Jerusalem: A life* (Weidenfeld & Nicolson, London 1978)

Kosler, Hans Christian, *Peter Altenberg: Leben und Werk in Texten und Bildern* (Matthes & Leitz Verlag, Munich, 1981)

Kraus, Karl, *Peter Altenberg*. Reading given at the grave of Peter Altenberg (Verlag Richard Lányi, Vienna, 1919)

Kraus, Karl, *The Last Days of Mankind*. Abridged and edited by Frederick Ungar (Frederick Ungar Publishing Co., New York, 1974)

Krellmann, Hans Peter, *Anton von Webern in Selbstzeugnissen und Bilddokumenten* (Rowohlts Monographien, Reinbek bei Hamburg, 1975)

Kremser, Eduard (ed.), *Wiener Lieder und Tänze*, Vol. I (Verlag Gerlach & Wiedling, Vienna, 1912)

Kuh, Anton, *Der Affe Zarathustras: Karl Kraus*. Transcript of talk given on 25 October 1925 at the Vienna Konzerthaus (Verlag J. Deibler, Vienna, undated)

Kühnelt, Harro H., *Österreich – England – Amerika: Verhandlungen zur Literatur-Geschichte*. Ed. by Sylvia M. Patsch (Verlag Christian Brandstätter, Vienna, 1986)

Le Rider, Jacques, *Der Fall Otto Weininger: Wurzeln des Antifeminismus und Antisemitismus* (Löcker Verlag, Vienna, 1985)

Leser, Norbert, *Genius Austriacus: Beiträge zur politischen Geschichte und Geistesgeschichte Österreichs* (H. Böhlaus Nachf., Vienna, 1986)

Lunzer Heinz, *Hofmannsthals politische Tätigkeit in den Jahren 1914–1917* (Verlag Peter D. Lang, Frankfurt am Main 1981)

Magris, Claudio, *Der habsburgische Mythos in der österreichischen Literatur* (Otto Müller Verlag, Salzburg, 1966)

Magris, Claudio, *Weit von wo: Verlorene Welt des Ostjudentums* (Europa Verlag, Vienna, 1974)

Mahler, Alma, *Gustav Mahler: Erinnerungen und Briefe* (Allert de Lange, Amsterdam, 1940). *See also* Mahler-Werfel, Alma.

Mahler, Gustav, *Briefe*. Ed. and revised by Herta Blaukopf (P. Zsolnay Verlag, Vienna, 1982)

Mahler-Werfel, Alma, *Mein Leben* (S. Fischer Verlag, Frankfurt, 1960)

Margutti, Albert Freiherr von, *Vom alten Kaiser: Persönliche Erinnerungen an Franz Joseph* I (Leonhardt-Verlag, Leipzig, 1921)

Mendelssohn, Peter de, *S. Fischer und sein Verlag* (S. Fischer Verlag, Frankfurt, 1970)

Meysels, Lucian O., *In meinem Salon ist Österreich: Berta Zuckerkandl und ihre Zeit* (Herold Verlag, Vienna, 1984)

Mozart, W. A., *Letters*. Ed. and introduced by Eric Blom (Penguin Books, Harmondsworth, 1956)

Museum moderner Kunst, Vienna *Otto Wagner: Möbel und Innenräume*. Includes contributions by Paul Asenbaum, Peter Haiko, Herbert Lachmayer and Reiner Zettl (Residenz Verlag, Salzburg/Vienna, 1984)

Musil, Robert, *Theater: Kritisches und Theoretisches*. Ed. by Marie-Louise Roth (Rowohlt Verlag, Reinbek bei Hamburg, 1965)

Nebehay, Christian M., *Egon Schiele 1890–1918: Leben, Briefe, Gedichte* (Residenz Verlag, Vienna, 1979)

Nebehay, Christian M., *Gustav Klimt: Sein Leben nach zeitgenössischen Berichten und Quellen* (dtv, Munich 1979)

Nebehay, Christian M., *Gustav Klimt/Dokumentations* (Verlag der Galerie Christian M. Nebehay, Vienna, 1969)

Nebehay, Christian M., *Wien Speziell: Architektur und Malerei um 1900* (Verlag Christian Brandstätter, Vienna, 1983)

Neumann, Robert., *Ein leichtes Leben: Bericht über mich selbst und Zeitgenossen* (Kurt Desch Verlag, Vienna, 1963)

Neumann, Robert, *Die Macht* (Paul Zsolnay Verlag, Vienna, 1932)

Nikitsch-Boulles, Paul, *Vor dem Sturm: Erinnerungen an Erzherzog Thronfolger Franz Ferdinand* (Verlag für Kulturpolitik, Berlin, 1925)

Oakeshott, Walter, *Egon Wellesz* (Oxford University Press, Oxford, 1975)

Pabst, Michael, *Wiener Grafik um 1900* (Verlag Silke Schreiber, Munich, 1984)

Pfabigan, Alfred (ed.), *Ornament und Askese im Zeitgeist des Wien der Jahrhundertwende* (Verlag Christian Brandstätter, Vienna, 1985)

Popper, Karl, *Unended Quest: An Intellectual Autobiography* (Fontana/Collins, London, 1976)

Powell, Nicholas, *The Sacred Spring: The Arts in Vienna 1898–1918* (Studio Vista, London 1974)

Prawy, Marcel, *Die Wiener Oper* (Verlag Fritz Molden, Vienna, 1969)

Reich, Willi, *Arnold Schoenberg, oder Der Konservative Revolutionär* (Molden Verlag, Vienna, 1968)

Rozenblit, Marsha L., *The Jews of Vienna, 1867–1915: Assimilation and Identity* (State University of New York Press, Albany, 1983)

Salten, Felix, *Das österreichische Antlitz* (S. Fischer Verlag, Berlin, 1910)

Schärliess, Volker, *Alban Berg in Selbstzeugnissen und Bilddokumenten* (Rowohlts Monographien, Reinbek bei Hamburg, 1975)

Schlick, Moritz, *Gesammelte Aufsätze 1926–1936*. With an introduction by Friedrich Waismann (Gerold, Vienna, 1938)

Schnitzler-Institut, Vienna, *Arthur Schnitzler (1862–1931): Materialien zur Ausstellung der Wiener Festwochen 1981*. Exhibition catalogue (1981)

Schollum, Robert, *Egon Wellesz: eine Studie* (Verlag der Österreichischen Musikzeitschrift, Elisabeth Lafite/Österreichischer Bundesverlag, Vienna, 1963)

Schönberg, Barbara Zeisl, *The Art of Peter Altenberg: Bedside Chronicles of a Dying World* (Unpublished dissertation, UCLA, Los Angeles, 1984)

Schönzeler, Hans-Hubert, *Bruckner* (Musikwissenschaftlicher Verlag, Vienna, 1974)

Schorske, Carl E., *Fin-de-siècle Vienna: Politics and Culture* (Alfred A. Knopf, New York; Weidenfeld & Nicolson, London, 1980)

Schreiber, Wolfgang (ed.), *Gustav Mahler in Selbstzeugnissen und Bilddokumenten* (Rowohlt Verlag, Reinbek bei Hamburg, 1971)

Schweiger, Werner J., *Wiener Werkstätte: Kunst und Handwerk 1903–1932* (Edition Christian Brandstätter, Vienna, 1982)

Sotriffer, Kristian (ed.), *Das grössere Österreich: geistiges und soziales Leben von 1880 bis zur Gegenwart* (Edition Tusch, Vienna, 1982)

Spiel, Hilde, *Fanny von Arnstein, oder Die Emanzipation: ein Frauenleben an der*

Zeitenwende 1758–1818 (S. Fischer Verlag, Frankfurt, 1962)

Spiel, Hilde, *In meinem Garten schlendernd*. Essays (Nymphenburger Verlagshandlung, Munich 1981)

Spiel, Hilde *Welt im Widerschein*. Essays (Verlag C. H. Beck, Munich, 1960)

Spiel, Hilde (ed.), *Wien: Spektrum einer Stadt*. Includes contributions by the editor, F. Achleitner, F. Heer, Hans Weigel and others (Biederstein Verlag, Munich, 1971)

Spiel, Hilde (ed.), *Die zeitgenössische Literatur Österreichs*. With an introduction by the editor (Kindler Verlag, Munich, 1976)

Staassamt für Äusseres in Wien, *Diplomatische Aktenstücke zur Vorgeschichte des Krieges 1914. Part 1, 28 Juni bis 23 Juli 1914* (National-Verlag, Berlin, 1922)

Staël, Mme de, *De l'Allemagne* (Ernst Flammarion, Paris, undated)

Steed, Wickham, *The Habsburg Monarchy*, (Constable, London, 1913)

Stefan, Paul, *Frau Doktor: Ein Bildnis aus dem unbekannten Wien* (Drei Masken Verlag A. G. Munich, 1922)

Stefan, Paul, *Gustav Mahler: eine Studie über Persönlichkeit und Werk* (R. Piper, Munich, 1912)

Stuckenschmidt, H. H., *Die Musik eines halben Jahrhunderts 1925–1975: Essay und Kritik* (R. Piper Verlag, Munich, 1976)

Stuckenschmidt, H. H., *Neue Musik*, Vol. II (Suhrkamp Verlag, Frankfurt, 1951)

Stuckenschmidt, H. H., *Schönberg: Leben, Umwelt, Werk* (Atlantis Verlag, Zürich, 1979)

Stuckenschmidt, H. H., *Schöpfer klassischer Musik: Bildnisse und Revisionen* (Siedler Verlag, Berlin, 1984)

Stuckenschmidt, H. H., *Schöpfer der neuen Musik: Porträts und Studien* (Suhrkamp Verlag, Frankfurt, 1958)

Szeps, Berta (Zuckerkandl), *Ich erlebte fünfzig Jahre Weltgeschichte* (Bermann-Fischer Verlag, Stockholm, 1939)

Tietze, Hans, *Die Juden Wiens: Geschichte – Wirtschaft – Kultur* (E. P. Tal Verlag, Vienna, 1933)

Tietze, Hans, *Wien: Kultur/Kunst/Geschichte* (Verlag Dr Hans Epstein, Vienna, 1931)

Trebitsch, Siegfried, *Chronik eines Lebens* (Artemis Verlag, Zürich, 1951)

Tschuppik, Karl, *Von Franz Joseph zu Adolf Hitler*. Ed. and introduced by Klaus Amann (Böhlau Verlag, Vienna, 1982)

Vajda, Stefan, *Felix Austria: Eine Geschichte Österreichs* (Verlag Carl Ueberreuter, Vienna 1980)

Wagner, Renate, and Vacha, Brigitte, *Wiener Schnitzler-Aufführungen, 1891–1970* (Prestel-Verlag, Munich, 1971)

Waismann, Friedrich, *Logik, Sprache, Philosophie*. With an introduction by Moritz Schlick (Philipp Reclam Jun., Stuttgart, 1976)

Waissenberger, Robert (ed.), *Wien 1870–1930: Traum und Wirklichkeit* (Historisches Museum der Stadt Wien/Residenz Verlag, Salzburg/Vienna, 1984)

Weigel, Hans, *Karl Kraus, oder Die Macht der Ohnmacht* (Molden Verlag, Vienna, 1968)

Weininger, Richard, *Exciting Years*. Ed. by Rodney Campbell (Exposition Press, Hicksville, N.Y., 1978)

Wellesz, Egon, *Arnold Schoenberg* (Galliard Ltd, London/Galaxy Music Corporation, New York, 1971)

Wellesz, Egon and Emmy, *Egon Wellesz: Leben und Werk*. Ed. by Franz Endler (Paul Zsolnay Verlag, Vienna, 1981)

Weys, Rudolf, *Wien bleibt Wien: und das geschieht ihm ganz recht*. Cabaret album, 1930–1945 (Europa Verlag, Vienna, 1974)

Wiesmann, Sigrid (ed.), *Gustav Mahler in Vienna*. With contributions by Pierre Boulez, Friedrich C. Heller, Hilde Spiel and others (Thames and Hudson, London, 1976)

Zeisel, Hans, *Austrian Socialism 1928 and 1978*. The first Paul F. Lazarsfeld lecture (Centre for Research on the Acts of Man, Philadelphia, 1978)

Zeller, Bernhard (ed.), *Jugend in Wien: Literatur um 1900*. Exhibition catalogue (Schiller-National-Museum, Marbach, 1974)

Zuckerkandl, Bertha [sic], *Österreich intim: Erinnerungen 1892–1942*. Ed. by Reinhard Federmann (Verlag Ullstein/Verlag Propyläen, Berlin, 1970) See also Szeps, Berta

Zweig, Stefan, *Aufsätze und Dokumente 1881/1981*. Ed. by Heinz Lunzer and Gerhard Renner (Dokumentationszelle für neuere österreichische Literatur, Vienna, 1981)

Zweig, Stefan, *Die Welt von Gestern: Erinnerungen eines Europäers* (Bermann-Fischer Verlag, Stockholm 1944)

INDEX

Numbers in *italics* refer to illustrations

Abend, Der (Wellesz) 175
Abenteurer und die Sängerin, Der (Hofmannsthal) 126
Abriss der Psychoanalyse (Freud) 137
Abschiedssouper (Schnitzler) 127
Adele Bloch-Bauer I (Klimt) *colour plate 5*
Adler, Alfred 137–9, 142
Adler, Friedrich 139
Adler, Guido 174
Adler, Victor 50, 56, 59, 139, 199
Adorno, Theodor W. 161, 163, 166
Akademietheater 124
Alescha (Theodor Allesch) 214
Alkandi's Lied (Schnitzler) 127
Alkestis (Wellesz) 175, 209
Allemagne, De l' (de Staël) 38
Allgemeine Erkenntnislehre (Schlick) 153
Alt, Rudolf von 92; *71*
Altenberg, Peter 100, 104, 118–20; associates 82, 98,
    108, 174; and cafés 59–60, 111, 112; personality 79,
    116, 125; quoted 58; *74*
Altenberg-Lieder (Berg) 172, 173, 175
Analyse der Empfindungen . . . (Mach) 133–4
Anatol (Schnitzler) 86, 91–2, 93, 112, 127
Andreas (Hofmannsthal) 90
Andrian, Leopold von 57, 88–9, 91, 93, 112, 224, 225
Anzengruber, Ludwig 129, 130, 132
Apostel, H. E. 208
Apponyi, Count Albert 166
Arabella (Hofmannsthal and Strauss) 181, 226
Arbeiterzeitung 198, 229
Arbeitslosen von Marienthal, Die (Lazarsfeld *et al.*) 141
Ariadne auf Naxos (Hofmannsthal) 122, 160
Armer Spielmann, Der (Grillparzer) 92
Armut (Wildgans) 132
army officers *203*
Arnstein, Baroness Fanny von 39, 40–1, 48; *44*
Artaria, Heinrich 42, 62; *70*
Arthaber family 42, 43, 48
Ashbee, Charles R. 67
Auden, W. H. 227
Auernheimer, Raoul 109, 131
Auersperg, Count (Anastasius Grün) 56
Augustin, Marx 180
'Austria's Answer' (Hofmannsthal) 198
Avenarius, Richard 139, 144, 145

Bach, David Josef 208, 210
Bach, Johann Sebastian 179, 180
Bahr, Hermann 85–6, 92, 97, 110, 111, 127, 129, 136;
    his circle 55, 57, 84, 95, 98, 108; quoted 27, 31, 33,
    64, 65, 86, 121–3
Bakchantinnen, Die (Wellesz) 209
Bambi (Salten) 96
Barbara oder die Frömmigkeit (*Barbara or Piety*) (Werfel)
    58, 229
Barrès, Maurice 85
Bartley, W. W. 151
Bartsch, R. H. 190, 200
Battyány, Count Lájos 21, 23, 206
Baudisch, Gertrud 81
Bauer, Felice 94; *222*
Bauer, Otto 59, 139, 230
Bauernfeld, Eduard von 48
Bechstein, Ludwig 164

Beckmann, Max 214–15
Beer-Hofmann, Richard 86, 92, 95, 96, 129, 131, 148–
    9, 224
Behrens, Peter 213
Békessy, Imre 116–17
Ben Gurion, David 149
Benatzky, Ralph 192
Benedict, Moritz 109, 148
Berchtold, Count Leopold 197
Berg, Alban 161, 168, 170–7 *passim*, 191, 208, 209, 211;
    159
Bergner, Elisabeth 235
Berkeley, Bishop George 83, 134
Bernfeld, Siegfried 139, 140, 142–3
Bernstein, Leonard 162–3, 164
Bestiarium Literaricum (Blei) 232
Bettelheim, Anton 130
Bettelstudent, Der (Millöcker) 188
Billroth, Theodor 59
Bismarck, Prince Otto von 24, 53
Blau, Tina 69
Blei, Franz 104, 108, 109, 232, 233
Blendung, Die (*Auto Da Fé*) (Canetti) 232
Bloch-Bauer, Adele 64; *colour plate 5*
Block, Maurus 197
Blue Danube, The (Strauss) 178, 188
Blum, Robert 21
Blümel, Johann 42
Böckl, Herbert 214
Bondy, François 207
Börne, Ludwig 101, 116
Bösendorfer, Ludwig 41
Bosniaken (regiment) *29*
Bottome, Phyllis 151
Boulez, Pierre 165–6, 168
Bourget, Paul 57, 85
Brahm, Otto 84
Brahms, Johannes 43, 161, 162, 164, 166, 169, 171, 189,
    191; *186*
Braun, Felix 199
Braun, Josef 185
Brecht, Bertolt 103, 118–19, 130, 150, 174, 209, 233
Brehm, Bruno 233
Breitner, Hugo 212; *222*
Breuer, Josef 97, 136
Brinckmann, Karl August von 41
Broch, Hermann 174, 189, 225, 228
Brock, Bazon 124
Brod, Max 224
Bruckner, Anton 161, 163, 164
Bruckner, Ferdinand 233
Bruderzwist in Habsburg, Ein (Grillparzer) 124
Brunngraber, Rudolf 230
Brunswik, Count Egon 140
Buch mit sieben Siegeln, Das (Schmidt) 211
Büchner, Georg 234
Bühler, Charlotte 139, 141
Bühler, Karl 139–41, 153, 154
Bürgerlichen Dramen, Die (Wildgans) 132
Burgtheater (Hofburgtheater) 34, 56, 63, 109, 121, 122–
    4, 129–30, 131; productions 126, 127, 148, 234

Calasso, Roberto 143
Calderon de la Barca, Pedro 83, 89, 90, 124

Canetti, Elias 114, 232
Carnap, Rudolf 153
Carnival in Rome (Strauss) 185
Castellio gegen Calvin (Zweig) 228
Castle, The (Kafka) 224
Central, Café 57–61, 98, 112, 119, 215, 229; *107*
Chalupka, O. F. 97
Chamberlain, Houston Stewart 30, 145
Chargaff, Erwin 114
Charles, Archduke (later Emperor) 53, 197
Charles I, Emperor 201, 206
Charles V, Holy Roman Emperor 7
Charles V (Krenek) 210
Charles VI, Holy Roman Emperor 8–9, 160
Chiavacci, Vinzenz 103–4
Chinesische Mauer, Die (Kraus) 115
Chotek, Countess Sophie 196, 197
Clemenceau, Georges 201, 206
Clemenceau, Paul 201
Clemenceau, Sophie (née Szeps) 201, 206
coffee-house 77
Conrad, Franz, Baron von Hötzendorf 197, 210
Corregidor (Wolf) 167
Crowds and Power (Canetti) 232
Csardasfürstin, Die (Kalman) 189
Csokor, Franz Theodor 191, 234
Custozza, Battle of 179
Czernin, Count Ottokar 59, 201, 206
Czeschka, C. O. 68, 181

Dachaulied (Soyfer) 230
Daffinger, Moritz Michael 19
D'Aguilar, Baron Diego 9
Dämonen, Die (*The Demons*) (Doderer) 232
Danhauser, Joseph 19, 43
Dedijer, Vladimir 196
Dehmel, Richard 89
Demel, Karl 62; *70*
'Demolierte Literatur, Die' ('The Demolished
   Literature') (Kraus) 57, 112
Diaghilev, Sergei 80, 206
Dies irae (Wildgans) 132
Dobrowsky, Josef 214
Doderer, Heimito von 232, 233
Dollfuss, Engelbert 115, 231
Don Giovanni (Mozart) 166, 185
Dörmann, Felix 57, 96–7, 104, 189
Draußen im Schönbrunner Park (Benatzky) 192
'Dream and Reality', exhibition 63, 236
Dreaming Youths, The (Kokoschka) 63, 68, 69, 78
Dreher, Anton 42
Dreimäderlhaus, Das (Berté and Schubert) 190
3 November 1918, Der (Csokor) 234
Dujardin, Edouard 93

Ebner-Eschenbach, Marie von 97, 98, 110, 129
Ehn, Karl 213
Ehrenstein, Albert 113, 193, 199, 228, 233
Ehrlich, Georg 213
Eisler, Hanns 208, 209
Ekstein, Rudolf 140
Elektra (Hofmannsthal and Strauss) 127
Elisabeth, Empress 23, 195
Elon, Amos 149
Eltz, Count August 54
Engelhart, Josef 64, 65, 81, 183; *71*

Engländer, Samuel 102
Enright, D. J. 111
Entry of Charles V into Antwerp, The (Makart) 62
Erdgeist (Wedekind) 104
Eros und Psyche (Weininger) 145
Erwartung (Schönberg) 172, 209
Evangelimann, Der (Kienzl) 211
Expectation and Fulfilment (Klimt) 80

Fackel, Die 113, 115, 146, 200
Faistauer, Anton 64, 214
Fall, Leo 189–90
Feigl, Herbert 153
Feldherrnhügel, Der (Roda Roda and Rössler) 132
Fendi, Peter 19, 43
Ferdinand I, Emperor (of Austria) 19–22
Ferdinand I, Holy Roman Emperor 7–8
Ferdinand II, Holy Roman Emperor 30, 37, 194
Ferstel, Heinrich von 183
Feuchtersleben, Baron 43
Fiakerlied (Pick) 182, 191; *187*
'Fiakermilli' 181, 182
Fidele Bauer, Der (Fall) 189
Fink und Fliederbusch (Schnitzler) 129
First Austrian Republic: monument to founders *223*
First World War: postcards *203*
Fischer, Samuel 118
Fischof, Adolf 20, 50, 102
Fledermaus, Die (cabaret) 108
Fledermaus, Die (operetta; Strauss) 184, 185–8
Flesch von Brunningen, Hans 228; *217*
Fliess, Wilhelm 136, 138, 146
Flöge, Emilie 64, 68
Florentinische Tragödie (Zemlinsky) 170
Franckenstein, Baron Georg 54, 91; *202*
Frank, Josef 212, 213
Frank, Philipp 154
Frankl, L. A. 20, 56, 102
Franz I, Emperor 10, 18, 19, 23, 33
Franz Ferdinand, Archduke 23, 115, 196–7; *202*
Franz Joseph I, Emperor 18, 22–4, 35–6, 48, 54–80, 92,
   115, 192, 195, 197, 200–1, 206, 234–5; *14, 71, 202,
   204–5*
Frau ohne Schatten, Die (Hofmannsthal and Strauss) 226
Fräulein Else (Schnitzler) 225
Free Typography 208, 209
Frege, Gottlob 153
Frenkel, Else 140
Freud, Anna 140, 141; *156*
Freud, Sigmund 134–41, 162; and associates 59, 98, 128,
   129, 134–5, 145, 146, 148, 163, 167, 225; *156*
Friedell, Egon 100, 104, 108–9, 116, 119, 126, 174, 233
Friedrich, Otto 71
Friedrich II (the Great), Emperor of Prussia 9, 40
Friedrich Wilhelm III, Emperor of Prussia 196
Fünf sakrale Lieder (Webern) 209

Gallmeyer, Josefine 185
Garten der Erkenntnis, Der (Andrian) 88
Gaulschreck im Rosennetz, Der (Herzmanovsky-
   Orlando) 234
Geheimnis des Reichs (Doderer) 232
Geoffroy, Abbé de 100–1
Gerhard, Roberto 208
'German Field-Post Greeting' (Schröder) 198
German Requiem (Brahms) 161

Gerstl, Richard 63, 68–9, 82, 175; *colour plate 10*
Gerstner, Anton 62; *70*
Geschlecht und Charakter (*Sex and Character*) (Weininger) 79, 143
Gessner, Hubert 213
Gestern (Hofmannsthal) 92, 97, 112, 125
Getupfte Ei, Das (Kokoschka) 108
Ginzkey, K. F. 200
Girardi, Alexander 123, 130, 182
Glances (Schönberg) 68
Globocnik, Odilo 31
Gluck, Christoph Willibald 10
Glückliche Hand, Die (Schönberg) 172, 209
Gödel, Kurt 153
Goethe, J. W. von 39, 41, 108, 144, 174
Gold (Korngold) 210
Goldmann, Paul 86, 92
Goldmark, Adolf 20
Goldoni, Carlo 32, 55, 122
Gomperz, Heinrich 48, 50
Gomperz, Julius von 166
Gomperz, Theodor 48, 50
Gould, Glenn 210
Gradiva (Jensen) 135, 136
Graf von Charolais, Der (Beer-Hofmann) 131
Graf von Luxemburg, Der (Lehár) 189
grandmothers, the author's *46*
'Great Formula, The' 18; *11*
Greek Thinkers (Gomperz) 48
Greiner, Franz von 39
Griensteidl, Café 55–8, 86, 87, 95, 97, 111–12, 191, 215, 227, 229
Grillparzer, Franz 18, 19–20, 31, 83–5, 92, 111, 124–5; funeral 102; quoted 32, 198; social life 41, 43, 56
Grimms' Fairy Tales 163
Gropius, Walter 229
Grosse Bestiarium der Literatur, Das (Blei) 109
Grossmann, Stephan 118
Grün, Anastasius (Count Auersperg) 56
Güdemann, Moritz, Chief Rabbi 149
Gurre-Lieder (Schönberg) 171, 172
Gütersloh, A. Paris 175, 214, 233–4

Habe, Hans 116
Habsburg Monarchy, The (Steed) 235
Hahn, Hans 153
Hainisch, Michael 56
Hall, Stanley 138
Hammerschlag, Peter 61
Handel-Mazzetti, Enrica von 110
Hanslick, Eduard 103, 162, 210
Harta, Felix A. 214
Hartmann, Heinz 140
Hartmann, Moritz 102
Hartung, Hermann 56
Hašek, Jaroslav 104
Hauer, Josef Matthias 170, 176
Hauptmann, Gerhart 85, 127, 129
Hauser, Carry 214
Haynau, Baron Julius 23
Heine, Heinrich 43, 101, 114
Henz, Rudolf 233
Herrenhof, Café 59–61, 215, 229
Herz, Henriette 39
Herzfeld, Marie 110
Herzgewächse (Schönberg) 172

Herzl, Theodor 91, 98, 112, 133; as writer 109–10, 113, 129, 131; and Zionism 51, 94, 147–9; *157*
Herzmanovsky-Orlando, Fritz von 214, 233–4
Hesse, Hermann 118
Hevesi, Ludwig 110
Hildebrandt, Lukas von 8
Hiob (Zeisl) 211
Hitler, Adolf 51, 52, 55, 84, 149, 234, 235
Hochzeit der Sobeide, Die (Hofmannsthal) 126
Hoffmann, Josef 63, 66–8, 78, 80–1, 82, 108, 113, 212, 213
Hofmann, Isak Löw 84, 91
Hofmann, Werner 79, 82
Hofmannsthal, Christiane von 115
Hofmannsthal, Gerty von (née Schlesinger) 89
Hofmannsthal, Hugo von 83–4, 86–92, 98, 110–36 *passim*, 144, 171, 174, 198–202 *passim*, 209, 224–7 *passim*; social life and friends 43, 48, 55, 95, 224; writings 31, 32, 83, 85, 97, 160, 175, 181, 189, 191; *106*
Hohenfels, Stella 129
Holtei, Karl von 43
Hölzel, Adolf 71
Holzer, Rudolf 102
Hornischer, Fanny 181
Horvath, Odön von 232
'Hunger' (Polgar) 104
Hus, Johann 194
Hutterstrasser, textile manufacturer 42

Ich und das Es, Das (Freud) 225
Im Prater blüh'n wieder die Bäume (Stolz) 191
In these Great Times (Kraus) 111
Indigo and the Forty Thieves (Strauss) 185
Instruction of Carnival Children 34
Interpretation of Dreams, The (Freud) 134, 136
Isherwood, Christopher 228
Italian Landscape (Merkel) *colour plate 9*
Itzig, Daniel 40
Izzet, Sultan of Turkey 148

Jahoda, Marie 141
Jakobs Traum (Beer-Hofmann) 129
Jakobsleiter, Die (Schönberg) 176
Jarno, Josef 130–1
Jedermann (Hofmannsthal) 90, 126
Jelusich, Mirko 233
Jensen, Wilhelm 135
Jeremias (Zweig) 200
Jesenská, Milena 61
Jettmar, Rudolf 81; *71*
Jews, Judaism 37, 39, 39–40, 42–51, 58, 90–1, 96, 212, 227, 234–6; anti-Semitism 20, 49, 51, 84, 96, 121; and Herzl 148–50; and literary figures 91, 94–5, 101–3; and Mahler 162–3; and Weininger 143–5; and the State 9, 10, 24
Jodl, Friedrich 144, 145
John Paul II, Pope 53
Jones, Ernest 135, 137
Jonny spielt auf (*Jonny strikes up*) (Krenek) 209
Joseph I, Emperor 8, 160
Joseph II, Emperor 10, 22, 23, 30, 39, 55, 100, 122, 130
Josephine Mutzenbacher (Salten) 96
Josephslegende (Hofmannsthal and Kessler) 206
Judastragödie (Friedell) 109

Juden und Deutsche (Kuh) 116
'Judenstaat, Der' (Herzl) 113, 149
Jung, Carl Gustav 137
Jungnickel, Ludwig 81

Kafka, Eduard Michael 97
Kafka, Franz 33, 61, 94, 215, 224
Kahn, Otto H. 146–7
Kainz, Josef 123
Kaiserhymne (Emperor's Hymn) (Haydn) 22, 179
Kalman, Emmerich 189, 190
Kammersymphonie (Chamber Symphony) (Schönberg) 171, 172
Kampf mit dem Dämon, Der (Zweig) 228
Kandinsky, Wassily 175
Karl Ludwig, Archduke 196
Karl Marx-Hof 213, 231; *colour plate 6*
Karlsplatz (Wagner) *colour plate 7*
Karlweis, C. 97
Kaunitz, Count Wenzel Anton 9
Kaus, Gina 117
Kernstock, Ottokar 198
Kerr, Alfred 98, 118, 125
Kessler, Count Harry 206
Khnopff, Fernand 65
Kienzl, Wilhelm 211
Kindertotenlieder (Mahler) 165, 168
Kirbisch (Wildgans) 232
Klagende Lied, Das (Mahler) 164
Klein, Melanie 140, 142
Klimt, Gustav 55, 62, 63–9 *passim*, 79–82 *passim*, 92, 113, 118, 150, 167; *colour plate 5, 71*
Knaben Wunderhorn, Des (Mahler) 163, 165
Knaben Wunderhorn, Des (Zeisl) 211
Klopstock, Friedrich Gottlieb 10
Köchert, Johannes 62; *70*
Kokoschka, Oskar 81–2, 175, 193–4, 196, 199, 214, 228; and associates 63, 65, 78, 118, 174; works 68, 69, 108; *colour plate 3, 216*
Kolig, Anton 214
Kolisch, Rudolf 208
Kollek, Teddy 235–6
Komtesse Mizzi (Schnitzler) 182
Königgrätz (Sadowa), Battle of 24, 42, 53, 95, 178
Königinhofer Handschrift 116
Körner, Theodor 41
Korngold, Erich Wolfgang 210
Korngold, Julius 171, 210
Kossuth, Lájos 21
Kraft, Viktor 153
Kramár, Karel 59
Kramer, Theodor 230
Kraus, Karl 79, 103, 110–18, 129–30, 146, 198, 200, 229, 233; as critic 32, 57, 143, 149; influence of 150, 174, 227; quoted 40, 57, 68, 82, 101, 197; social life and friends 60, 120; *106*
Krauss, Clemens 209
Kreisky, Bruno 200
Kremser, Eduard 183–4, 191
Krenek, Ernst 114, 209–10; *219*
Krise der Psychologie, Die (Bühler) 140, 141
Krone für Zion, Eine (Kraus) 112–3
Krzyzanowski, Otfried (café habitué) 60–1
Krzyzanowski, Rudolf 164
Kubin, Alfred 214
Kuh, Anton 57, 58, 59, 116–18; *106*

Kuh, Emil 102, 116
Kulka, G. Ch. 113
Kulsczycki, Franz Georg 55
Kupelwieser, Leopold 43
Kunwald, Gottfried 232; *222*
Kürnberger, Ferdinand 32, 101–3, 114, 116, 119
Kurzweil, Max 81

Lament of the Gracious Ladies of this Day and Age 10
Land des Lächelns, Das (Lehár) 189
Ländler (Bruckner) 161
Lanner, Josef 183
Lanz von Liebenfels, Jörg 30, 51
Larwin, Hans 183
Lasker-Schüler, Else 113
Lazarsfeld, Paul F. 139, 141
Lazarsfeld, Sophie 139
Lebenslied (Hofmannsthal) 191
Lederer, August 68
Lehár, Franz 55, 161, 188–9, 191
Lenau, Nikolaus 19–20; *16*
Lenneis, lacemaker 42
Lenz, Maximilien *colour plate 4*
Leonce und Lena (Büchner) 211
Leonce und Lena (Zeisl) 211
Leopold I, Holy Roman Emperor 8, 30, 36
Leopold II, Holy Roman Emperor 10
Leopoldi (Kohn), Hermann 192
Lernet-Holenia, Alexander 227–8, 233; *218*
Leser, Norbert 207
Lessing, Gotthold Ephraim 10, 40, 43
'Letter of Lord Chandos' (Hofmannsthal) 86, 87, 88, 89
Letzten Tage der Menschheit, Die (*The Last Days of Mankind*) (Kraus) 115, 118, 200
Leutnant Gustl (Schnitzler) 93, 94, 98, 134
Liebe (Wildgans) 132
Liebelei (Schnitzler) 127
Liebesliederwalzer (Brahms) 161
Lied von Bernadette, Das (Werfel) 224
Lied von der Erde (Mahler) 167, 168
Lieder (Berg) 172, 173
Life is a Dream (Hofmannsthal) 136
Liliom (Molnár) 131
Lipiner, Siegfried 165
Literarische Herzenssachen (Kürnberger) 101
Little Café Down the Street, A (Leopoldi) 192
Lloyd George, David 206
Löffler, E. 81
Logik der Forschung (Popper) 154
Loos, Adolf 78–9, 115; friends and associates 63, 81, 82, 118, 150, 174, 193, 200; writings 66, 68
Loos, Lina 108
Loos-Haus ('house without eyebrows') 78–9, 81; *75*
Los Angeles City College Opera Workshop 211
Lothar, Rudolf 97
Löwenfeld, Leopold 145
Lucka, Emil 199
Lueger, Karl 49, 59, 96, 183, 195
Luitpold, Josef 229
Lumpazivagabundus (Nestroy) 33
Lustige Krieg, Der (Strauss) 188
'Luxury Vehicle, The' (Loos) 78

Maazel, Lorin 32
MacDonald, Frances and Margaret 67
Mach, Ernst 83, 99, 128, 133–4, 139, 144

Macht, Die (Neumann) 232
Mackintosh, Charles Rennie 67
McNair, Herbert 67
Maeterlinck, Maurice 98, 99, 171
Magic Flute, The (Schikaneder) 160
Mahler, Anna 210
Mahler, Gustav 68, 82, 162–8, 170, 171–2, 180, 191, 210; works 161, 169, 188; *159*
Mahler-Werfel, Alma 64, 82, 180, 193–4, 209, 229, 231, 233; quoted 162, 171–2, 210; *220*
Magris, Claudio 82, 233
Makart, Hans 53–4, 55, 62–3
'Manche freilich . . .' (Hofmannsthal) 84
Mann, Thomas 93, 118, 224, 226
Mann ohne Eigenschaften, Der (*The Man without Qualities*) (Musil) 98, 228
Mannsfeld, Antonie 181
Maria Theresia, Empress 9, 30, 49, 62, 121, 122, 132
Marienleben (Rilke) 224
Marriage of Figaro, The (Mozart) 190
Marx, Joseph 210
Marx, Karl 21, 139; Marxism 142–3
Masaryk, Thomas Garrigue 27, 59, 116, 198
Mass Psychology and Fascism (Reich) 143
Maximilian I, Emperor 54
Maximilian, Emperor of Mexico 23, 195
Mayreder, Rosa 110
Mehring, Walter 233
Meistersinger, Die (Wagner) 8, 162
Mell, Max 233
Mendelssohn, Moses 40, 43, 115
Mendelssohn-Bartholdy, Felix 189
Menger, Karl 153
Mental Development of the Child (Bühler) 140
Merkel, Georg 214, 235; *colour plate 9*
Merry Widow, The (Lehár) 55, 188, 191
Metternich, Prince Clement 18, 20, 36, 40
Metternich, Princess Pauline 54, 55
Meyerbeer, Giacomo 88
Milani, Johann Ev. 55–6
Mildenburg, Anna von 165
Mill, John Stuart 48
Miller von Aichholz family 43
Millöcker, Karl 188
Mit fremden Federn (Neumann) 232
Modern Architecture (Wagner) 66
Moderne, Die 57, 65
Modersohn-Becker, Paula 215
Moll, Carl 64, 81, 171; *71*
Molnár, Ferenc 131
Moltke, Count Helmuth James von 233
Montag, Louise 181
Montenuovo, Prince Alfred 167
Moore, G. E. 151, 152
Morality and Criminality (Kraus) 79
Mord, den jeder begeht, Ein (Doderer) 232
Morgenstern, Christian 209
Morris, William 67
Moser, Hans 33
Moser, Koloman (Kolo) 65, 67, 68, 80–1; *71*
Moses und Aron (Schönberg) 175
Motesiczky, Marie Louise von 214–15; *colour plate 2*
Mozart, W. A. 10, 55, 160, 164, 165, 184, 185
Müller, Hans 199
Müller, Josef 188
Müllner, Lorenz 145

Museum, Café 57, 59, 60, 78
Musikblätter des Anbruchs (*Music Sheets of Departure*) 208
Musikverein 169, 172; *colour plate 7*
Musil, Robert 98–9, 125, 132, 228, 232, 233; *218*

Nacht in Venedig, Eine (Strauss) 188
Nachts unter der steinernen Brücke (Perutz) 224
Nadler, Josef 226
Napoleon I, Emperor 10, 18, 25, 39, 52
Napoleon III, Emperor 23
Nestroy, Johann 19–20, 57, 114, 122, 129, 130; quoted 31, 32, 33; *16*
Neue Freie Presse 56, 59, 109, 111, 115, 117, 148, 149, 198, 210
Neue Ghetto, Das (Herzl) 131
Neue Wiener Tagblatt 201
Neumann, Robert 232
Neurath, Otto 153
Neurotica (Dörmann) 96
Neutra, Richard 212
Nicholas I, Tsar 22–3
Niese, Hansi 130
Nietzsche, Friedrich 117, 145, 165
Nowak, Heinrich 228

Oberwinder, Heinrich 56
Offenbach, Jacques 114, 167, 184, 185, 188
O'Kelly, Michael 55, 184
Olbrich, Joseph Maria 63, 65, 66, 67, 78, 80, 110, 213; *71*
Oppenheimer, Baron Felix 91
Oppenheimer, Max 69; portrait of Webern *159*
'Origins of Schönberg's Twelve-Tone System' (Wellesz) 176
Orlik, Emil 81
Ornament and Crime (Loos) 63, 78
Ornament und Askese (symposium) 63
Österreichische Antlitz, Das (Salten) 96
Overcoming of Naturalism, The (Bahr) 85–6

Palácky, František 195
Palmström (Eisler and Morgenstern) 209
Paoli, Betty 110
Pappenheim, Bertha 172
Pappenheim, Marie 172, 208
Paracelsus (Schnitzler) 128–9
Pastoral Symphony (Beethoven) 160
Peche, Dagobert 81
Pelleas und Melisande (Schönberg) 171, 172
Pensionat, Das (Suppé) 188
Pereira, Baron Eliseus von 41
Pereira-Arnstein, Baroness Henriette 41, 43; *44*
Perkonig, Josef Friedrich 233
Pernerstorfer, Engelbert 56
Perutz, Leo 215, 224, 228
Petzold, Alfons 229
Peymann, Claus 124
Philip II, King of Spain 7
Philosophical Investigations (Wittgenstein) 151, 153
Pichler, Caroline 39, 43
Pick, Gustav 182–3, 191; *44–5*
Pierrot Lunaire (Schönberg) 170, 172–3
Pirandello, Luigi 130
Pisk, Paul A. 208, 211
Pius X, Pope 148
Poincaré, Raymond 206

Polak, Ernst 61; *106*
Polgar, Alfred 58, 104, 109, 116, 118, 131, 199, 233
Popper, Sir Karl 154–5
postcards, multilingual *203*
Postsparkasse (Wagner) 66; *73*
Pötzl, Eduard 93
'Prague Circle' 224
Prater *28, 47*
Prater Violet (Isherwood) 228
Prediger (The Preacher) (Schiele) *colour plate 1*
Prinčip, Gavrilo 196, 197
Professor Bernhardi (Schnitzler) 94, 127–8
Prutscher, O. 81

Quelle des Übels (Polgar) 104
'Question, A' (Hofmannsthal) 86
Quintet with Piano in C Major (Webern) 173

Radetzky, Count Johann Joseph 54, 178, 181
Radetzky March (Strauss) 178
Radetzkymarsch (Roth) 227–8, 234
Raimund, Ferdinand 19, 56, 122, 129, 130; *16*
Raimundtheater 130
Rastelbinder, Der (Lehár) 189
Rauhe Leben, Das (Petzold) 229
Reich, Wilhelm 142–3
Reigen (La Ronde) (Schnitzler) 127, 134
Reinhardt, Max 109, 226, 233
Reinhold, Ernst 69
Renner, Karl 59
Requiem Concertante (Zeisl) 211
Requiem Ebraico (Zeisl) 211
Resurrection symphony (Mahler) 165
Rilke, Rainer Maria 96, 199, 200, 215, 224, 227
Rivarol, Antoine 103
Roda Roda 132, 233
Rodin, Auguste 89
Roller, Alfred 65, 166, 167
Rose von Stambul, Die (Fall) 189
Rosenkavalier, Der (Hofmannsthal and Strauss) 126, 171, 184
Rössler, Carl 132
Roth, Joseph 227–8, 232–3, 234, 235; *218*
Rothschild, Salomon 20
Rudolf, Crown Prince 23, 49, 182, 196
Rudolf I, King (the Founder) 54
Rudolf of Habsburg 54
Rufer, Josef 208–9
Ruskin, John 67
Russell, Bertrand 142, 150, 151, 152, 153
Russell, John 78
'Russian Invasion of Galicia, The' (Zweig *et al.*) 200

Saar, Ferdinand von 48, 92–3, 97–8, 129
Sacre du Printemps (Stravinsky) 172
Salome (Strauss) 167
Salten, Felix 86, 96, 98, 104, 112, 123, 131
Salzburger grosse Welttheater, Das (Hofmannsthal) 126
San Stefano, Peace of 195
Saphir, Moritz 103
Schatz, Otto Rudolf 214
Scheibelreiter, Ernst 233
Schey, Baron Josef 48
Schiele, Egon 63, 64, 65, 69–78, 79, 81, 82; *colour plate 1, 217*
Schiele, Melanie 78

Schikaneder, Emanuel 160
Schiller, Friedrich 41, 43, 53, 112
'Schlaflied für Miriam' (Beer-Hofmann) 96
Schlaf-Wandler, Die (The Sleepwalkers) (Broch) 225, 228
Schlagobers (Strauss) 171
Schlegel, August Wilhelm von 40, 41
Schlegel, Dorothea von 39, 41
Schlegel, Karl Wilhelm Friedrich von 40
Schlenther, Paul 129
Schlesinger, Hans 150
Schlick, Moritz 61, 153–5, 170; *158*
Schlögl, Friedrich 103–4
Schmeltzl, Wolfgang 26, 180
Schmidt, Franz 211
Schneemann, Der (Korngold) 210
Schnitzler, Arthur 91–5, 97, 98, 99, 126–30, 133, 198; and Freud 134–6, 148, 225; quoted 104, 112; social life and friends 55, 86, 167, 224; works 34, 83, 182, 225–6; *105*
Schober, Johann 230, 233
Schöffel, Joseph 101
Schönberg, Arnold 68–9, 143, 161, 168–76 *passim*, 188, 191, 198–9, 208–9, 211; *159*
Schönbichler, J. 62; *71*
Schöne Galathee, Die (Suppé) 188
Schönerer, Georg von 49, 51, 56
Schönherr, Karl 129
Schopenhauer, Arthur 111, 145, 150
Schrammel, Johann and Josef 184
Schratt, Katharina 129, 201
Schreker, Franz 171, 210
Schrifttum als geistiger Raum der Nation, Das (Hofmannsthal) 226
Schröder, Rudolf Alexander 198
Schubert, Franz 19, 160, 161, 164, 165, 178, 183, 184, 190
Schulmeister, Otto 42–3
Schuschnigg, Kurt (von) 115, 229, 231, 233, 234
Schwammerl (Bartsch) 190
Schwarzenberg, Prince Felix 21, 22
Schwarzkopf, Gustav 81
Schwarzwald, Eugenie 81, 174, 175, 208, 233; *220*
Schwierige, Der (The Difficult Man) (Hofmannsthal) 31, 125, 126
Secession 62, 63, 80–1, 86, 92, 115, 166, 201, 213, 214; building 59, 110, 150; *colour plate 8, 76*
Second Vienna School 161, 170–7 *passim*
Seipel, Ignaz 207, 230; *220*
Seitz, Karl 230
Self-portrait (Gerstl) *colour plate 10*
Self-portrait with Comb (Motesiczky) *colour plate 2*
Selim, Josma 192
Sensationen (Dörmann) 96
Serkin, Rudolf 208
Servus Du . . . (Stolz) 191
Seventh Symphony (Mahler) 188
Sexual Revolution, The (Reich) 143
Shakespeare, William 9, 114, 129, 134
Shaw, George Bernard 114, 165
Siegelringe (Kürnberger) 101
Sigismund, Holy Roman Emperor 194
Sigismund I, King of Poland 51
Simplicissimus (cabaret) 192
Sintflut, Die (Neumann) 232
Sirk-Ecke (Lenz) *colour plate 4*

Sittlichkeit und Kriminalität (Kraus) 115
Sixtus, Prince, of Parma 206
Slovakian peddlers *28*
Solferino, Battle of 23
Sonne und Mond (Gütersloh) 233
Sonnenfels, Joseph von 9, 121–2; *15*
Sonnenfels, Liebmann Berlin von 9
Sonnenschein, Hugo 228
Sophie, Archduchess 21
Soyfer, Jura 230
Soyka, Otto 131
Specht, Richard 95, 97, 98, 111
Speidel, Ludwig 103, 109
Spengler, Oswald 150
Sperber, Manès 138–9, 200, 232–3
Spitz, René 140
Spitzer, Daniel 32, 103, 114
Srbik, Heinrich Ritter von 31
Staël, Germaine de 38–9, 40
Standarte, Die (Lernet-Holenia) 227
Starhemberg, Rüdiger von 230
Steed, Henry Wickham 235
Stefan, Paul 208
Stein, Erwin 176, 208
Stekel, Wilhelm 137
Stern, J. P. 113
Stiebitz, Franz Joseph 42
Stifter, Adalbert 19, 41, 43, 83, 92; *16*
Still Life with Ewe and Hyacinths (Kokoschka) 69
Stoclet, Palais 80, 82
Stolz, Robert 191, 192
Stoppard, Tom 111
Straus, Oscar 97, 172, 183, 189, 191
Strauss, Adele 188
Strauss, Eduard 179
Strauss, Johann, the elder 178–80, 183
Strauss, Johann, the younger 84, 136, 161, 178–80, 183, 184–8, 191; *186*
Strauss, Josef 185
Strauss, Richard 161, 162, 167, 170–1, 173, 184, 210; and Hofmannsthal 90, 126, 127, 181, 226
Stravinsky, Igor 80, 172
Strindberg, August 131, 143
String Quartet in D minor (Schönberg) 188
String Quartet in F sharp minor (Schönberg) 171, 177
String Quartet op. 3 (Berg) 175
String Trio op. 20 (Webern) 209
Strnad, Oskar 81, 213
Strzygowski, Josef 30
Studien über Hysterie (Freud) 136
Suchenwirt, Peter 100
Sullivan, Louis 65
Suppé, Franz von 185, 188
Suttner, Bertha von 110, 149, 197
Swarofsky, Hans 208
Swoboda, Hermann 146
Symphony op. 21 (Webern) 175
System of Logic (Mill) 48
Szeps, Moritz 201

Tagebuch (Eisler) 209
Tales of Hoffmann (Offenbach) 167
Tandler, Julius 212
'Terzinen über Vergänglichkeit' (Hofmannsthal) 84
Theater an der Wien 132, 188
Theater in der Josefstadt 130, 233

Therese (Schnitzler) 225–6
This Kiss to the Whole World (Klimt) 68
Thöny, Wilhelm 214
Thorsch family 183
Three Essays on the Theory of Sexuality (Freud) 136
Thus spake Zarathustra (Nietzsche) 117
Tichy, Hans *71*
Tieck, Ludwig 41
Times Literary Supplement 110–11
Tisza, Count Stefan 197
To my Peoples (Emperor Franz Joseph I) 197
Tod Georgs, Der (Beer-Hofmann) 95
Tod des Tizian, Der (Hofmannsthal) 125
Todesco, Baron Eduard 48
Todesco, Baron Moritz 185
Todesco, Baroness Sophie 48, 88, 91, 102, 126, 185, 214; *45*
Todesco, Palais *46*
Toorop, Jan 65
Tor und der Tod, Der (Death and the Fool) (Hofmannsthal) 125
Torberg, Friedrich 215, 236
Tote Stadt, Die (Korngold) 210
Tractatus Logico-Philosophicus (Wittgenstein) 151–2
Trakl, Georg 228
Trance Actor (Kokoschka) 69
Traum ein Leben, Der (Grillparzer) 124
Traumnovelle (Schnitzler) 225
Treffz-Strauss, Henriette (Jetty) 185, 188
Tristan und Isolde (Wagner) 161
Trial, The (Kafka) 224
Trotsky, Leon 197
Tucholsky, Kurt 233
Turm, Der (The Tower) (Hofmannsthal) 83, 90, 226
Twilight of the Gods (Wagner) 164

Unbestechliche, Der (The Incorruptible) (Hofmannsthal) 126, 130, 226
Union 197
Unruh, Fritz von 233
Urzidil, Johannes 224

Van de Velde, Henry 65
Varnhagen, August and Rahel von 40
Ver Sacrum 65, 98
Verklärte Nacht (Schönberg) 169, 171, 172, 209
Verwirrung der Gefühle (Zweig) 228
Verwirrungen des Zöglings Törless (Musil) 98–9
Vetsera, Baroness Marie 182
Vida es Sueño, La (Calderon) 83, 89, 124
Vienna (map, *c.* 1873) *12–13*
Vienna Circle 61, 88, 152–4
Vienna Festival (1985) 63
Vienna High School of Arts and Crafts 81
Vienna Kunstschau 68, 69
Vienna Philharmonic Orchestra 169, 184, 209
'Vienna Rambles' (Spitzer) 103
Vienna State Opera (earlier Hofoper) 32, 166, 171, 209, 210
Vienna Stock Exchange 48–9, 188
'Vienna and the Viennese' (Stifter) 92
Vier Lieder für Gesang und Orchester (Schönberg) 173, 176
Viertel, Berthold 113, 147, 174, 228
Vierzig Tage des Musa Dagh, Die (Werfel) 229
Visions (Schönberg) 68

Vogelhändler, Der (Zeller) 188
Vogelweide, Walther von der 7, 83, 100
Volksoper 209
Volkstheater (Deutsches) 129, 130
Vorlesungen zur Einführung in die Psychoanalyse (Freud) 140

Wacker, Rudolf 214
Waffen nieder, Die (Suttner) 110
Waggerl, Karl Heinrich 233
Wagner, Cosima 166
Wagner, Otto 65–7, 78, 81, 196, 212; *colour plate 7, 72, 73*
Wagner, Richard 8, 103, 145, 148, 161–7 *passim*, 171, 191
Waismann, Friedrich 153
Waldeck, Heinrich Suso 233
Waldinger, Ernst 230
Waldmüller, Ferdinand Georg 43
Walter, Bruno 163, 210
Walzertraum, Ein (Dörmann and Straus) 96–7, 172, 183, 189
Wärndorfer, Fritz 68
washerwomen's ball (Gause) *186*
Wassermann, Jakob 200, 224–5
Weber, Carl Maria von 163, 183
Weber, Die (Hauptmann) 85
Webern, Anton von 161, 168, 170, 172, 173, 174–5, 191, 208, 209; *159*
Wedekind, Frank 60, 104, 131
Weg ins Freie, Der (Schnitzler) 94, 95
Weh dem der lügt (Grillparzer) 124
Weigel, Hans 160
Weinheber, Josef 227
Weininger, Otto 58, 68, 79, 138, 143–7; *156*
Weininger, Richard 144, 146–7, 150; *156*
Weite Land, Das (Schnitzler) 127, 129
Wellesz, Egon 80, 168, 172, 173–4, 175, 176–7; *158*
Wellesz, Emmy (née Stross) 174
Weltfreund, Der (Werfel) 228
Werfel, Franz 58, 113, 114, 199, 215, 224, 228–9
Wertheimstein, Josephine von 48, 88, 126; *45*
Wertheimstein, Leopold von 48
Wertheimstein (Wertheimer) family 30
Weyl, Josef 178
White Horse Inn, The (Benatzky) 192
White Mountain, Battle on the 194
Wiegele, Franz 214

Wien wird bei Nacht erst schön (Stolz) 191
Wiener Blut (Strauss) 188
Wiener Rundschau 112
Wiener Werkstätte 67, 69, 78, 80–1
Wieselthier, Vally 81
Wildgans, Anton 132, 232
Wilhelm II, Emperor of Germany 148, 206
Wimmer-Wisgrill, E. J. 81
Windischgrätz, Prince Alfred 21, 22
Windsbraut, Die (*The Tempest*) (Kokoschka) 193; *colour plate 3*
Wittgenstein, Karl 150
Wittgenstein, Ludwig 82, 88, 113, 133, 143, 146, 150–4, 170; *158*
Wittgenstein, Margarete 64, 82, 133, 150
Wittgenstein, Paul 150
Wlach, Oskar 213
Wolf, Hugo 161, 163, 164, 167
Wolf, Käthe 140
Women Workers' Paper 110
World Exhibition, Vienna 48
Woyzeck (Büchner) 173, 211
Wozzeck (Berg) 173, 175, 209, 211
Wydenbruck, Countess Mysa 167

Xavier, Prince of Parma 206

'Zarathustra's Ape' (Kuh) 117
Zeisel, Hans 141
Zeisl, Erich 211; *219*
Zeitungsausschnitte (Eisler) 209
Zeller, Karl 188
Zemlinsky, Alexander von 68, 167, 168, 169, 171, 172, 210
Zernatto, Guido 233
Zigeunerbaron, Der (*The Gipsy Baron*) (Strauss) 188, 189
Zita, Empress 201, 206
Zohn, Professor Harry 111
Zsolnay, Paul, Verlag 215, 229
Zuckerkandl, Berta (née Szeps) 64, 110, 201, 206, 233; *221*
Zuckerkandl, Emil 201
Zuckmayer, Carl 174
Zur Kritik der Moderne (Bahr) 85
Zwei Herzen im 3/4 Takt (Stolz) 191
Zweig, Stefan 94–5, 114, 144, 167, 197, 199–200, 228, 232
Zwerg, Der (Zemlinsky) 170

PICTURE ACKNOWLEDGMENTS

Illustrations have been supplied and are reproduced by kind permission of the following:

Archiv Hubmann: pp 11, 14, 15, 16 (above left), 17, 29 (above & below), 47 (above), 75 (above), 76, 77, 106 (above right, below right & left), 107, 156 (all photos), 157, 158 (all photos), 159 (below right; von der Heydt Museum, Wuppertal), 202 (above left & right), 204–5 (above), 216 (below), 218 (above right, below), 220 (above right, below), 222 (all photos), 223.

Bildarchiv Österreiches National Bibliothek: pp 16

(above right, below left & right), 44 (above left, below), 72, 105, 106 (above left), 159 (above left & right, below left), 186 (below), 202 (below), 204–5 (below), 218 (above left), 220 (above left), 221.

Hilde Spiel: pp 44–5, 46 (below left & right), 187, 203 (above & below), 216 (above), 217, 219 (below).

Historisches Museum der Stadt Wien: pp 12, 70 (all photos), 71 (above & below), 74, 186 (above).

Hubmann/Nechansky: pp 45 (above right, below), 46.

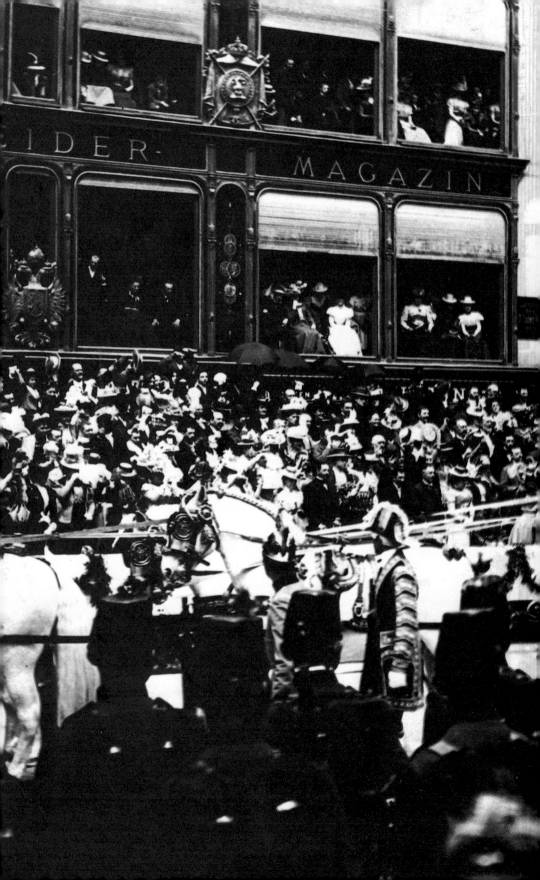